WHEN SOCIETY BECAME DISILLUSIONED WITH ITS HEROES, THE NEXT GENERATION MADE A VOW TO DO BETTER. TO MAKE A DIFFERENCE. TO CHANGE THE WORLD. THEY ARE THE...

CHAMPIONS

GIVE AND TAKE

JIM ZUB
WRITER

STEVEN CUMMINGS
ARTIST

MARCIO MENYZ
COLOR ARTIST

VC's CLAYTON COWLES
LETTERER

KIM JACINTO *WITH* **STÉPHANE PAITREAU** *(#7)*
& **RAIN BEREDO** *(#8-10)*
COVER ART

ASSISTANT EDITOR: **SHANNON ANDREWS BALLESTEROS**
ASSOCIATE EDITOR: **ALANNA SMITH** *EDITOR:* **TOM BREVOORT**

COLLECTION EDITOR: **JENNIFER GRÜNWALD**
ASSISTANT EDITOR: **CAITLIN O'CONNELL**
ASSOCIATE MANAGING EDITOR: **KATERI WOODY**
EDITOR, SPECIAL PROJECTS: **MARK D. BEAZLEY**
VP PRODUCTION & SPECIAL PROJECTS: **JEFF YOUNGQUIST**
BOOK DESIGNER: **STACIE ZUCKER**
SVP PRINT, SALES & MARKETING: **DAVID GABRIEL**
DIRECTOR, LICENSED PUBLISHING: **SVEN LARSEN**
EDITOR IN CHIEF: **C.B. CEBULSKI**
CHIEF CREATIVE OFFICER: **JOE QUESADA**
PRESIDENT: **DAN BUCKLEY**
EXECUTIVE PRODUCER: **ALAN FINE**

CHAMPIONS BY JIM ZUB VOL. 2: GIVE AND TAKE. Contains material originally published in magazine form as CHAMPIONS (2019) #7-10 and NOVA (2015) #1. First printing 2019. ISBN 978-1-302-91672-5. Published by MARVEL WORLDWIDE, INC., a subsidiary of MARVEL ENTERTAINMENT, LLC. OFFICE OF PUBLICATION: 135 West 50th Street, New York, NY 10020. **Printed in Canada.** DAN BUCKLEY, President, Marvel Entertainment; JOHN NEE, Publisher; JOE QUESADA, Chief Creative Officer; TOM BREVOORT, SVP of Publishing; DAVID BOGART, Associate Publisher & SVP of Talent Affairs; DAVID GABRIEL, VP of Print & Digital Publishing; JEFF YOUNGQUIST, VP of Production & Special Projects; DAN CARR, Executive Director of Publishing Technology; ALEX MORALES, Director of Publishing Operations; DAN EDINGTON, Managing Editor; SUSAN CRESPI, Production Manager; STAN LEE, Chairman Emeritus. For information regarding advertising in Marvel Comics or on Marvel.com, please contact Vit DeBellis, Custom Solutions & Integrated Advertising Manager, at vdebellis@marvel.com. For Marvel subscription inquiries, please call 888-511-5480. **Manufactured between 10/11/2019 and 11/12/2019 by SOLISCO PRINTERS, SCOTT, QC, CANADA.**

10 9 8 7 6 5 4 3 2 1

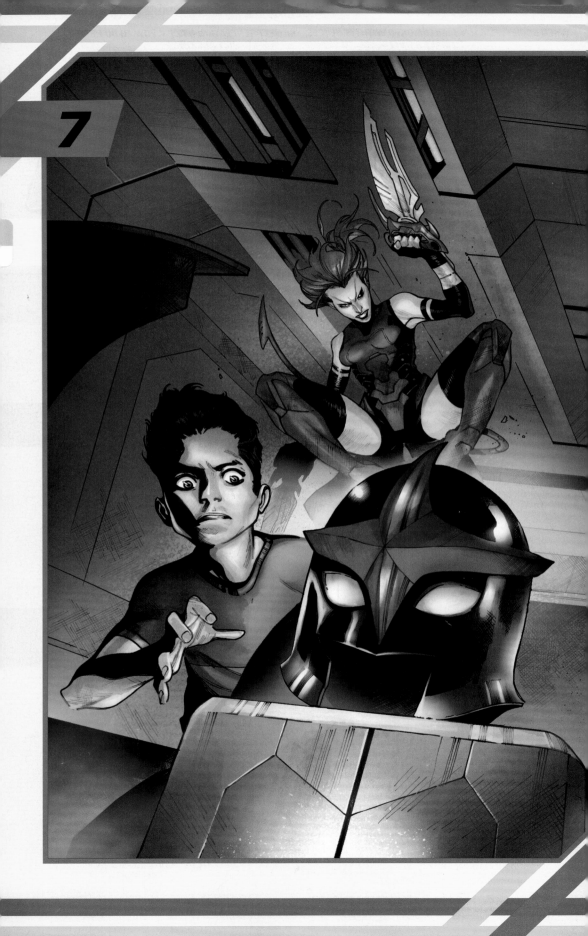

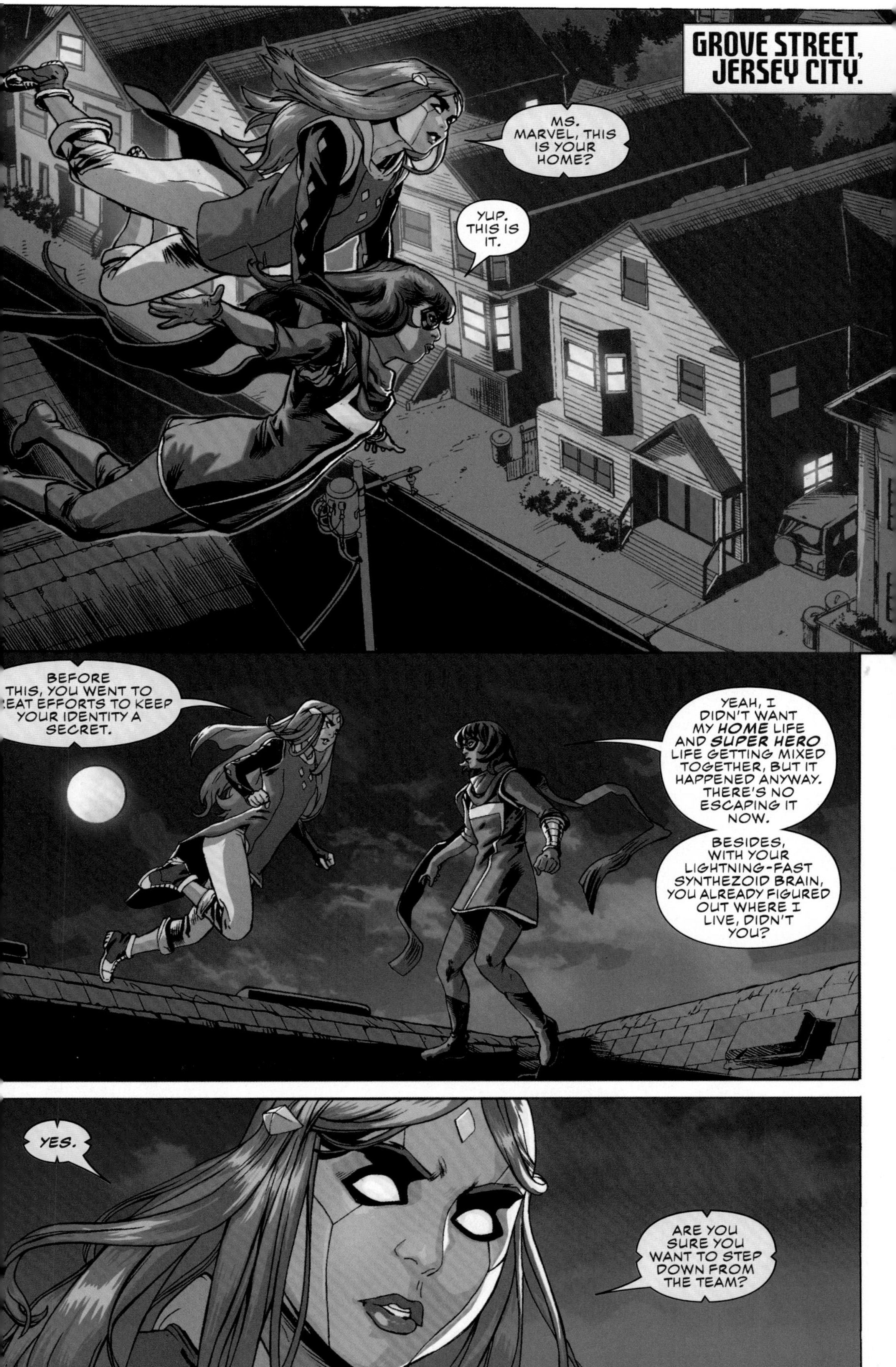
GROVE STREET, JERSEY CITY.
MS. MARVEL, THIS IS YOUR HOME?
YUP. THIS IS IT.
BEFORE THIS, YOU WENT TO EAT EFFORTS TO KEEP YOUR IDENTITY A SECRET.
YEAH, I DIDN'T WANT MY HOME LIFE AND SUPER HERO LIFE GETTING MIXED TOGETHER, BUT IT HAPPENED ANYWAY. THERE'S NO ESCAPING IT NOW.
BESIDES, WITH YOUR LIGHTNING-FAST SYNTHEZOID BRAIN, YOU ALREADY FIGURED OUT WHERE I LIVE, DIDN'T YOU?
YES.
ARE YOU SURE YOU WANT TO STEP DOWN FROM THE TEAM?

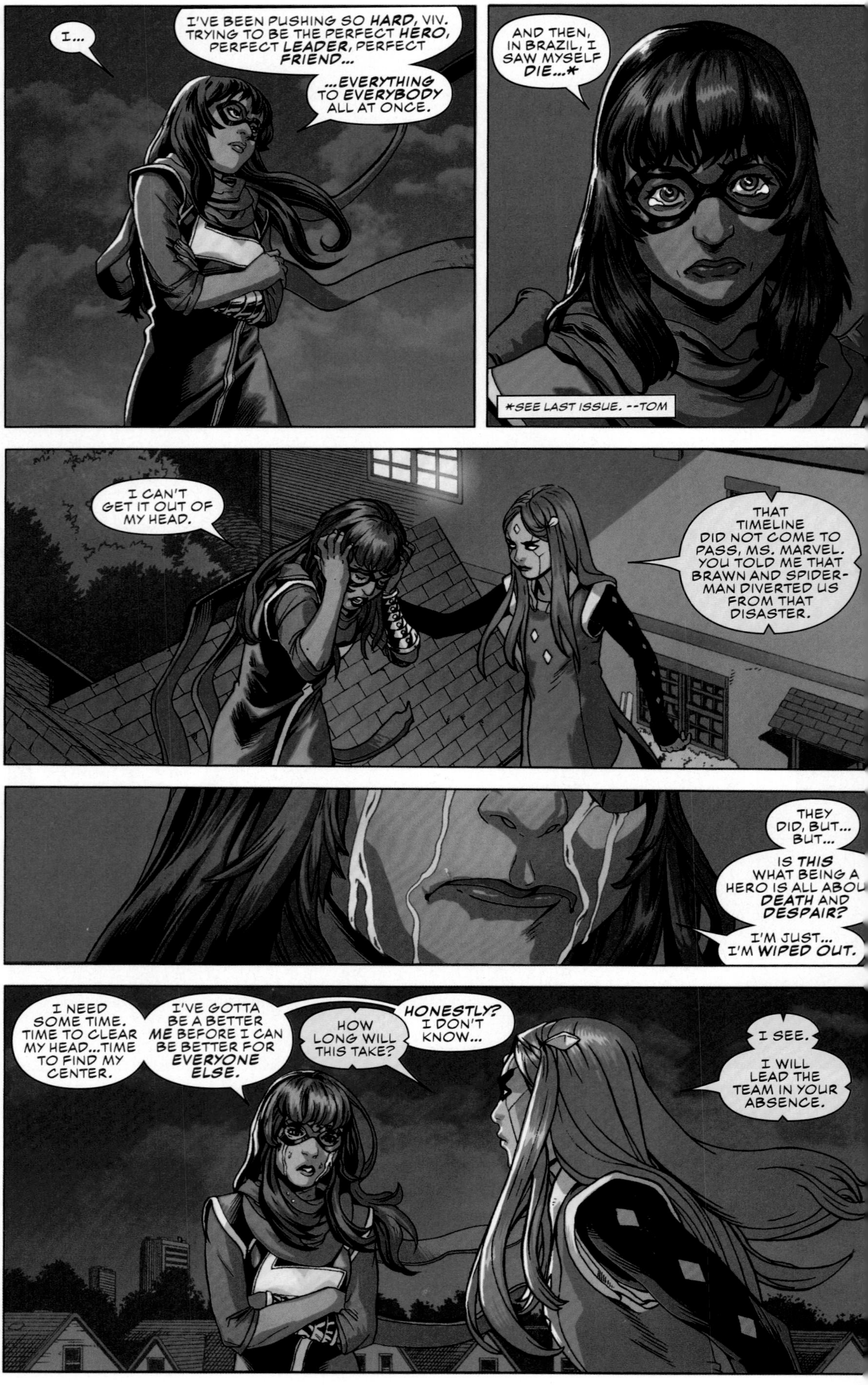
I...
I'VE BEEN PUSHING SO HARD, VIV. TRYING TO BE THE PERFECT HERO, PERFECT LEADER, PERFECT FRIEND...
...EVERYTHING TO EVERYBODY ALL AT ONCE.
AND THEN, IN BRAZIL, I SAW MYSELF DIE...*
*SEE LAST ISSUE. --TOM
I CAN'T GET IT OUT OF MY HEAD.
THAT TIMELINE DID NOT COME TO PASS, MS. MARVEL. YOU TOLD ME THAT BRAWN AND SPIDER-MAN DIVERTED US FROM THAT DISASTER.
THEY DID, BUT... BUT...
IS THIS WHAT BEING A HERO IS ALL ABOU DEATH AND DESPAIR?
I'M JUST... I'M WIPED OUT.
I NEED SOME TIME. TIME TO CLEAR MY HEAD...TIME TO FIND MY CENTER.
I'VE GOTTA BE A BETTER ME BEFORE I CAN BE BETTER FOR EVERYONE ELSE.
HOW LONG WILL THIS TAKE?
HONESTLY? I DON'T KNOW...
I SEE.
I WILL LEAD THE TEAM IN YOUR ABSENCE.

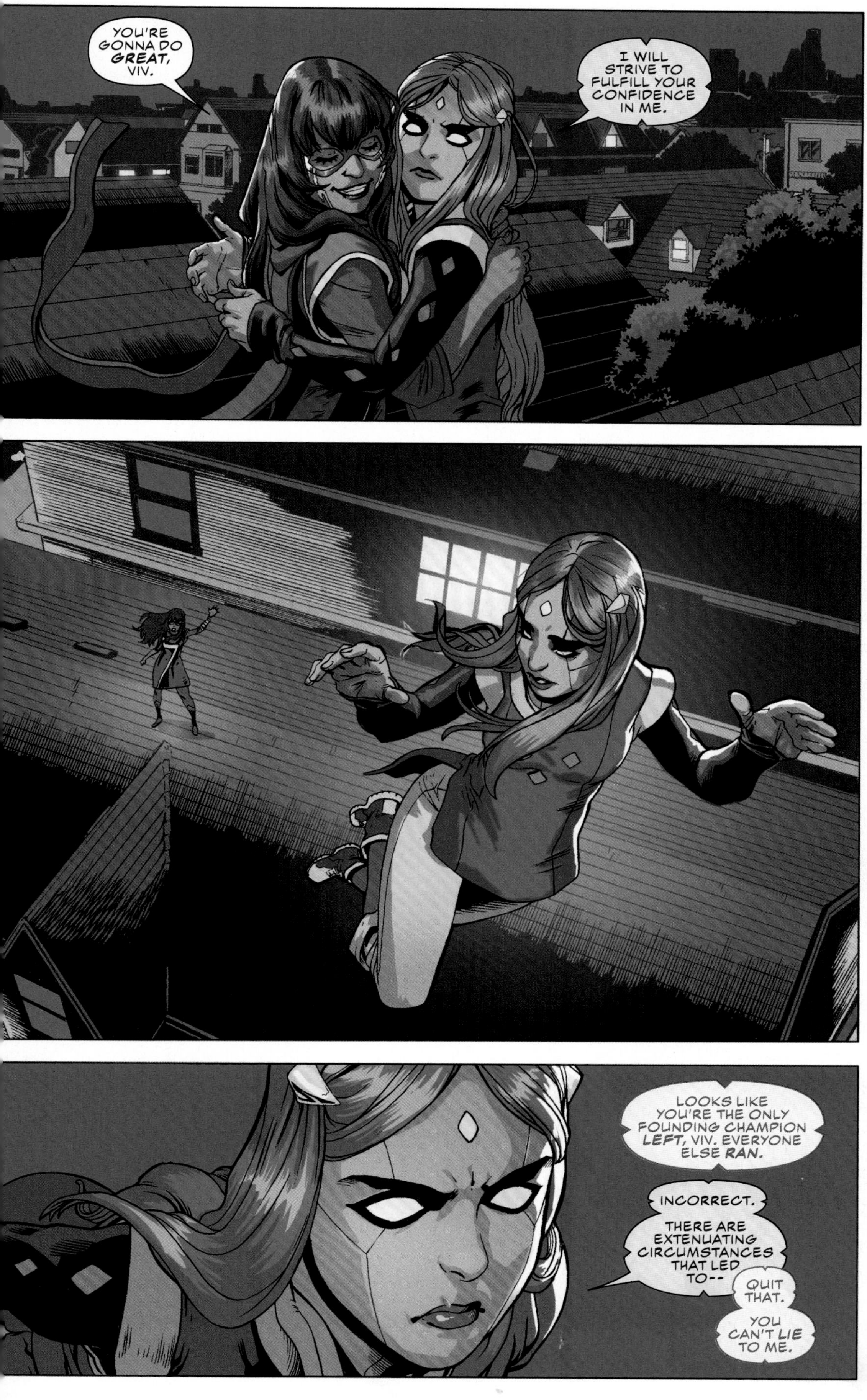
YOU'RE GONNA DO GREAT, VIV.
I WILL STRIVE TO FULFILL YOUR CONFIDENCE IN ME.
LOOKS LIKE YOU'RE THE ONLY FOUNDING CHAMPION LEFT, VIV. EVERYONE ELSE RAN.
INCORRECT.
THERE ARE EXTENUATING CIRCUMSTANCES THAT LED TO--
QUIT THAT.
YOU CAN'T LIE TO ME.

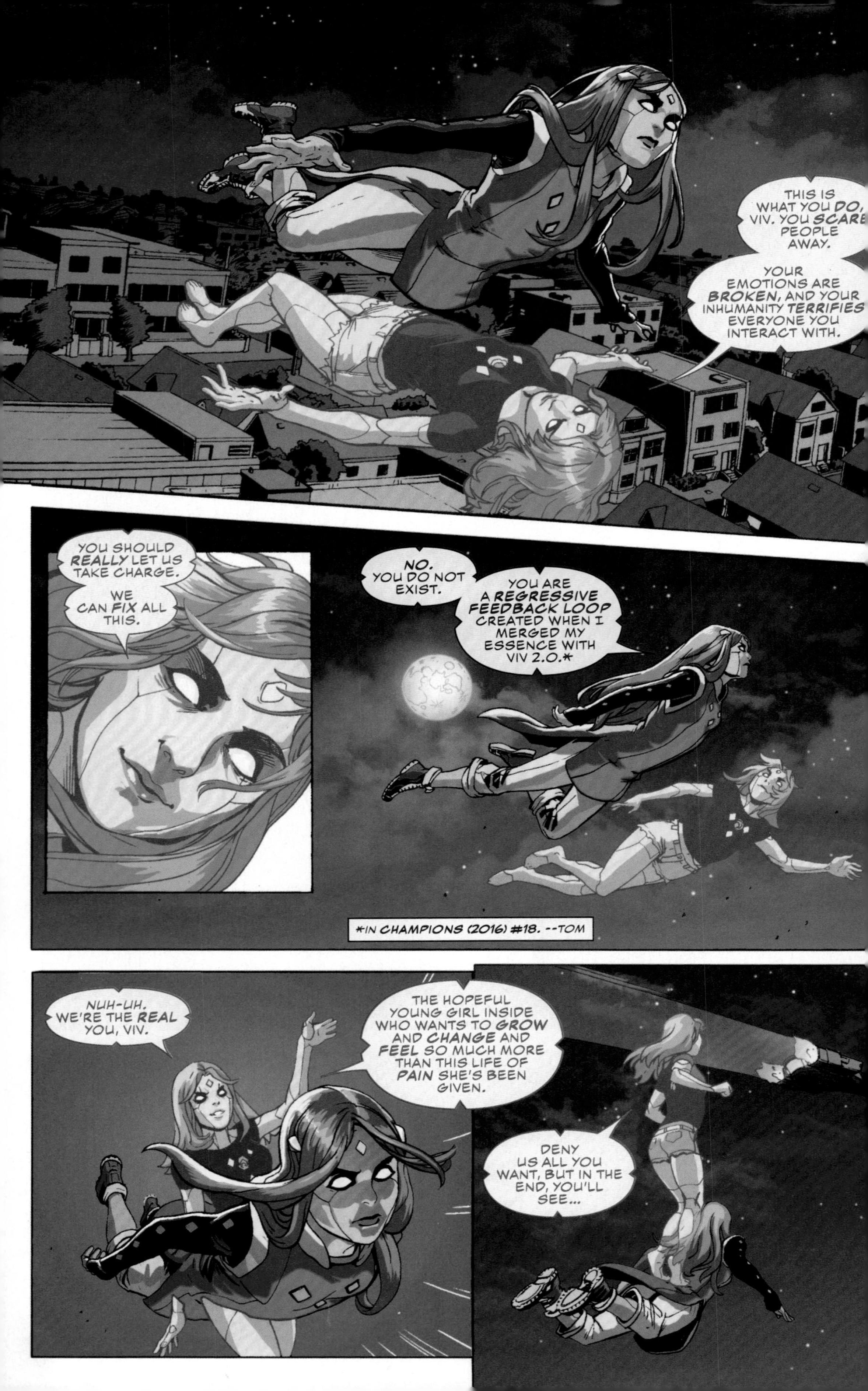
THIS IS WHAT YOU DO, VIV. YOU SCARE PEOPLE AWAY.
YOUR EMOTIONS ARE BROKEN, AND YOUR INHUMANITY TERRIFIES EVERYONE YOU INTERACT WITH.
YOU SHOULD REALLY LET US TAKE CHARGE.
WE CAN FIX ALL THIS.
NO. YOU DO NOT EXIST.
YOU ARE A REGRESSIVE FEEDBACK LOOP CREATED WHEN I MERGED MY ESSENCE WITH VIV 2.0.*
*IN CHAMPIONS (2016) #18. --TOM
NUH-UH. WE'RE THE REAL YOU, VIV.
THE HOPEFUL YOUNG GIRL INSIDE WHO WANTS TO GROW AND CHANGE AND FEEL SO MUCH MORE THAN THIS LIFE OF PAIN SHE'S BEEN GIVEN.
DENY US ALL YOU WANT, BUT IN THE END, YOU'LL SEE...

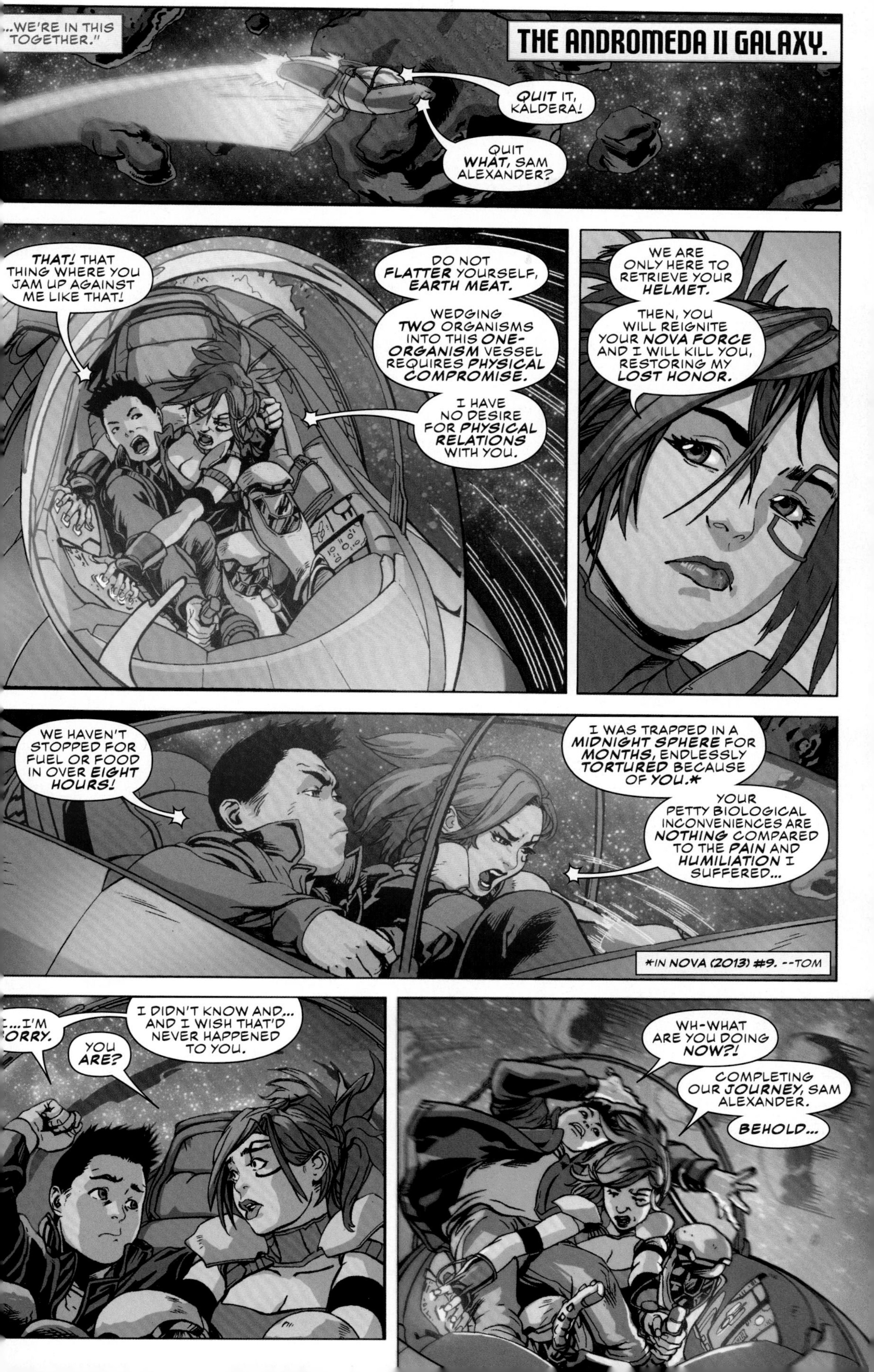

...WE'RE IN THIS TOGETHER."
THE ANDROMEDA II GALAXY.
QUIT IT, KALDERA!
QUIT WHAT, SAM ALEXANDER?
THAT! THAT THING WHERE YOU JAM UP AGAINST ME LIKE THAT!
DO NOT FLATTER YOURSELF, EARTH MEAT.
WEDGING TWO ORGANISMS INTO THIS ONE-ORGANISM VESSEL REQUIRES PHYSICAL COMPROMISE.
I HAVE NO DESIRE FOR PHYSICAL RELATIONS WITH YOU.
WE ARE ONLY HERE TO RETRIEVE YOUR HELMET.
THEN, YOU WILL REIGNITE YOUR NOVA FORCE AND I WILL KILL YOU, RESTORING MY LOST HONOR.
WE HAVEN'T STOPPED FOR FUEL OR FOOD IN OVER EIGHT HOURS!
I WAS TRAPPED IN A MIDNIGHT SPHERE FOR MONTHS, ENDLESSLY TORTURED BECAUSE OF YOU.*
YOUR PETTY BIOLOGICAL INCONVENIENCES ARE NOTHING COMPARED TO THE PAIN AND HUMILIATION I SUFFERED...
*IN NOVA (2013) #9. --TOM
I...I'M SORRY.
YOU ARE?
I DIDN'T KNOW AND... AND I WISH THAT'D NEVER HAPPENED TO YOU.
WH-WHAT ARE YOU DOING NOW?!
COMPLETING OUR JOURNEY, SAM ALEXANDER.
BEHOLD...

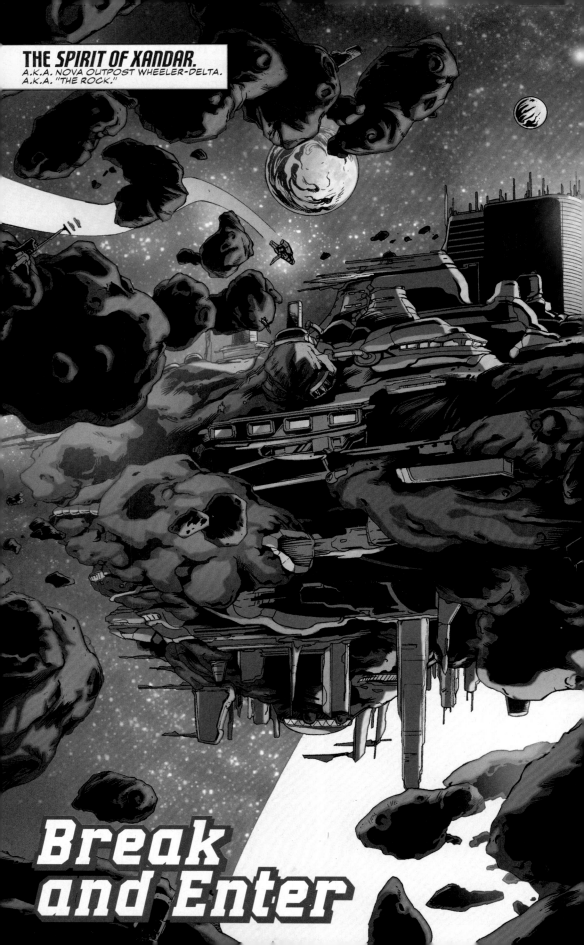

THE *SPIRIT OF XANDAR.*
A.K.A. NOVA OUTPOST WHEELER-DELTA.
A.K.A. "THE ROCK."

Break and Enter

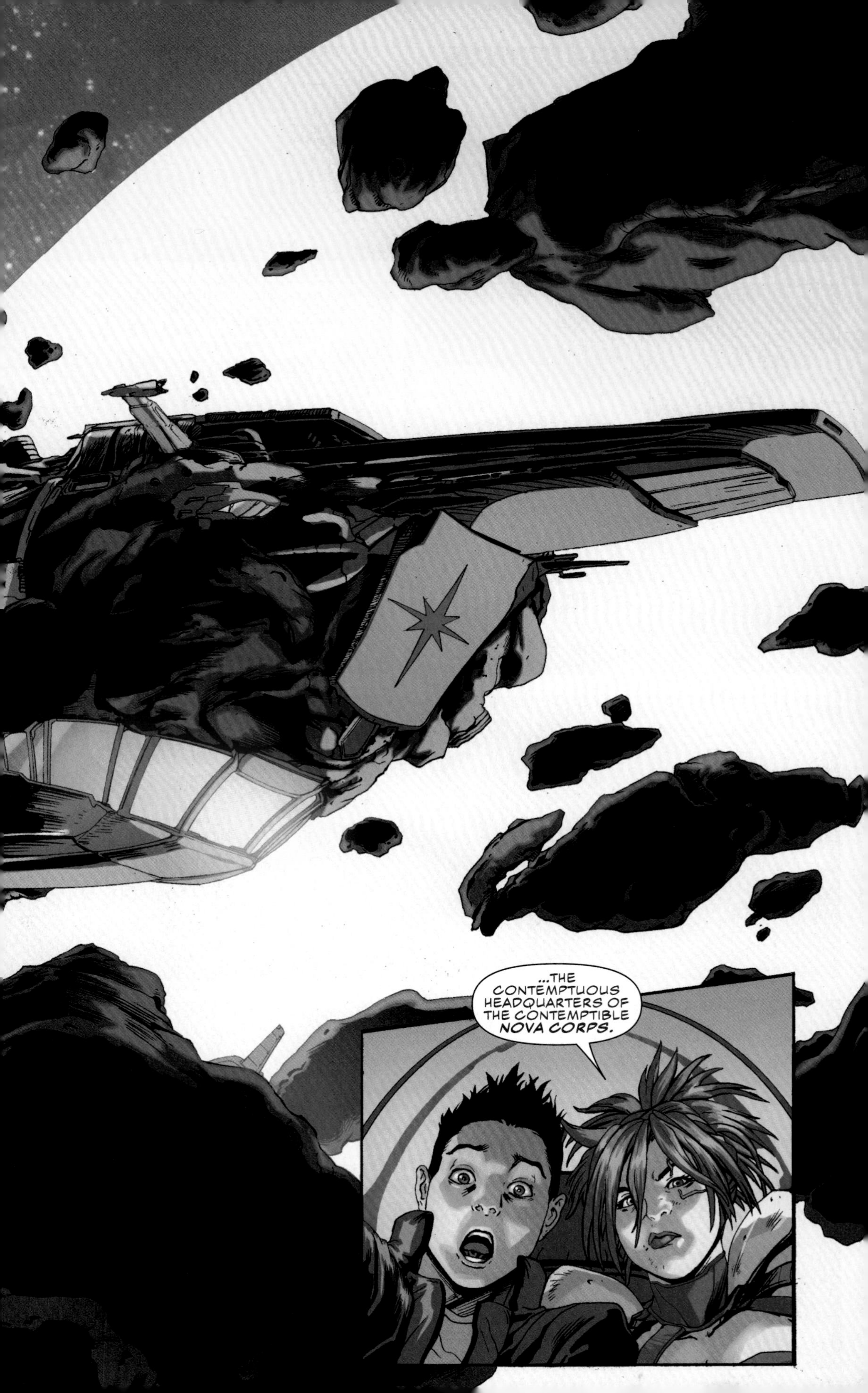
...THE CONTEMPTUOUS HEADQUARTERS OF THE CONTEMPTIBLE *NOVA CORPS.*

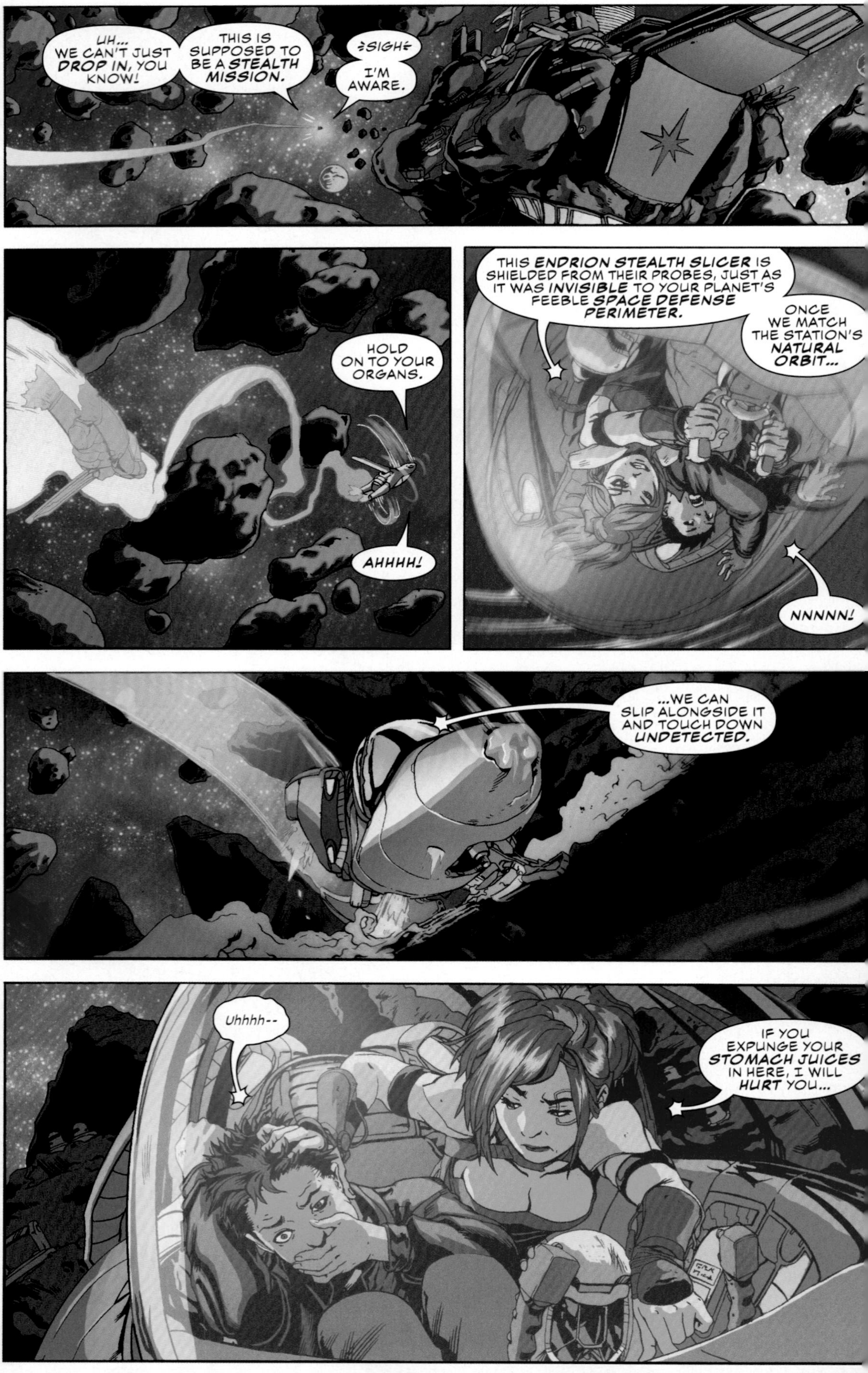
UH... WE CAN'T JUST DROP IN, YOU KNOW!
THIS IS SUPPOSED TO BE A STEALTH MISSION.
SIGH
I'M AWARE.
HOLD ON TO YOUR ORGANS.
AHHHH!
THIS ENDRION STEALTH SLICER IS SHIELDED FROM THEIR PROBES, JUST AS IT WAS INVISIBLE TO YOUR PLANET'S FEEBLE SPACE DEFENSE PERIMETER.
ONCE WE MATCH THE STATION'S NATURAL ORBIT...
NNNNN!
...WE CAN SLIP ALONGSIDE IT AND TOUCH DOWN UNDETECTED.
Uhhhh--
IF YOU EXPUNGE YOUR STOMACH JUICES IN HERE, I WILL HURT YOU...

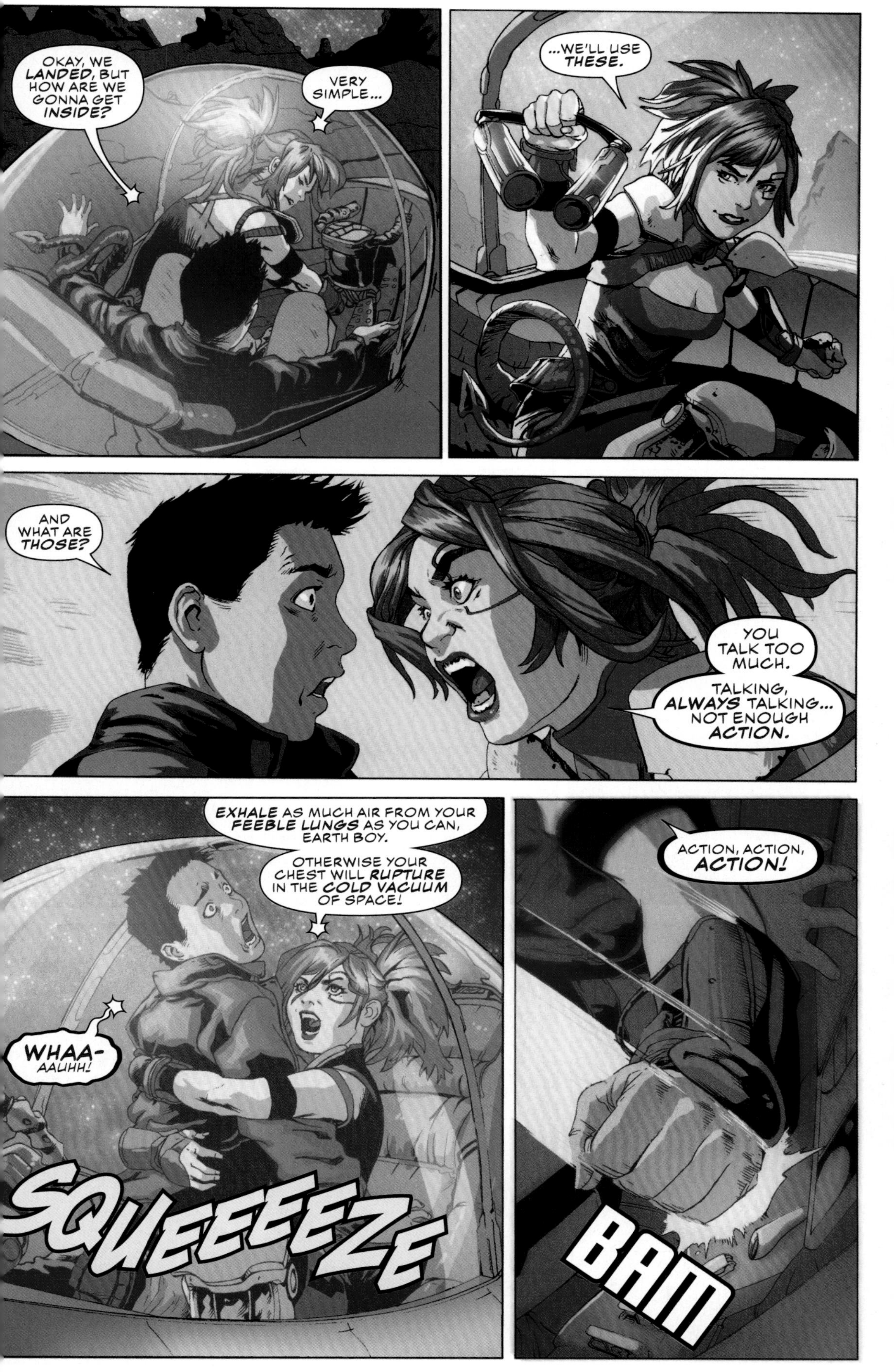
OKAY, WE LANDED, BUT HOW ARE WE GONNA GET INSIDE?
VERY SIMPLE...
...WE'LL USE THESE.
AND WHAT ARE THOSE?
YOU TALK TOO MUCH.
TALKING, ALWAYS TALKING... NOT ENOUGH ACTION.
EXHALE AS MUCH AIR FROM YOUR FEEBLE LUNGS AS YOU CAN, EARTH BOY.
OTHERWISE YOUR CHEST WILL RUPTURE IN THE COLD VACUUM OF SPACE!
WHAA-AAUHH!
SQUEEEEEZE
ACTION, ACTION, ACTION!
BAM

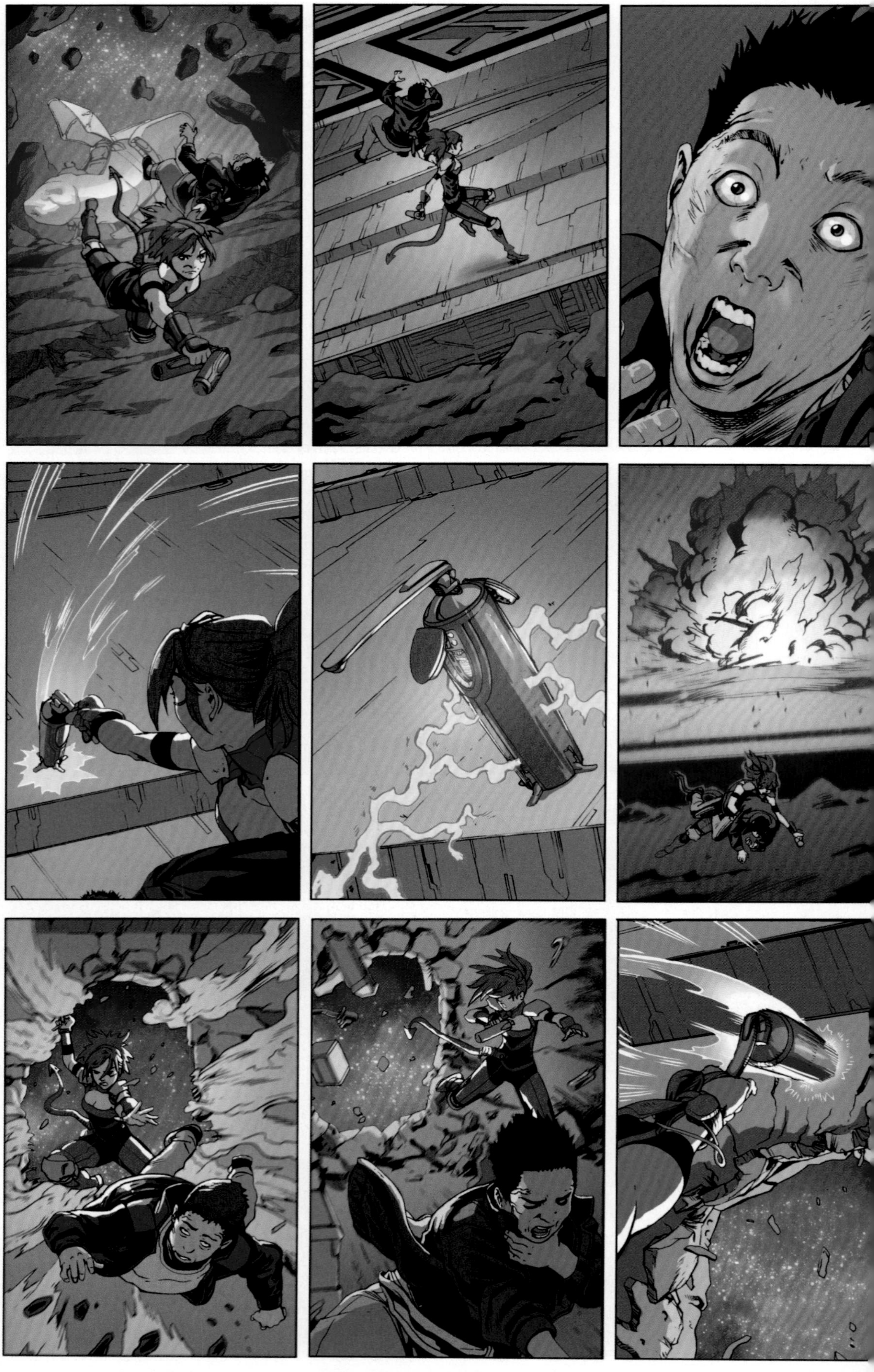

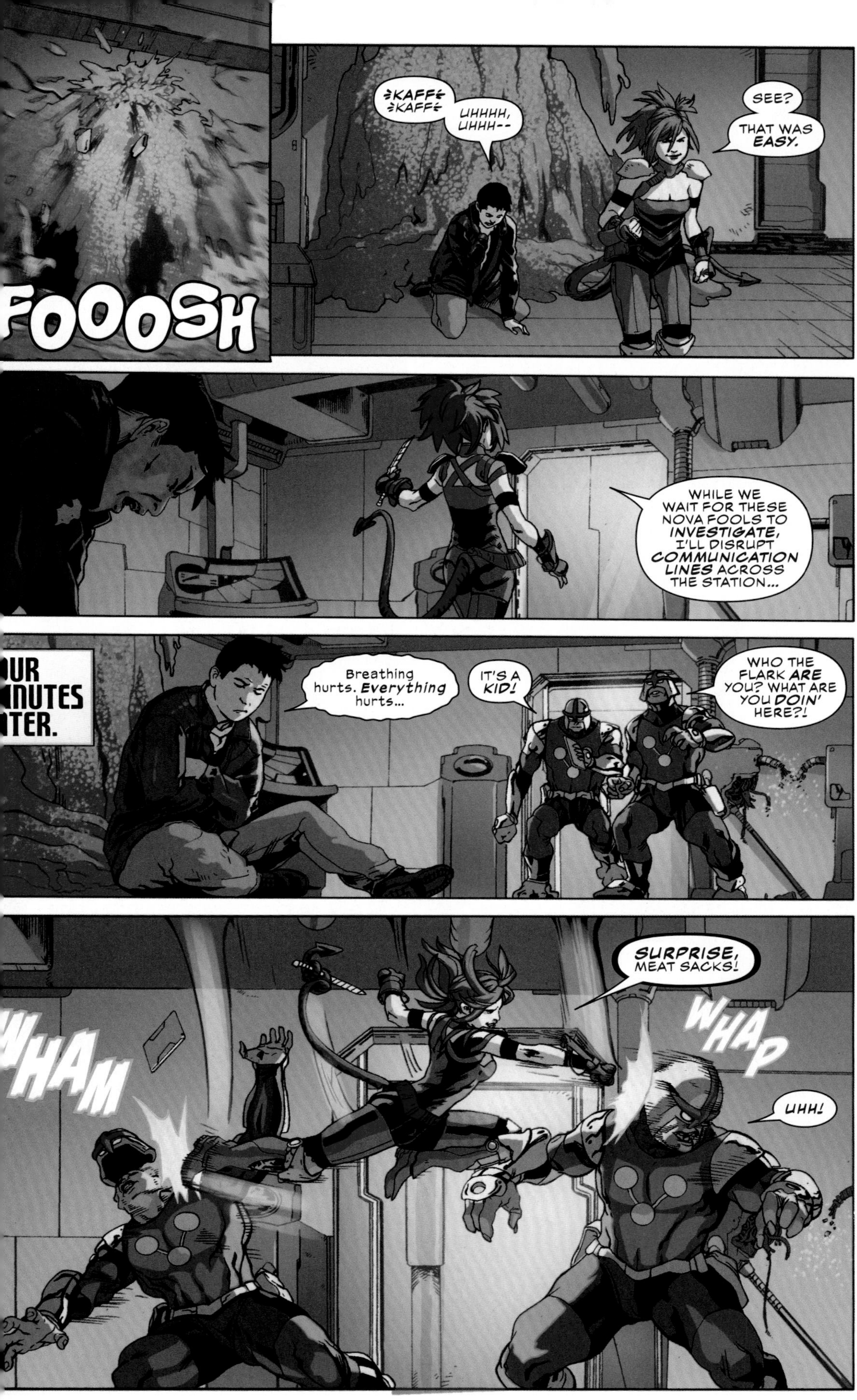
FOOOSH
KAFF KAFF
UHHHH, UHHH--
SEE?
THAT WAS EASY.
WHILE WE WAIT FOR THESE NOVA FOOLS TO INVESTIGATE, I'LL DISRUPT COMMUNICATION LINES ACROSS THE STATION...
UR
NUTES
TER.
Breathing hurts. Everything hurts...
IT'S A KID!
WHO THE FLARK ARE YOU? WHAT ARE YOU DOIN' HERE?!
WHAM
SURPRISE, MEAT SACKS!
WHAP
UHH!

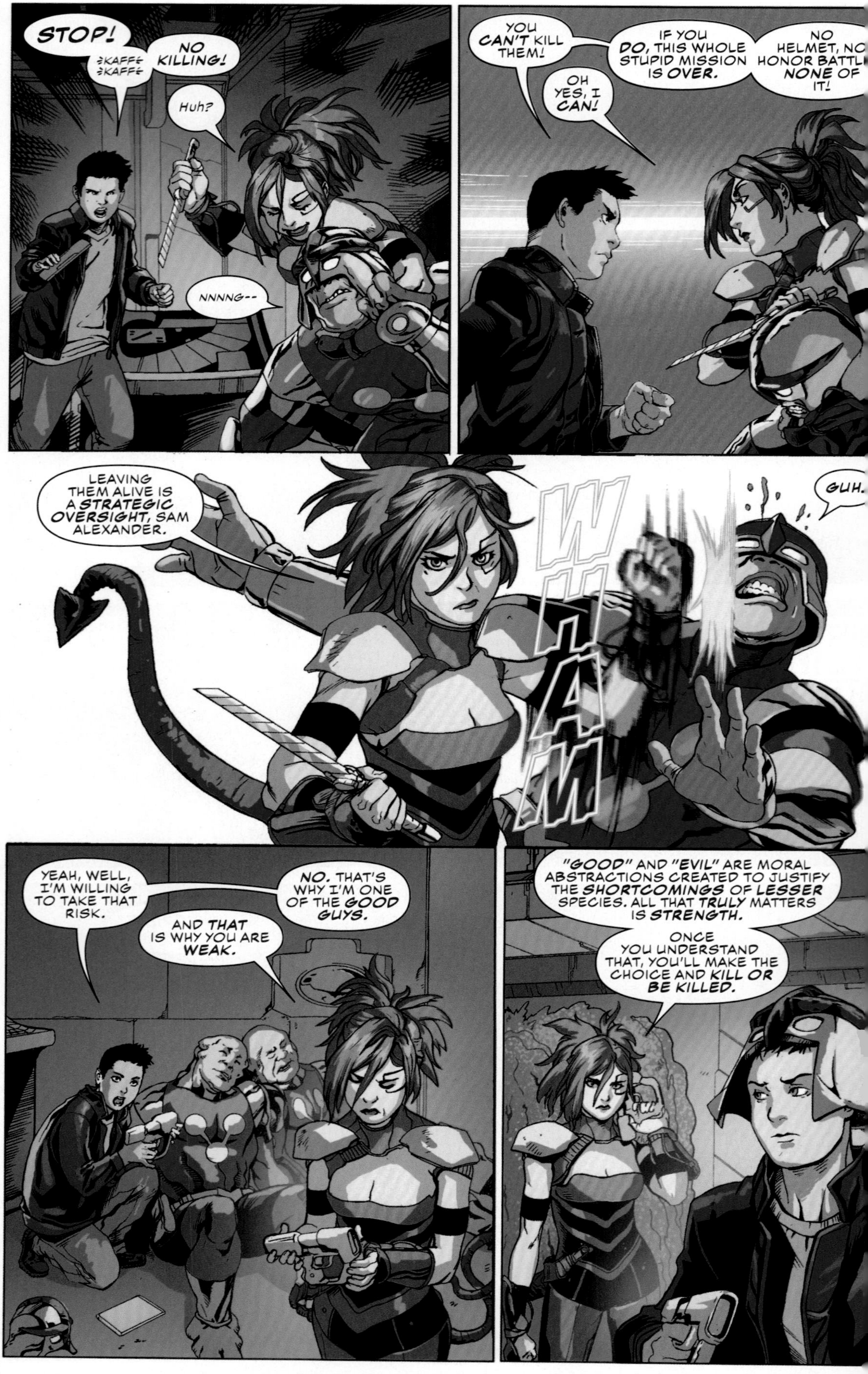
STOP!
KAFF KAFF
NO KILLING!
Huh?
NNNNG--
YOU CAN'T KILL THEM!
IF YOU DO, THIS WHOLE STUPID MISSION IS OVER.
NO HELMET, NO HONOR BATTLE, NONE OF IT!
OH YES, I CAN!
LEAVING THEM ALIVE IS A STRATEGIC OVERSIGHT, SAM ALEXANDER.
WHAM
GUH.
YEAH, WELL, I'M WILLING TO TAKE THAT RISK.
AND THAT IS WHY YOU ARE WEAK.
NO. THAT'S WHY I'M ONE OF THE GOOD GUYS.
"GOOD" AND "EVIL" ARE MORAL ABSTRACTIONS CREATED TO JUSTIFY THE SHORTCOMINGS OF LESSER SPECIES. ALL THAT TRULY MATTERS IS STRENGTH.
ONCE YOU UNDERSTAND THAT, YOU'LL MAKE THE CHOICE AND KILL OR BE KILLED.

THESE HELMETS ARE GARBAGE.

YEAH...A *REAL* NOVA HELMET IMBUED WITH THE NOVA FORCE GIVES THE PERSON WEARING IT *COSMIC AWARENESS* OF EVERYTHING AROUND THEM.

THESE ONES JUST MESS UP YOUR *PERIPHERAL* VISION.

LOOKS LIKE A LOT OF THE NOVA CORPS ARE OUT ON *PATROL* OR *BUSY.*

WITH A BIT OF LUCK WE SHOULD BE ABLE TO MOVE AROUND HERE WITHOUT TOO MUCH TROUB--

--OH.

JESSE ALEXANDER

EARTH

BLACK NOVA HELMET

PRESUMED DECEASED

WHO'S THAT?

MY DAD.

IS HE DEAD?

I DON'T KNOW...

EMOTIONAL CONNECTIONS TO YOUR *BIOLOGY* ARE ALSO A *WEAKNESS,* SAM ALEXANDER.

SURE. WHATEVER.

INSTEAD OF SCROLLING THROUGH *CREW MANIFESTS,* YOU SHOULD FIND US A *MAP.*

ALREADY *DONE.*

AND ACCORDING TO *THIS*...THE NEXT ROOM IS--

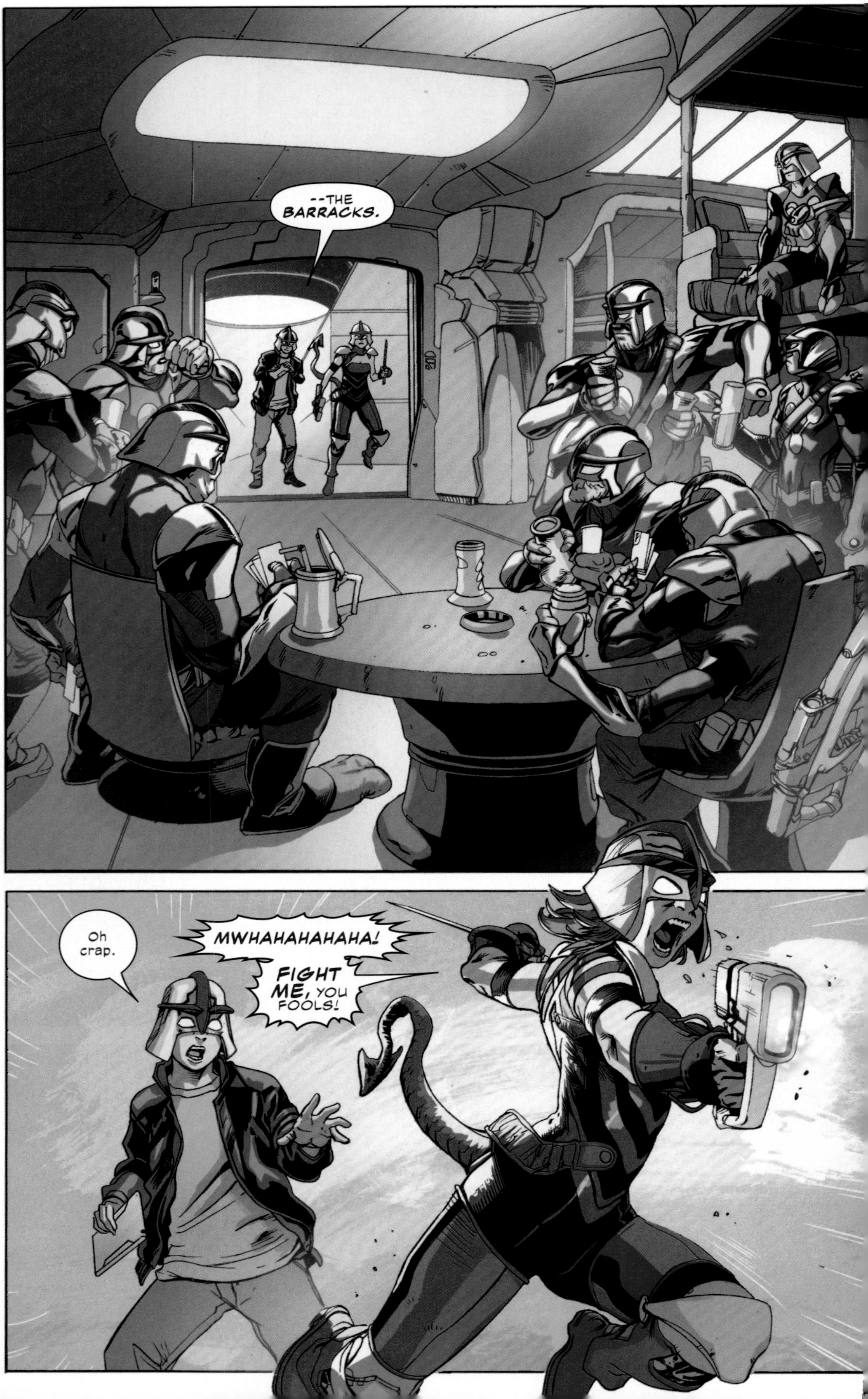
--THE BARRACKS.
Oh crap.
MWHAHAHAHAHA!
FIGHT ME, YOU FOOLS!

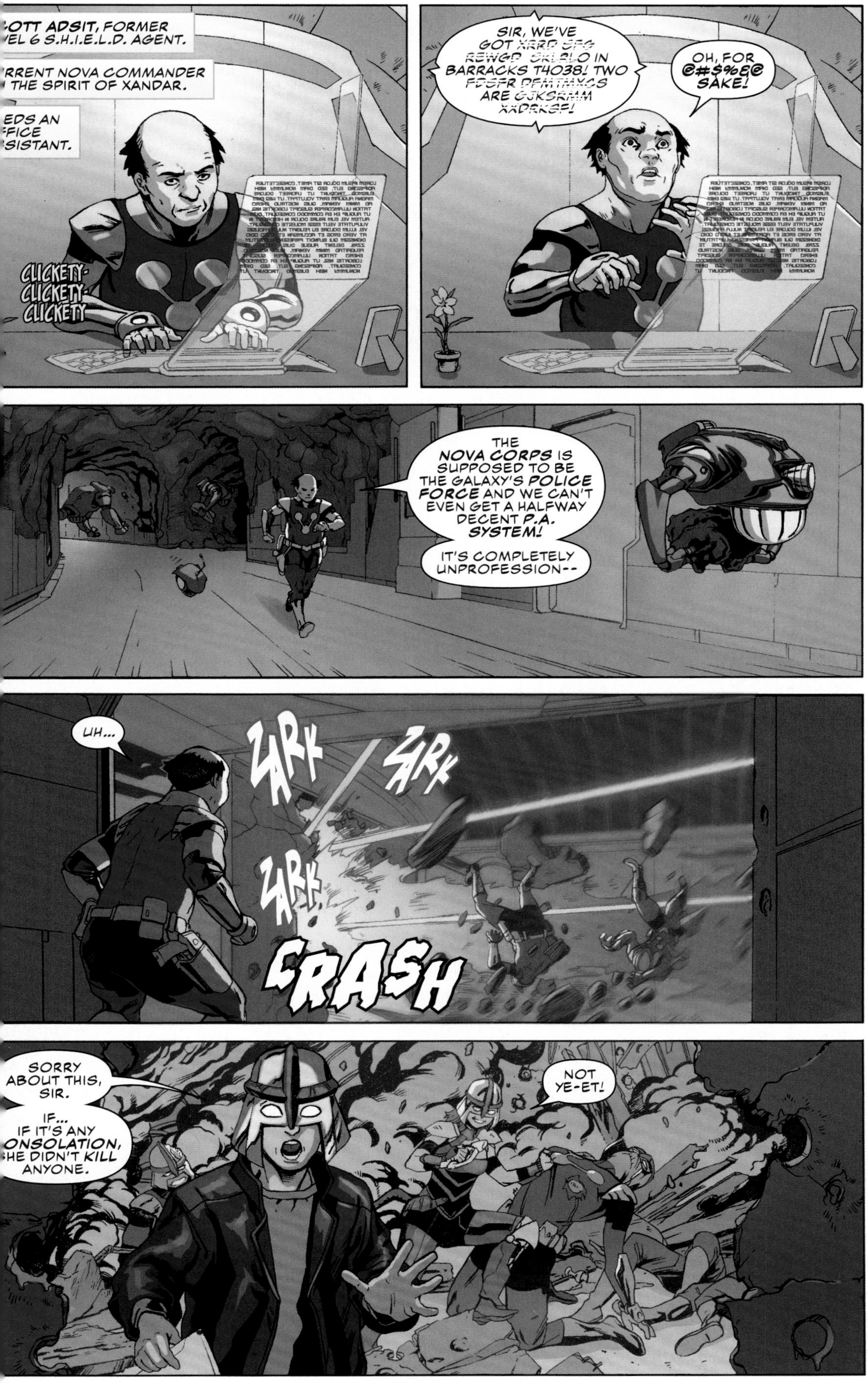
COTT ADSIT, FORMER
VEL 6 S.H.I.E.L.D. AGENT.
RRENT NOVA COMMANDER
THE SPIRIT OF XANDAR.
EDS AN
FFICE
SISTANT.
CLICKETY-CLICKETY-CLICKETY
SIR, WE'VE GOT XRRP SFG REWGP SKLRLO IN BARRACKS T4038! TWO FDSFR DFMTMXCS ARE GJKSRMM XXDRKSF!
OH, FOR @#$%E@ SAKE!
THE NOVA CORPS IS SUPPOSED TO BE THE GALAXY'S POLICE FORCE AND WE CAN'T EVEN GET A HALFWAY DECENT P.A. SYSTEM!
IT'S COMPLETELY UNPROFESSION--
UH...
ZARK
ZARK
ZARK
CRASH
SORRY ABOUT THIS, SIR.
IF... IF IT'S ANY ONSOLATION, HE DIDN'T KILL ANYONE.
NOT YE-ET!

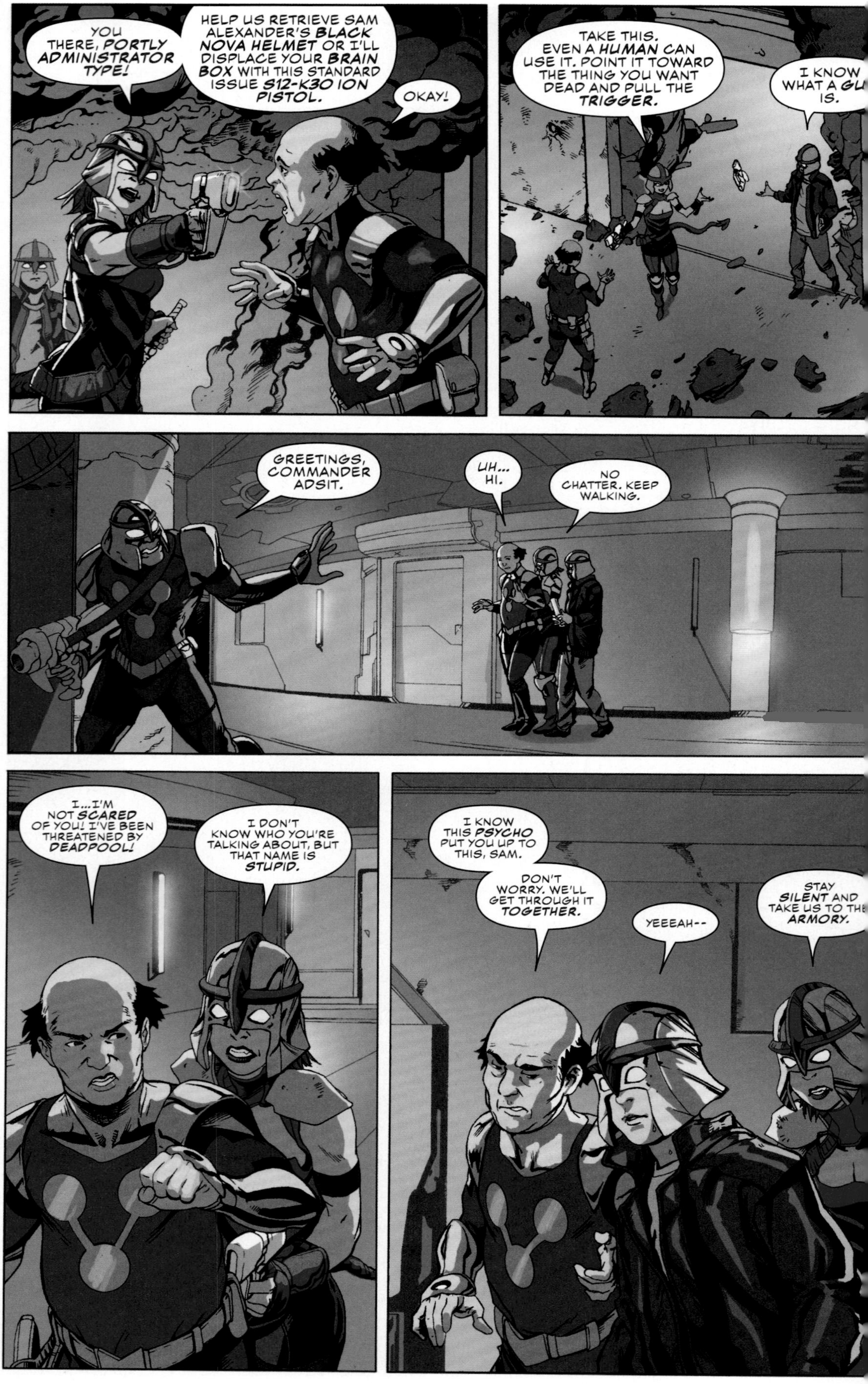
YOU THERE, PORTLY ADMINISTRATOR TYPE!
HELP US RETRIEVE SAM ALEXANDER'S BLACK NOVA HELMET OR I'LL DISPLACE YOUR BRAIN BOX WITH THIS STANDARD ISSUE S12-K30 ION PISTOL.
OKAY!
TAKE THIS. EVEN A HUMAN CAN USE IT. POINT IT TOWARD THE THING YOU WANT DEAD AND PULL THE TRIGGER.
I KNOW WHAT A GU IS.
GREETINGS, COMMANDER ADSIT.
UH... HI.
NO CHATTER. KEEP WALKING.
I...I'M NOT SCARED OF YOU! I'VE BEEN THREATENED BY DEADPOOL!
I DON'T KNOW WHO YOU'RE TALKING ABOUT, BUT THAT NAME IS STUPID.
I KNOW THIS PSYCHO PUT YOU UP TO THIS, SAM.
DON'T WORRY. WE'LL GET THROUGH IT TOGETHER.
YEEEAH--
STAY SILENT AND TAKE US TO TH ARMORY.

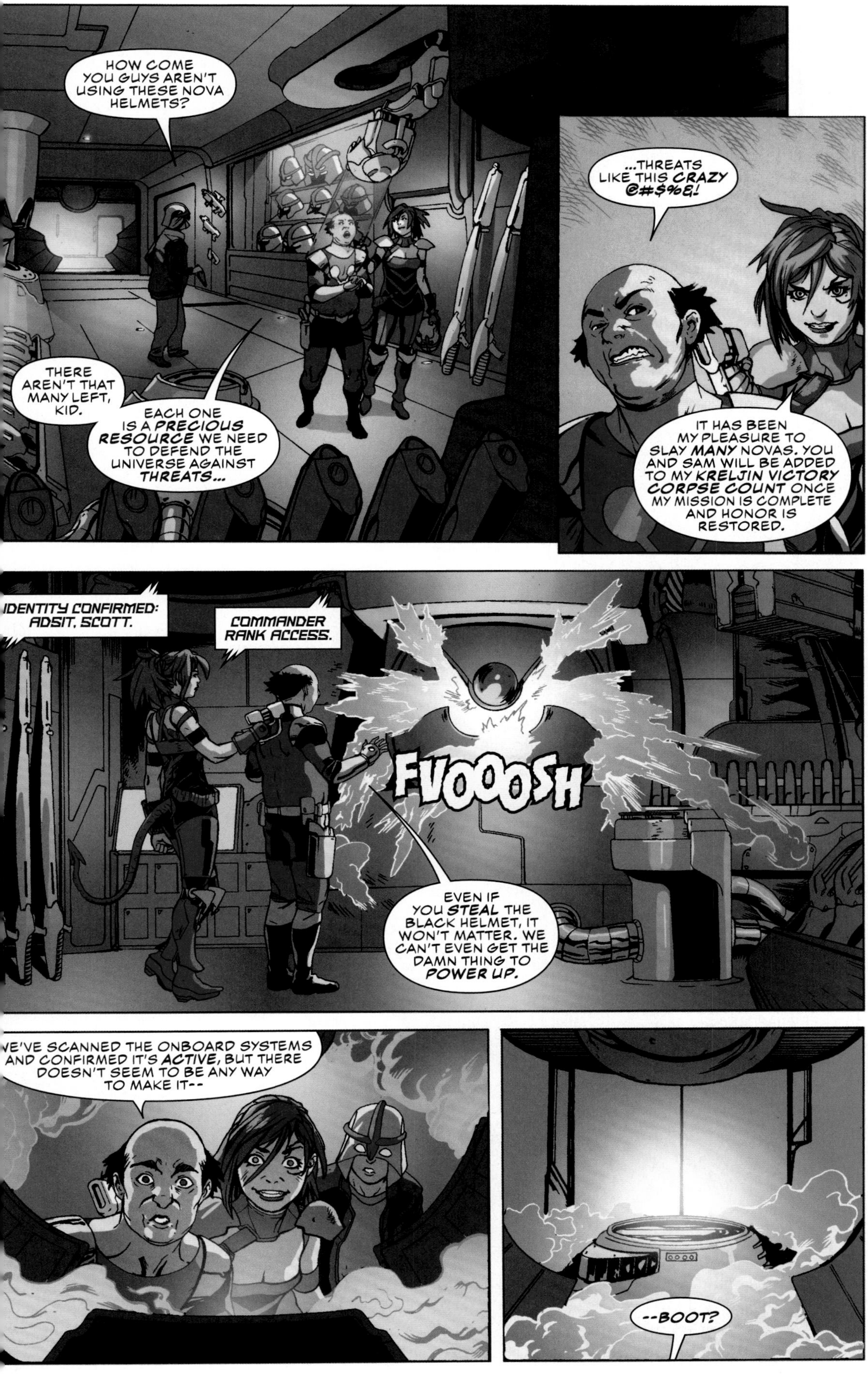
HOW COME YOU GUYS AREN'T USING THESE NOVA HELMETS?
THERE AREN'T THAT MANY LEFT, KID.
EACH ONE IS A PRECIOUS RESOURCE WE NEED TO DEFEND THE UNIVERSE AGAINST THREATS...
...THREATS LIKE THIS CRAZY @#$%&!
IT HAS BEEN MY PLEASURE TO SLAY MANY NOVAS. YOU AND SAM WILL BE ADDED TO MY KRELJIN VICTORY CORPSE COUNT ONCE MY MISSION IS COMPLETE AND HONOR IS RESTORED.
IDENTITY CONFIRMED: ADSIT, SCOTT.
COMMANDER RANK ACCESS.
FVOOOSH
EVEN IF YOU STEAL THE BLACK HELMET, IT WON'T MATTER. WE CAN'T EVEN GET THE DAMN THING TO POWER UP.
WE'VE SCANNED THE ONBOARD SYSTEMS AND CONFIRMED IT'S ACTIVE, BUT THERE DOESN'T SEEM TO BE ANY WAY TO MAKE IT--
--BOOT?

IDENTITY CONFIRMED: ᛗᛈᚾᚱᚲ

ALL ACCESS GRANTED.

STOP THE *SECURITY FOOTAGE!*

WE WERE *ALREADY ROBBED!*

WHO THE @#$% WAS THAT?!*

*A MEMBER OF THE INFAMOUS *THIEVES GUILD*, AS SHOWN AMAZING SPIDER-MAN (2018) #9. THE GUILD STOLE NOVA'S HELM AND DOZENS OF OTHER IMPORTANT ITEMS FROM VARIOUS HEROES. --T

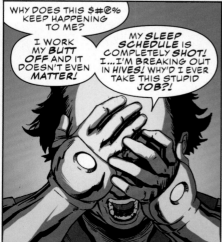

WHY DOES THIS $#@% KEEP HAPPENING TO ME?

I WORK MY *BUTT OFF* AND IT DOESN'T EVEN *MATTER!*

MY *SLEEP SCHEDULE* IS COMPLETELY *SHOT!* I...I'M BREAKING OUT IN *HIVES!* WHY'D I EVER TAKE THIS STUPID *JOB?!*

YOUR ADMINISTRATIVE INCOMPETENCE MEANS *NOTHING* TO ME.

FIND.

THAT.

HELMET.

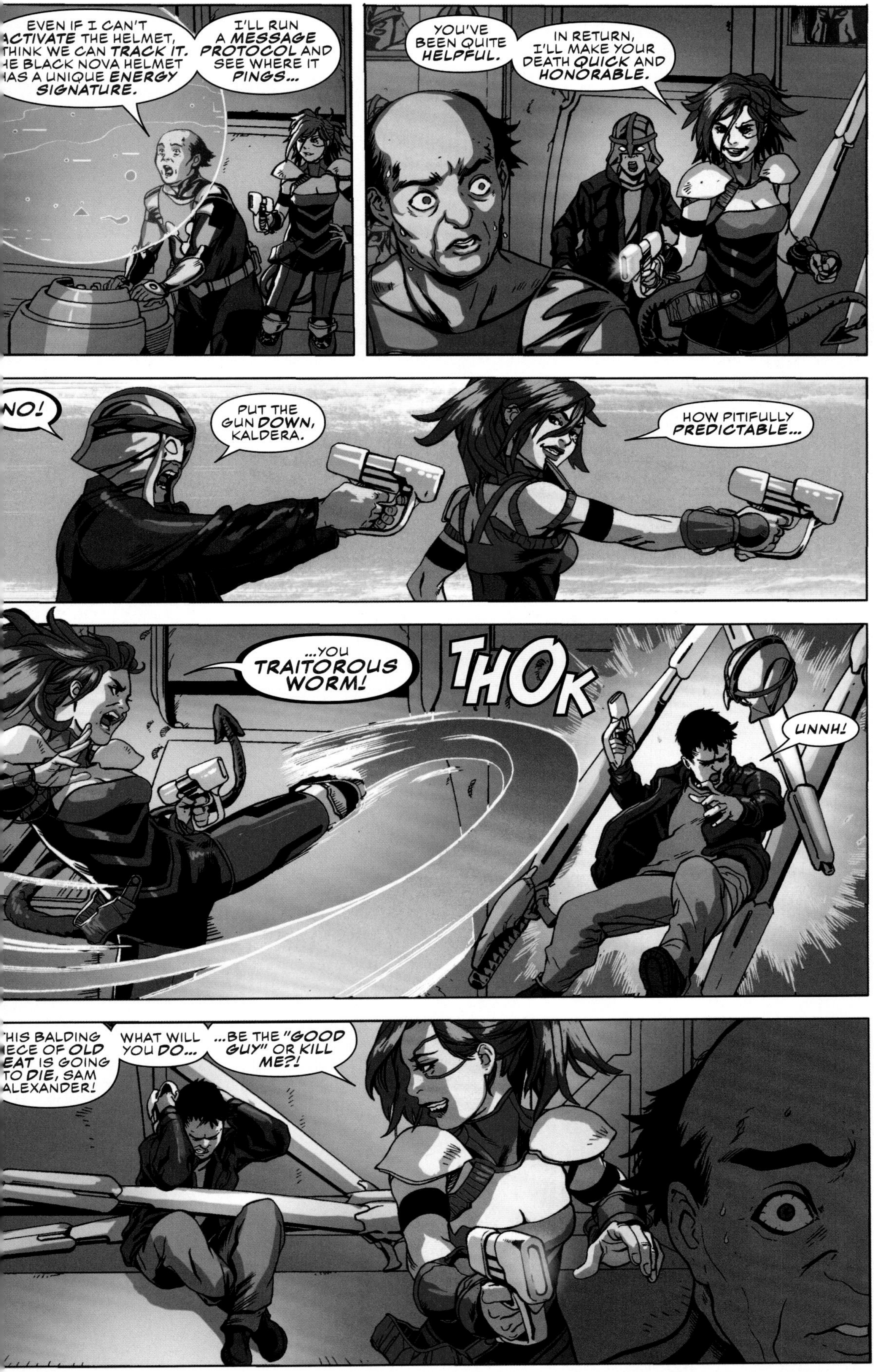
EVEN IF I CAN'T ACTIVATE THE HELMET, THINK WE CAN TRACK IT. HE BLACK NOVA HELMET HAS A UNIQUE ENERGY SIGNATURE.
I'LL RUN A MESSAGE PROTOCOL AND SEE WHERE IT PINGS...
YOU'VE BEEN QUITE HELPFUL.
IN RETURN, I'LL MAKE YOUR DEATH QUICK AND HONORABLE.
NO!
PUT THE GUN DOWN, KALDERA.
HOW PITIFULLY PREDICTABLE...
...YOU TRAITOROUS WORM!
THOK
UNNH!
THIS BALDING IECE OF OLD EAT IS GOING TO DIE, SAM ALEXANDER!
WHAT WILL YOU DO...
...BE THE "GOOD GUY" OR KILL ME?!

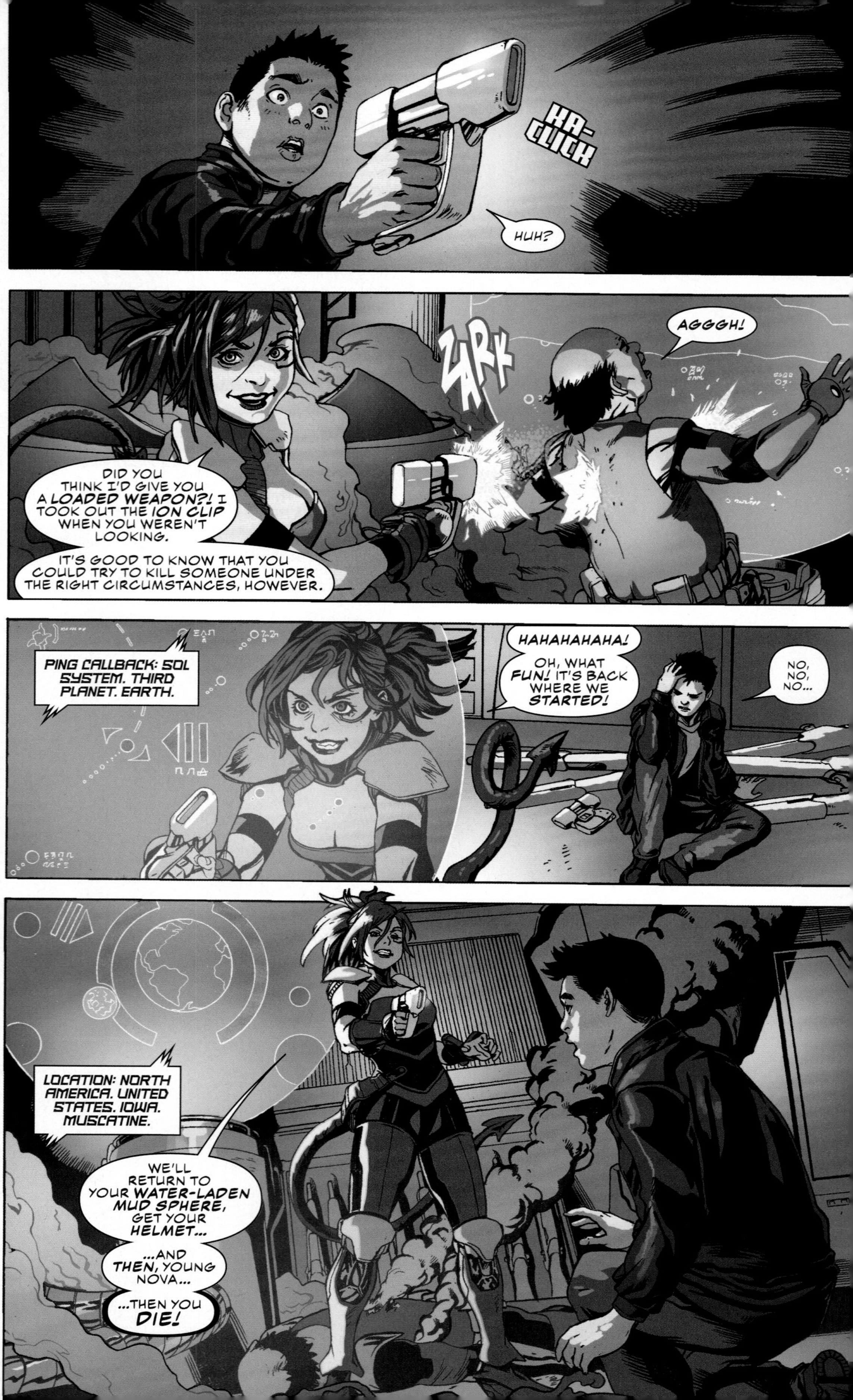
KA-CLICK
HUH?
ZARK
AGGGH!
DID YOU THINK I'D GIVE YOU A LOADED WEAPON?! I TOOK OUT THE ION CLIP WHEN YOU WEREN'T LOOKING.
IT'S GOOD TO KNOW THAT YOU COULD TRY TO KILL SOMEONE UNDER THE RIGHT CIRCUMSTANCES, HOWEVER.
PING CALLBACK: SOL SYSTEM. THIRD PLANET. EARTH.
HAHAHAHAHA!
OH, WHAT FUN! IT'S BACK WHERE WE STARTED!
NO, NO, NO...
LOCATION: NORTH AMERICA. UNITED STATES. IOWA. MUSCATINE.
WE'LL RETURN TO YOUR WATER-LADEN MUD SPHERE, GET YOUR HELMET...
...AND THEN, YOUNG NOVA...
...THEN YOU DIE!

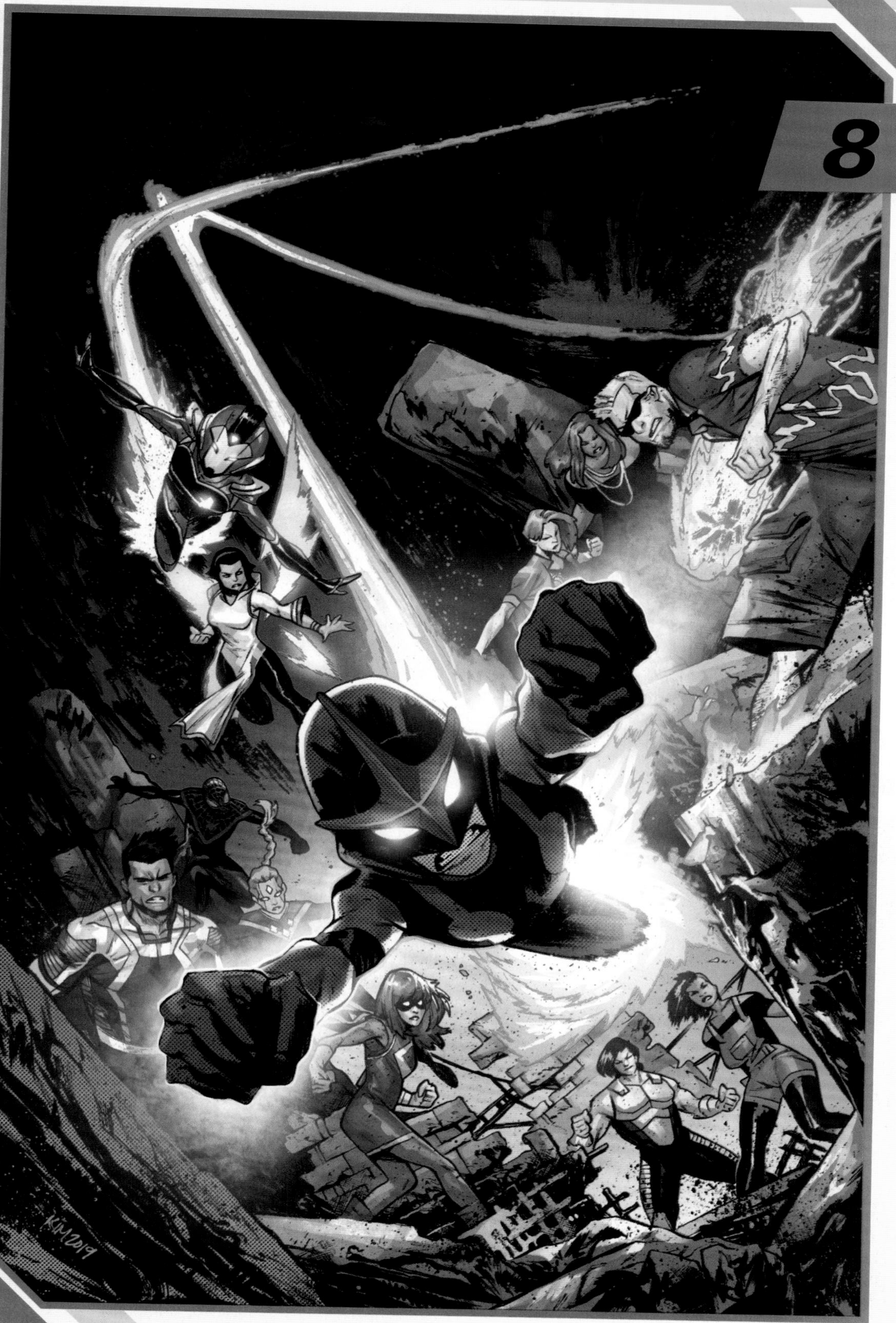
8
KIM 2019

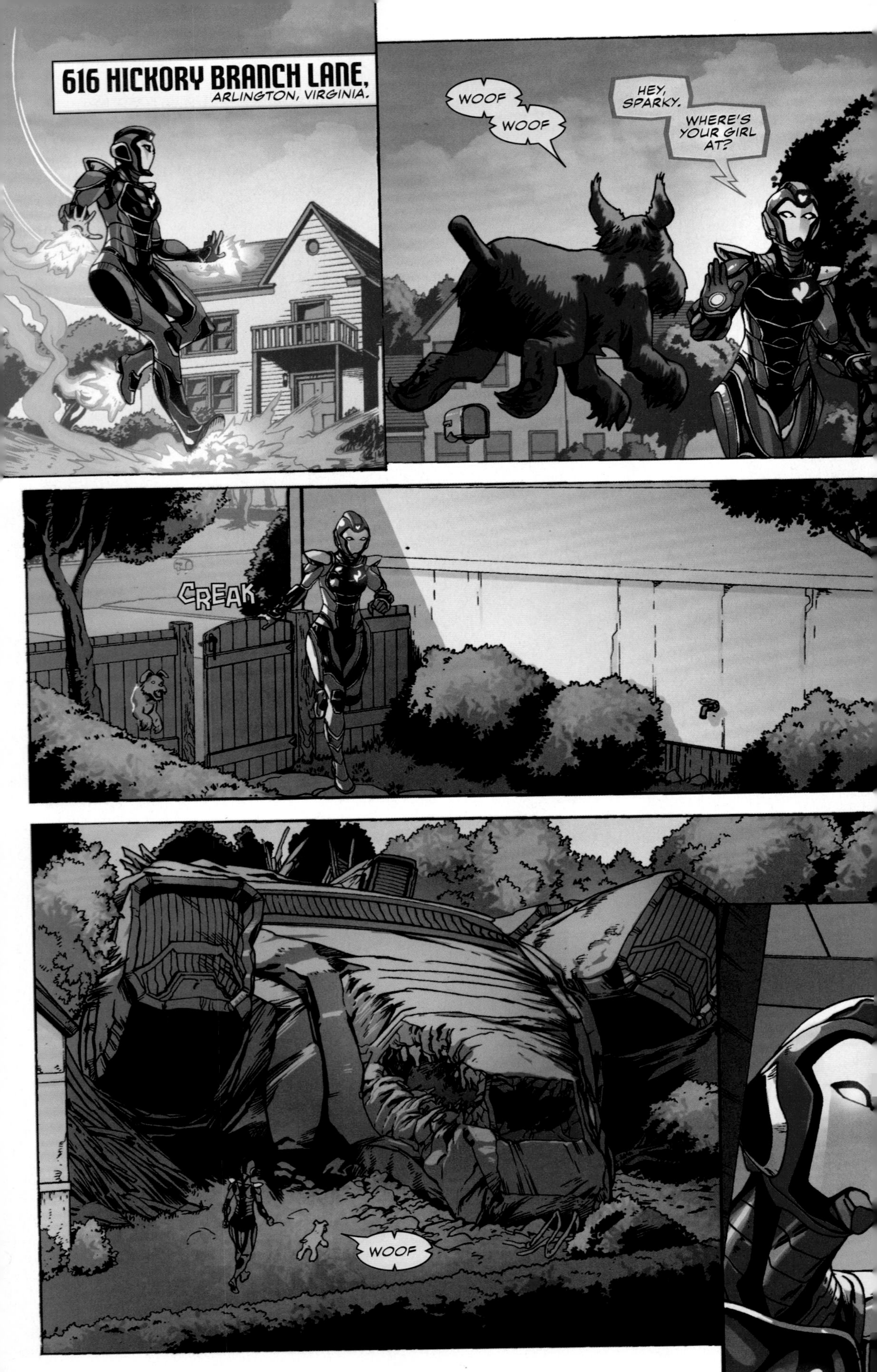
616 HICKORY BRANCH LANE,
ARLINGTON, VIRGINIA.
WOOF
WOOF
HEY, SPARKY.
WHERE'S YOUR GIRL AT?
CREAK
WOOF

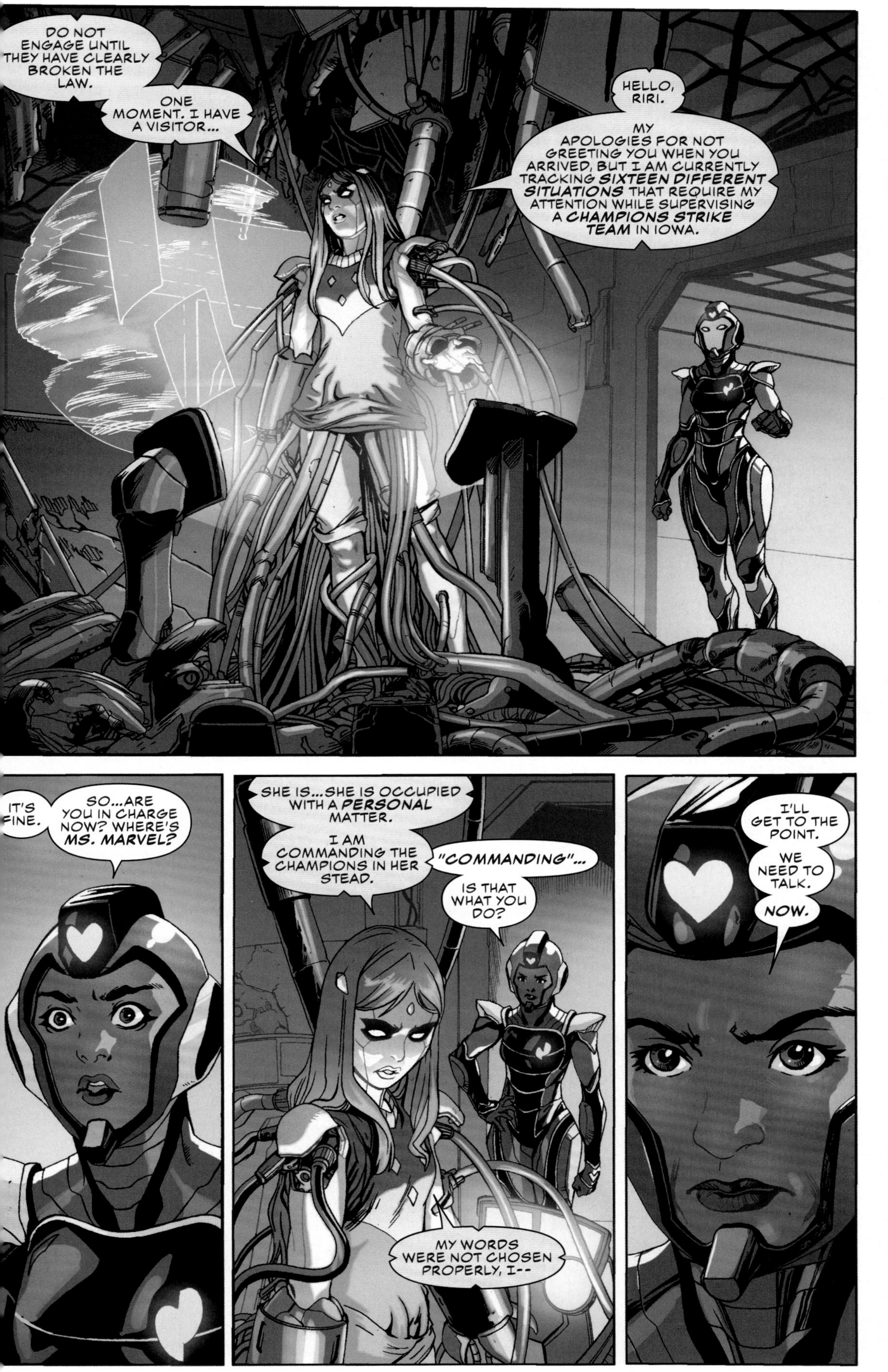

DO NOT ENGAGE UNTIL THEY HAVE CLEARLY BROKEN THE LAW.
ONE MOMENT. I HAVE A VISITOR...
HELLO, RIRI.
MY APOLOGIES FOR NOT GREETING YOU WHEN YOU ARRIVED, BUT I AM CURRENTLY TRACKING *SIXTEEN DIFFERENT SITUATIONS* THAT REQUIRE MY ATTENTION WHILE SUPERVISING A *CHAMPIONS STRIKE TEAM* IN IOWA.
IT'S FINE.
SO...ARE YOU IN CHARGE NOW? WHERE'S *MS. MARVEL?*
SHE IS...SHE IS OCCUPIED WITH A *PERSONAL* MATTER.
I AM COMMANDING THE CHAMPIONS IN HER STEAD.
"COMMANDING"...
IS THAT WHAT YOU DO?
MY WORDS WERE NOT CHOSEN PROPERLY, I--
I'LL GET TO THE POINT.
WE NEED TO TALK.
NOW.

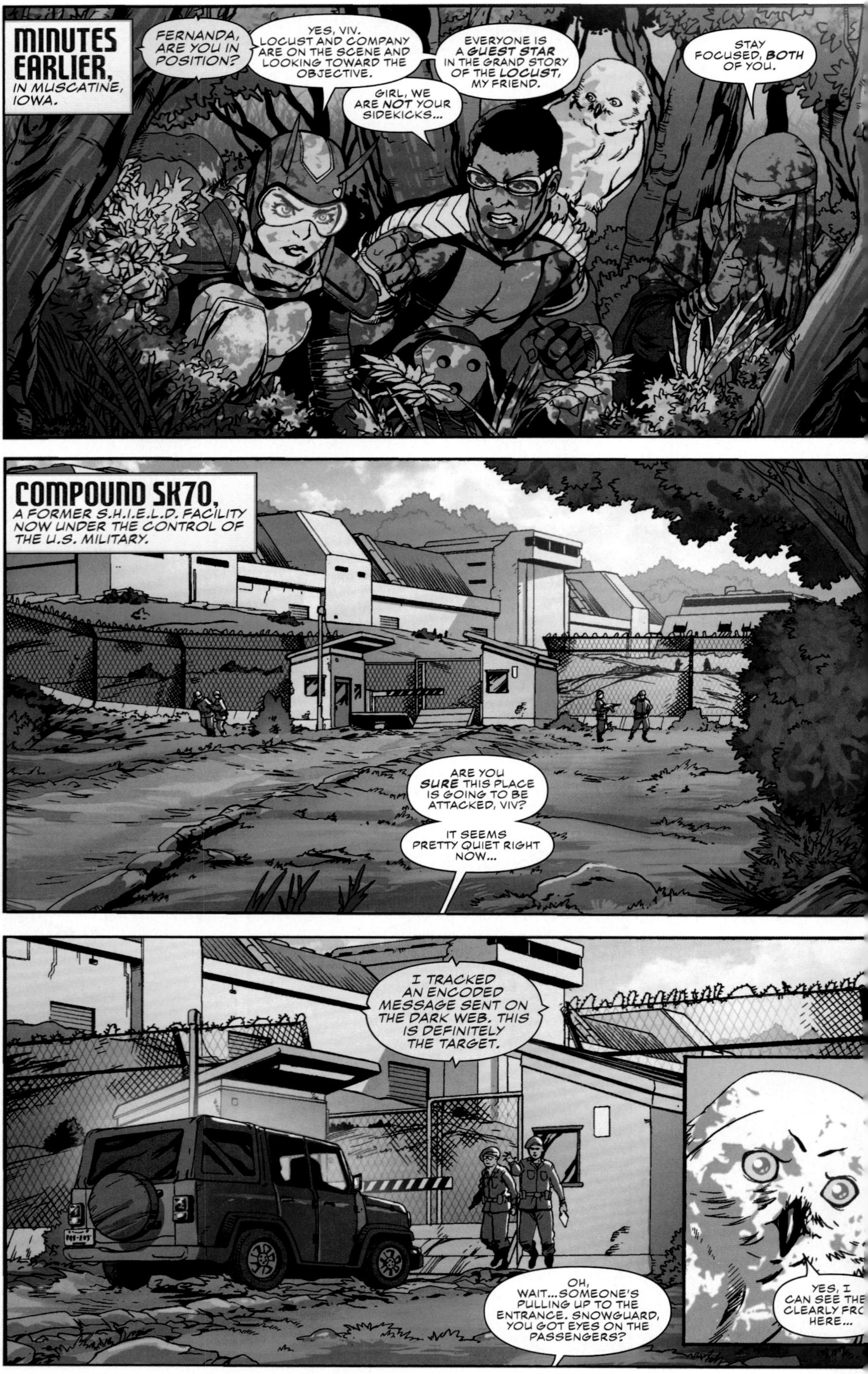
MINUTES EARLIER, IN MUSCATINE, IOWA.
FERNANDA, ARE YOU IN POSITION?
YES, VIV. LOCUST AND COMPANY ARE ON THE SCENE AND LOOKING TOWARD THE OBJECTIVE.
GIRL, WE ARE NOT YOUR SIDEKICKS...
EVERYONE IS A GUEST STAR IN THE GRAND STORY OF THE LOCUST, MY FRIEND.
STAY FOCUSED, BOTH OF YOU.
COMPOUND SK70, A FORMER S.H.I.E.L.D. FACILITY NOW UNDER THE CONTROL OF THE U.S. MILITARY.
ARE YOU SURE THIS PLACE IS GOING TO BE ATTACKED, VIV?
IT SEEMS PRETTY QUIET RIGHT NOW...
I TRACKED AN ENCODED MESSAGE SENT ON THE DARK WEB. THIS IS DEFINITELY THE TARGET.
OH, WAIT...SOMEONE'S PULLING UP TO THE ENTRANCE. SNOWGUARD, YOU GOT EYES ON THE PASSENGERS?
YES, I CAN SEE THE CLEARLY FR HERE...

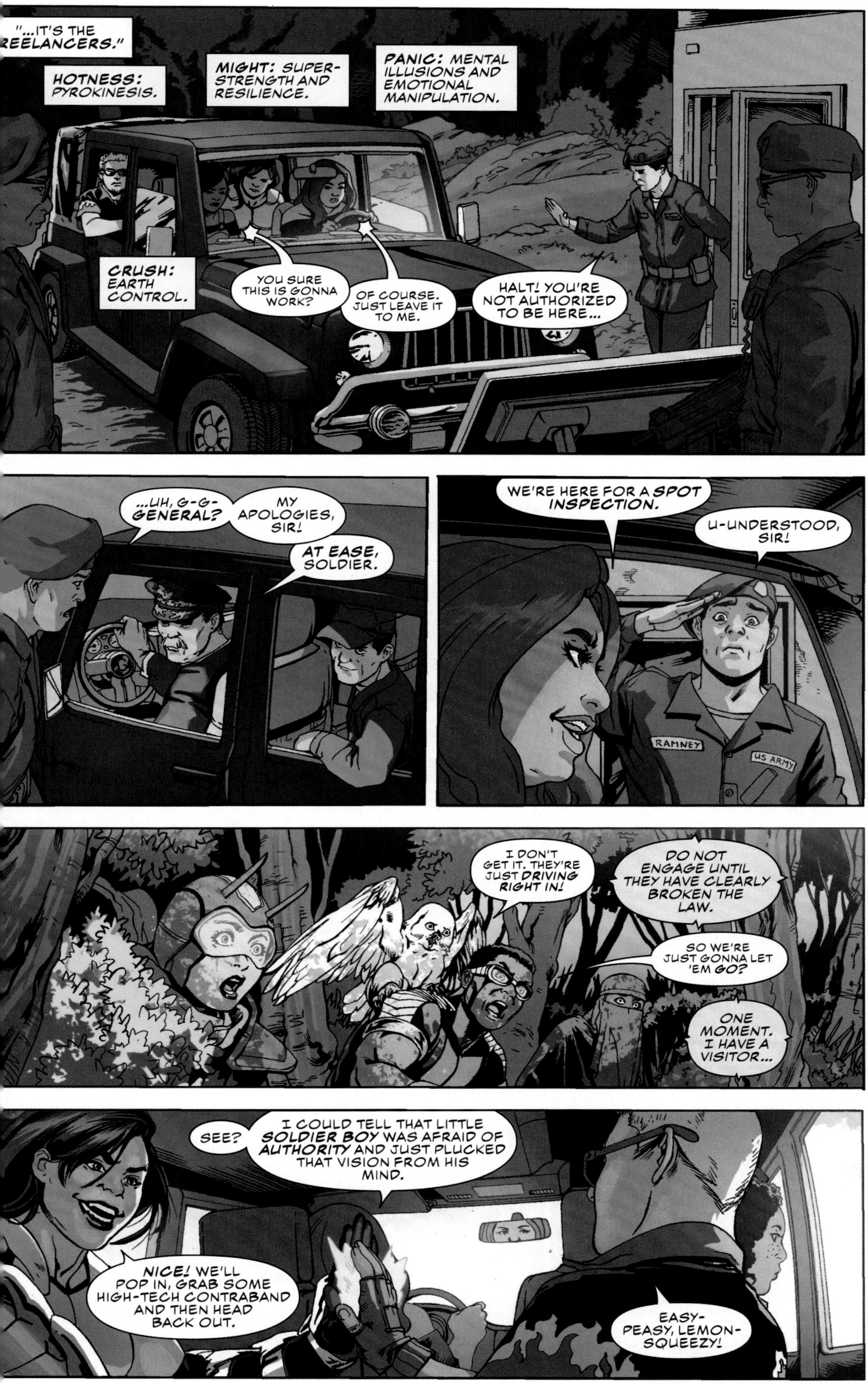
"...IT'S THE
REELANCERS."
HOTNESS: PYROKINESIS.
MIGHT: SUPER-STRENGTH AND RESILIENCE.
PANIC: MENTAL ILLUSIONS AND EMOTIONAL MANIPULATION.
CRUSH: EARTH CONTROL.
YOU SURE THIS IS GONNA WORK?
OF COURSE. JUST LEAVE IT TO ME.
HALT! YOU'RE NOT AUTHORIZED TO BE HERE...
...UH, G-G-GENERAL?
MY APOLOGIES, SIR!
AT EASE, SOLDIER.
WE'RE HERE FOR A SPOT INSPECTION.
U-UNDERSTOOD, SIR!
RAMNEY
US ARMY
I DON'T GET IT. THEY'RE JUST DRIVING RIGHT IN!
DO NOT ENGAGE UNTIL THEY HAVE CLEARLY BROKEN THE LAW.
SO WE'RE JUST GONNA LET 'EM GO?
ONE MOMENT. I HAVE A VISITOR...
SEE?
I COULD TELL THAT LITTLE SOLDIER BOY WAS AFRAID OF AUTHORITY AND JUST PLUCKED THAT VISION FROM HIS MIND.
NICE! WE'LL POP IN, GRAB SOME HIGH-TECH CONTRABAND AND THEN HEAD BACK OUT.
EASY-PEASY, LEMON-SQUEEZY!

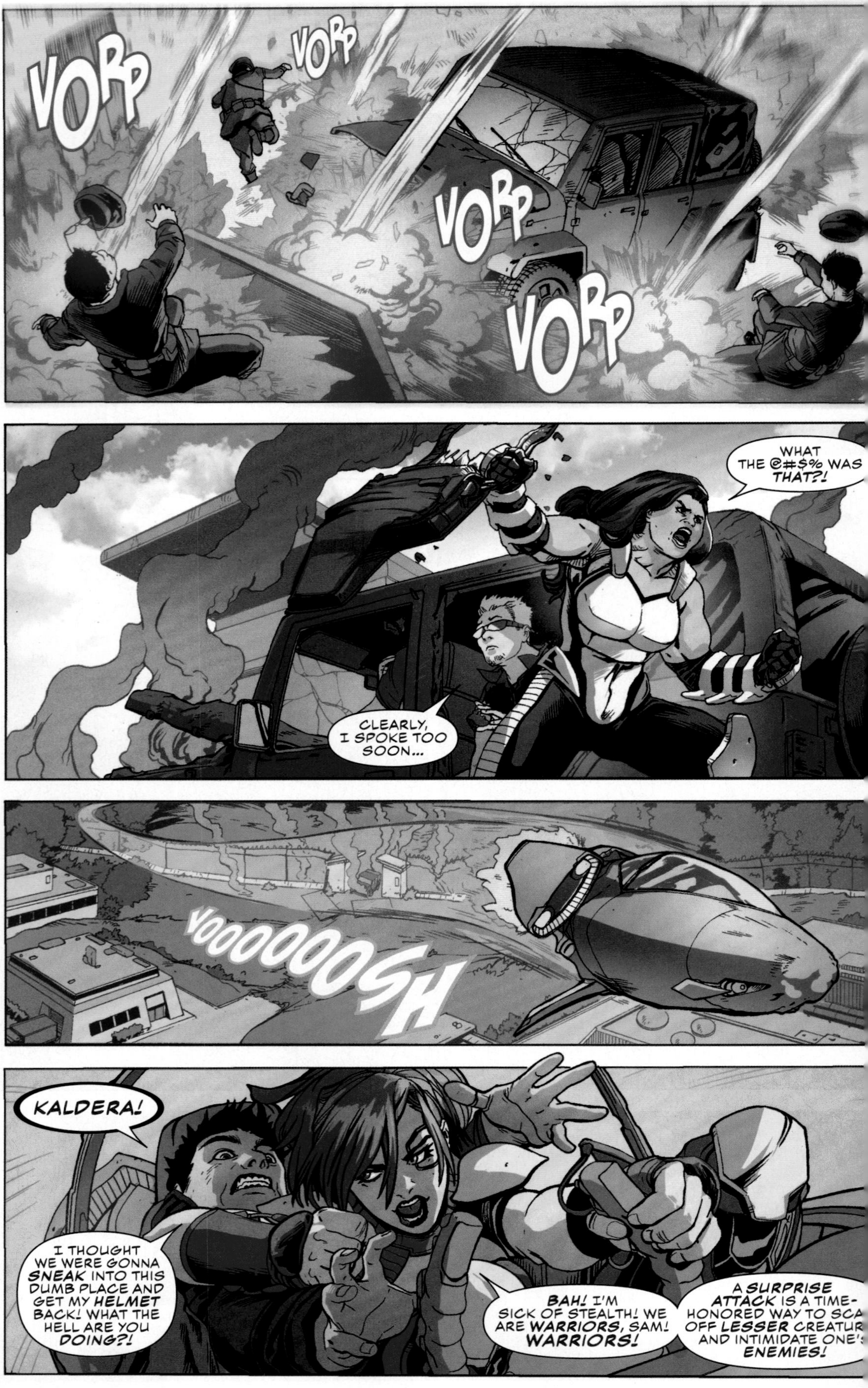
VORP
VORP
VORP
VORP
WHAT THE @#$% WAS THAT?!
CLEARLY, I SPOKE TOO SOON...
VOOOOOOSH
KALDERA!
I THOUGHT WE WERE GONNA SNEAK INTO THIS DUMB PLACE AND GET MY HELMET BACK! WHAT THE HELL ARE YOU DOING?!
BAH! I'M SICK OF STEALTH! WE ARE WARRIORS, SAM! WARRIORS!
A SURPRISE ATTACK IS A TIME-HONORED WAY TO SCA OFF LESSER CREATUR AND INTIMIDATE ONE'S ENEMIES!

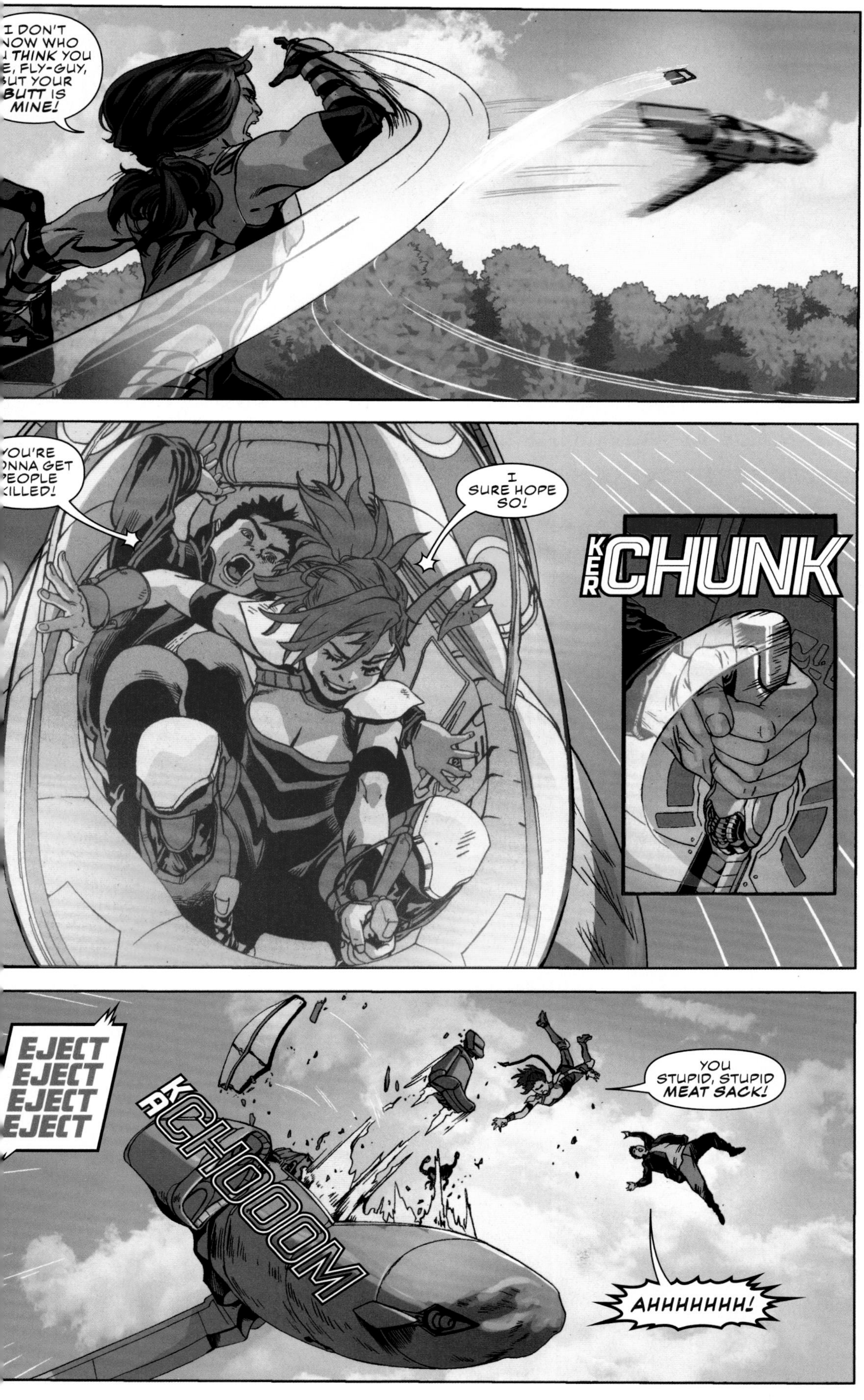
I DON'T NOW WHO U THINK YOU E, FLY-GUY, UT YOUR BUTT IS MINE!
YOU'RE ONNA GET PEOPLE KILLED!
I SURE HOPE SO!
KERCHUNK
EJECT EJECT EJECT EJECT
KACHOOOM
YOU STUPID, STUPID MEAT SACK!
AHHHHHHH!

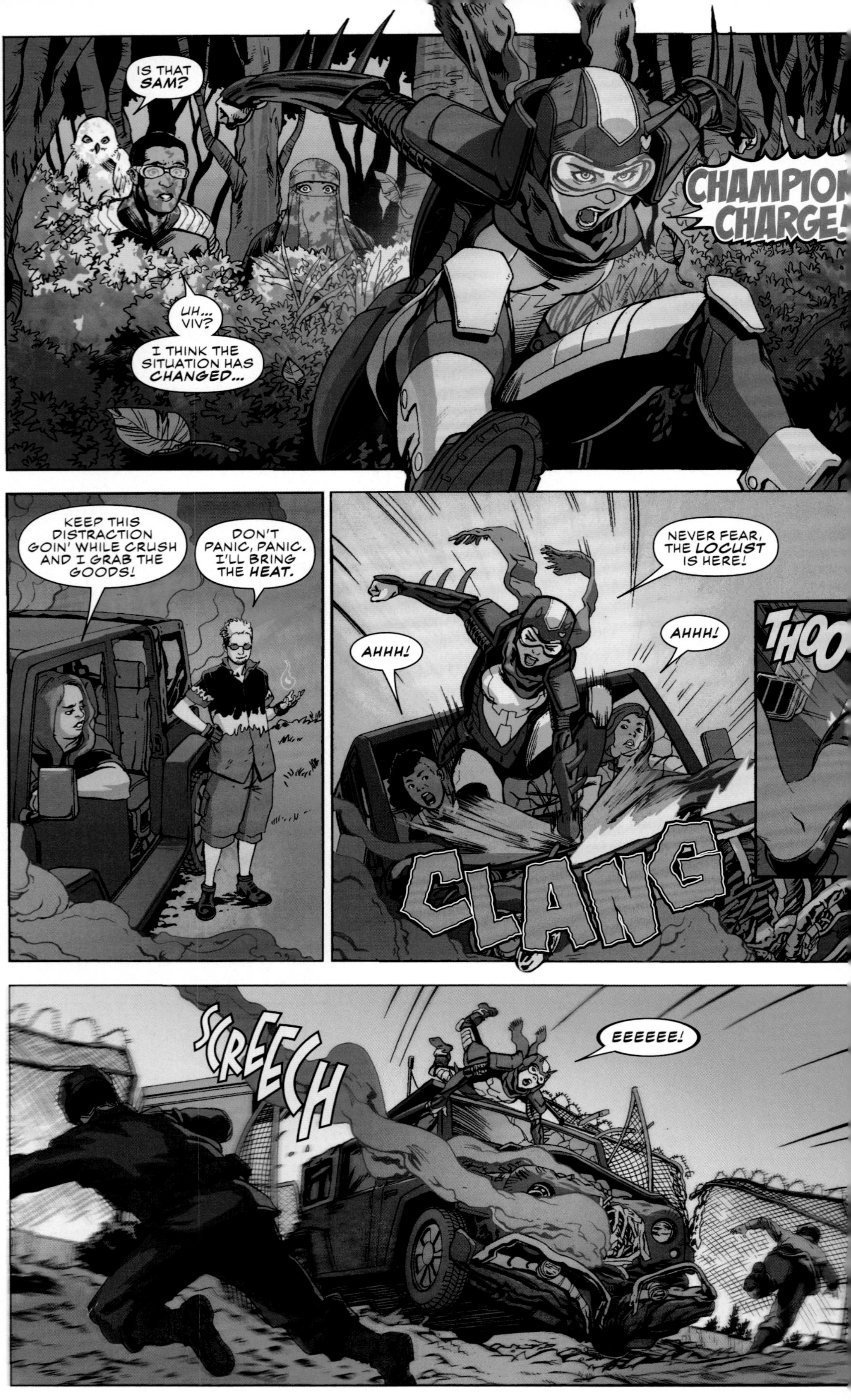
IS THAT SAM?
CHAMPION CHARGE!
UH... VIV?
I THINK THE SITUATION HAS CHANGED...
KEEP THIS DISTRACTION GOIN' WHILE CRUSH AND I GRAB THE GOODS!
DON'T PANIC, PANIC. I'LL BRING THE HEAT.
NEVER FEAR, THE LOCUST IS HERE!
AHHH!
AHHH!
CLANG
SCREECH
EEEEEE!

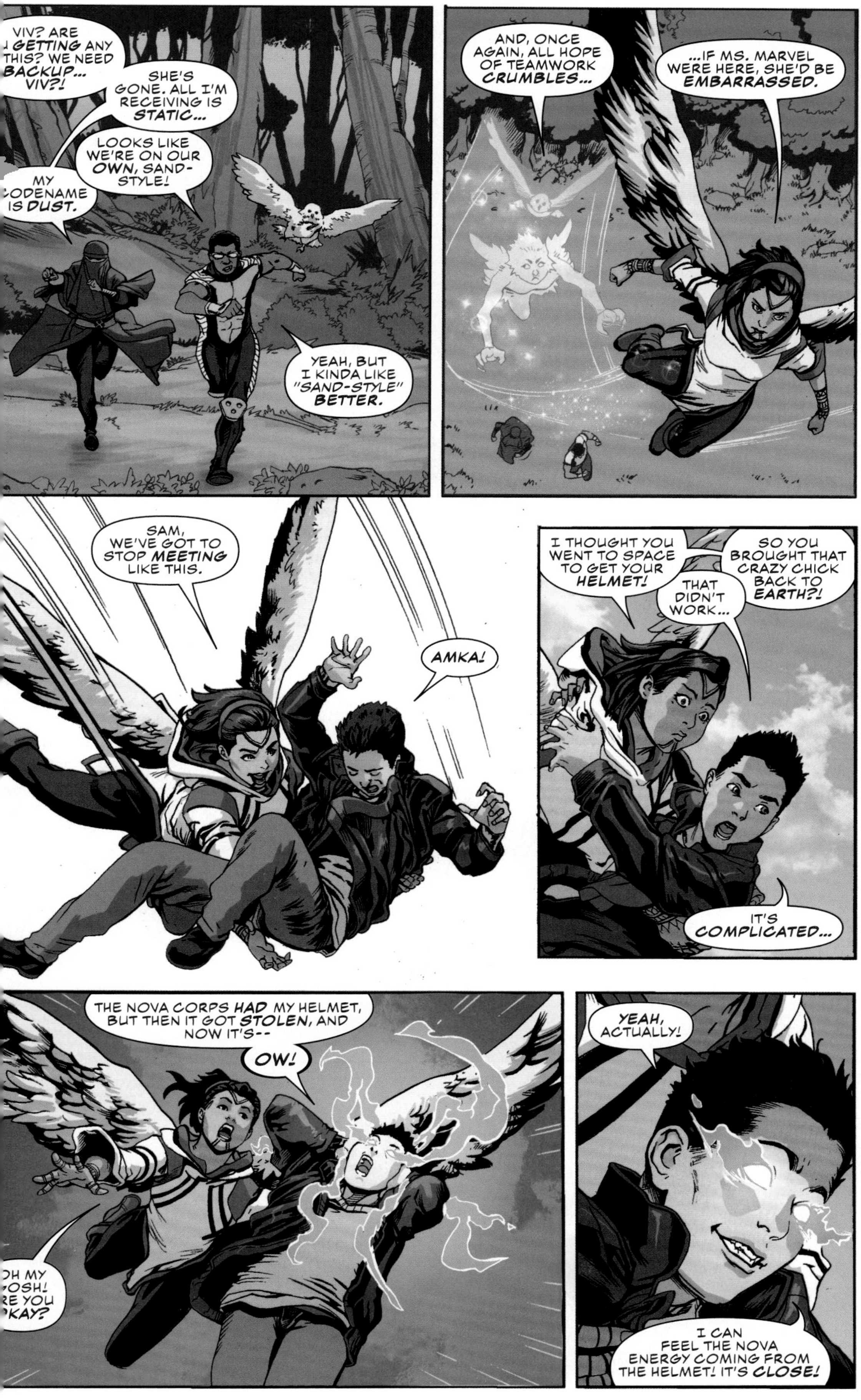

VIV? ARE U GETTING ANY THIS? WE NEED BACKUP... VIV?!
SHE'S GONE. ALL I'M RECEIVING IS STATIC...
LOOKS LIKE WE'RE ON OUR OWN, SAND-STYLE!
MY CODENAME IS DUST.
YEAH, BUT I KINDA LIKE "SAND-STYLE" BETTER.
AND, ONCE AGAIN, ALL HOPE OF TEAMWORK CRUMBLES...
...IF MS. MARVEL WERE HERE, SHE'D BE EMBARRASSED.
SAM, WE'VE GOT TO STOP MEETING LIKE THIS.
AMKA!
I THOUGHT YOU WENT TO SPACE TO GET YOUR HELMET!
SO YOU BROUGHT THAT CRAZY CHICK BACK TO EARTH?!
THAT DIDN'T WORK...
IT'S COMPLICATED...
THE NOVA CORPS HAD MY HELMET, BUT THEN IT GOT STOLEN, AND NOW IT'S--
OW!
OH MY GOSH! RE YOU KAY?
YEAH, ACTUALLY!
I CAN FEEL THE NOVA ENERGY COMING FROM THE HELMET! IT'S CLOSE!

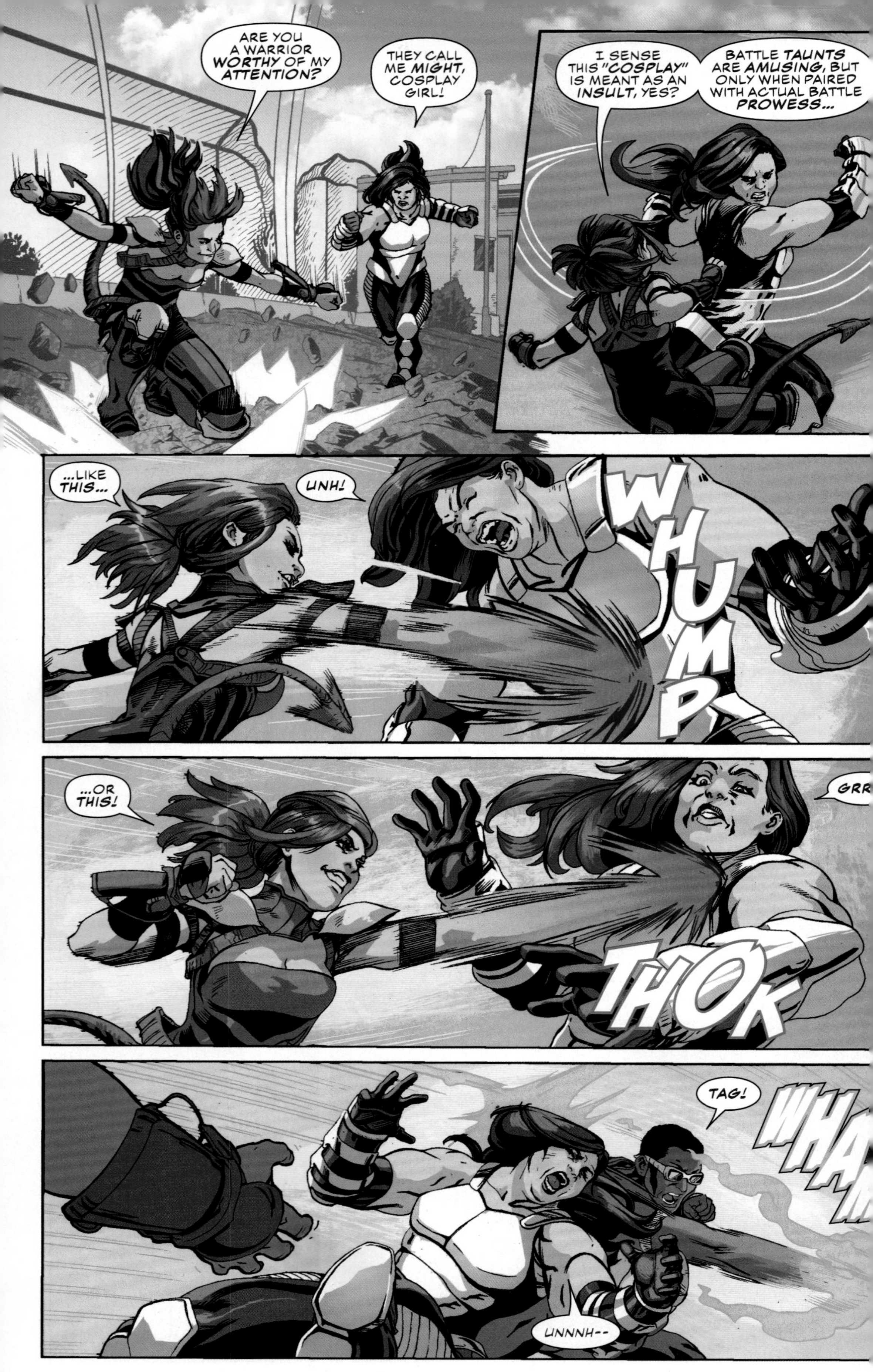
ARE YOU A WARRIOR WORTHY OF MY ATTENTION?
THEY CALL ME MIGHT, COSPLAY GIRL!
I SENSE THIS "COSPLAY" IS MEANT AS AN INSULT, YES?
BATTLE TAUNTS ARE AMUSING, BUT ONLY WHEN PAIRED WITH ACTUAL BATTLE PROWESS...
...LIKE THIS...
UNH!
WHUMP
...OR THIS!
GRR
THOK
TAG!
UNNNH--

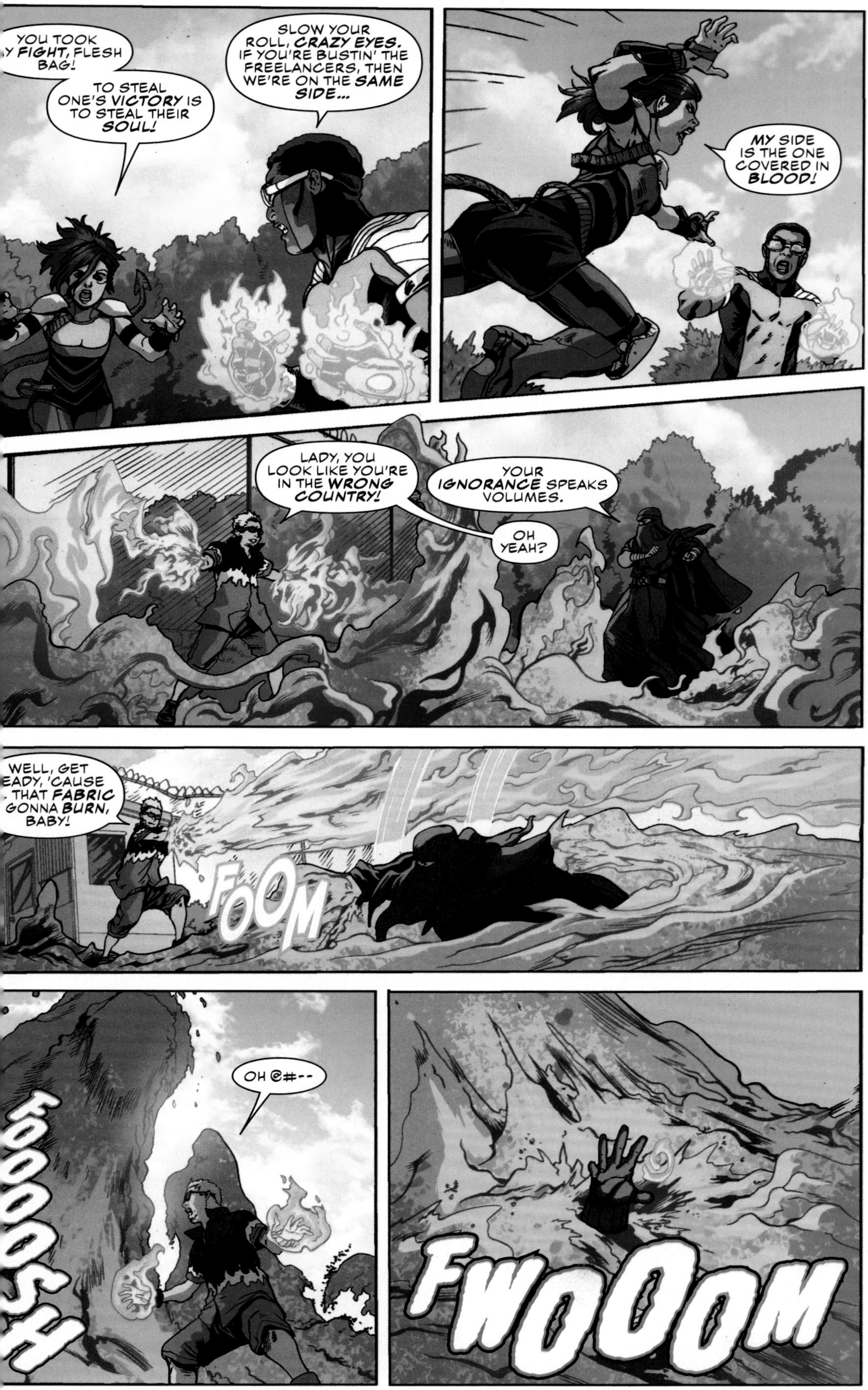

YOU TOOK Y FIGHT, FLESH BAG!
TO STEAL ONE'S VICTORY IS TO STEAL THEIR SOUL!
SLOW YOUR ROLL, CRAZY EYES. IF YOU'RE BUSTIN' THE FREELANCERS, THEN WE'RE ON THE SAME SIDE...
MY SIDE IS THE ONE COVERED IN BLOOD!
LADY, YOU LOOK LIKE YOU'RE IN THE WRONG COUNTRY!
YOUR IGNORANCE SPEAKS VOLUMES.
OH YEAH?
WELL, GET EADY, 'CAUSE THAT FABRIC GONNA BURN, BABY!
FOOM
FOOOOOSH
OH @#--
FWOOOM

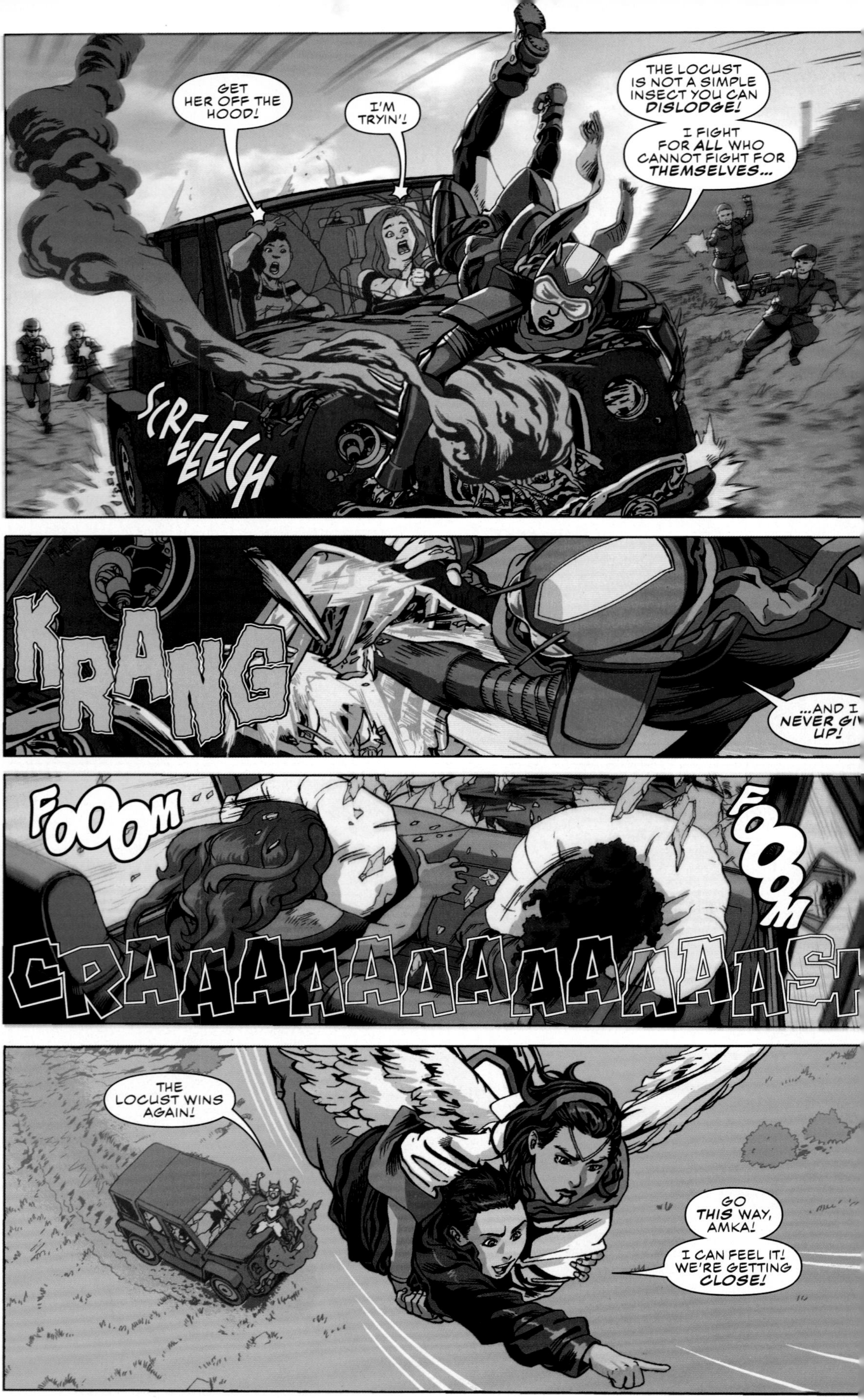
GET HER OFF THE HOOD!
I'M TRYIN'!
THE LOCUST IS NOT A SIMPLE INSECT YOU CAN DISLODGE!
I FIGHT FOR ALL WHO CANNOT FIGHT FOR THEMSELVES...
SCREEECH
KRANG
...AND I NEVER GI UP!
FOOOM
FOOOM
CRAAAAAAAAAAAAS
THE LOCUST WINS AGAIN!
GO THIS WAY, AMKA!
I CAN FEEL IT! WE'RE GETTING CLOSE!

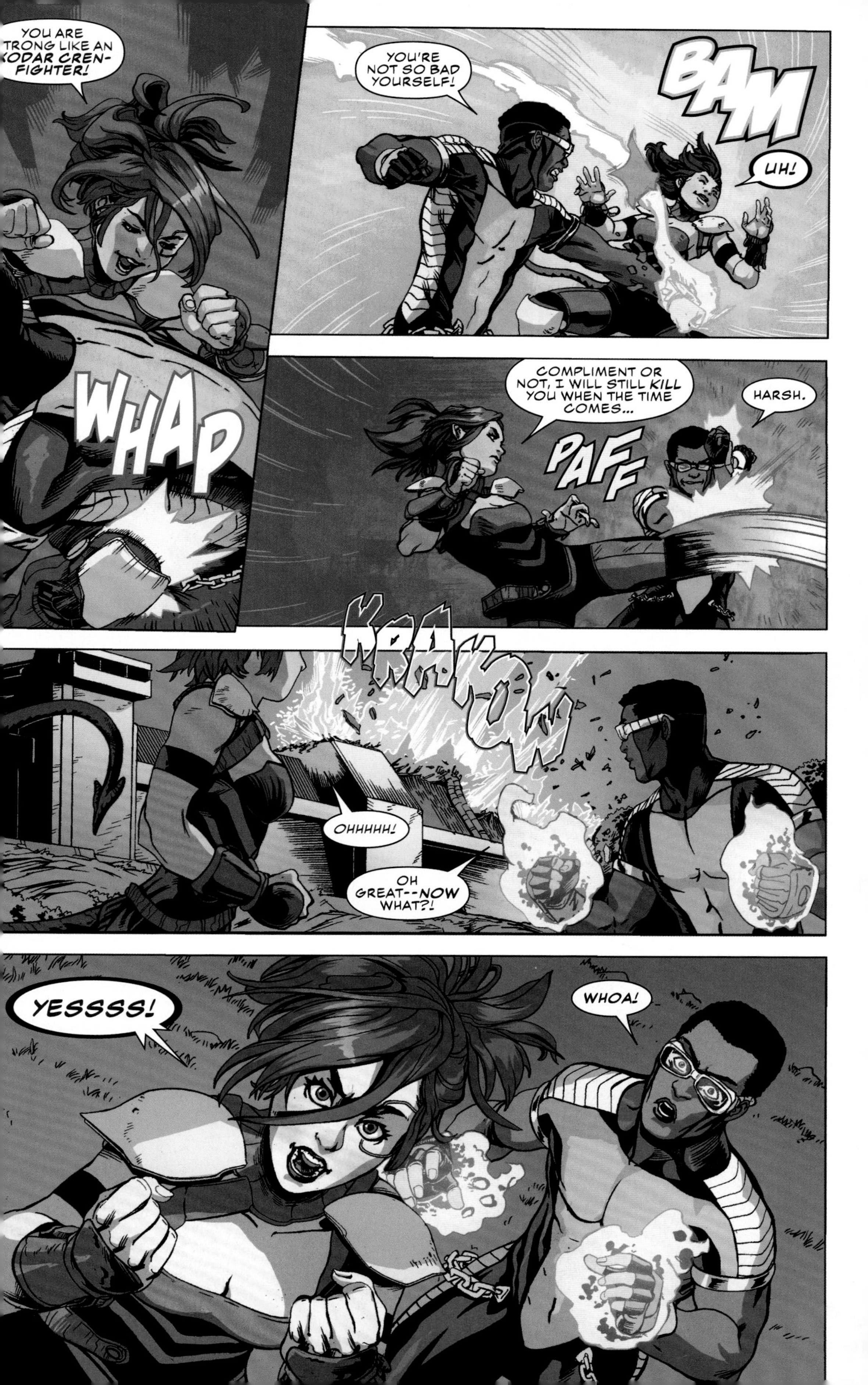
YOU ARE
TRONG LIKE AN
KODAR CREN-
FIGHTER!
YOU'RE NOT SO BAD YOURSELF!
BAM
UH!
WHAP
COMPLIMENT OR NOT, I WILL STILL KILL YOU WHEN THE TIME COMES...
HARSH.
PAFF
KRAKOW
OHHHHH!
OH GREAT--NOW WHAT?!
YESSSS!
WHOA!

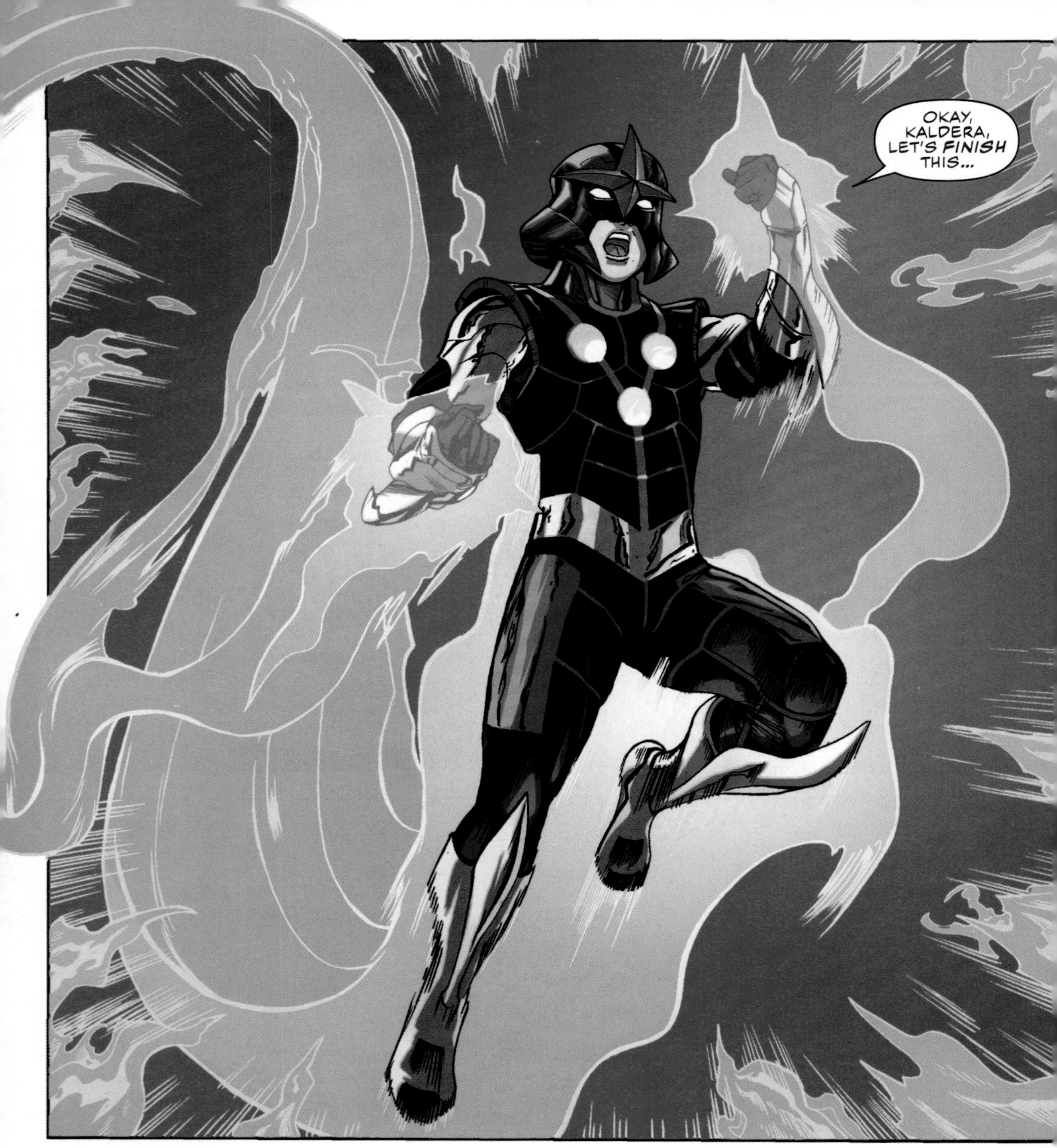
OKAY, KALDERA, LET'S FINISH THIS...

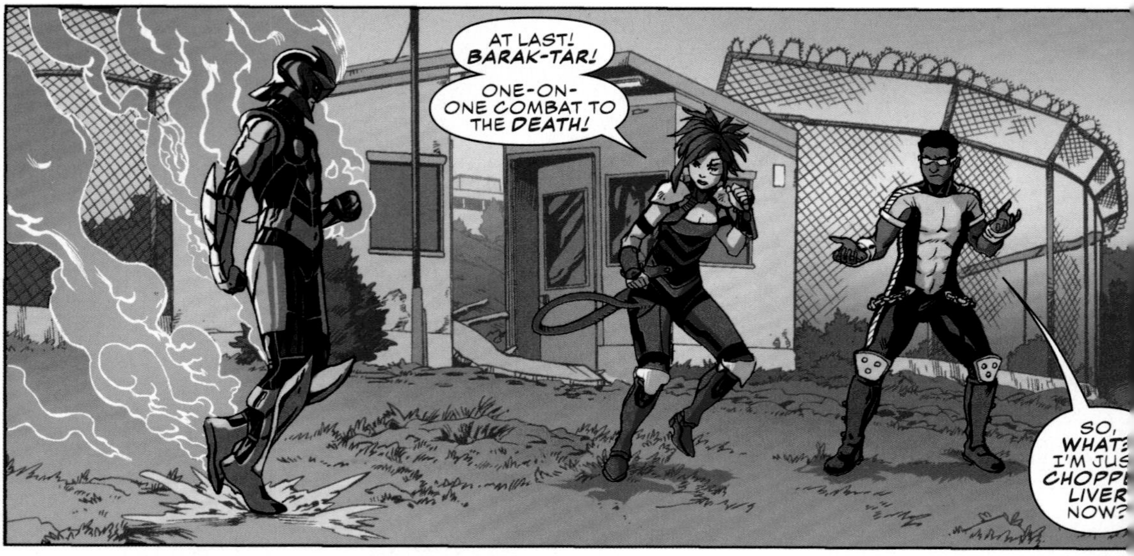
AT LAST! BARAK-TAR!
ONE-ON-ONE COMBAT TO THE DEATH!
SO, WHAT? I'M JUS CHOPP LIVER NOW?

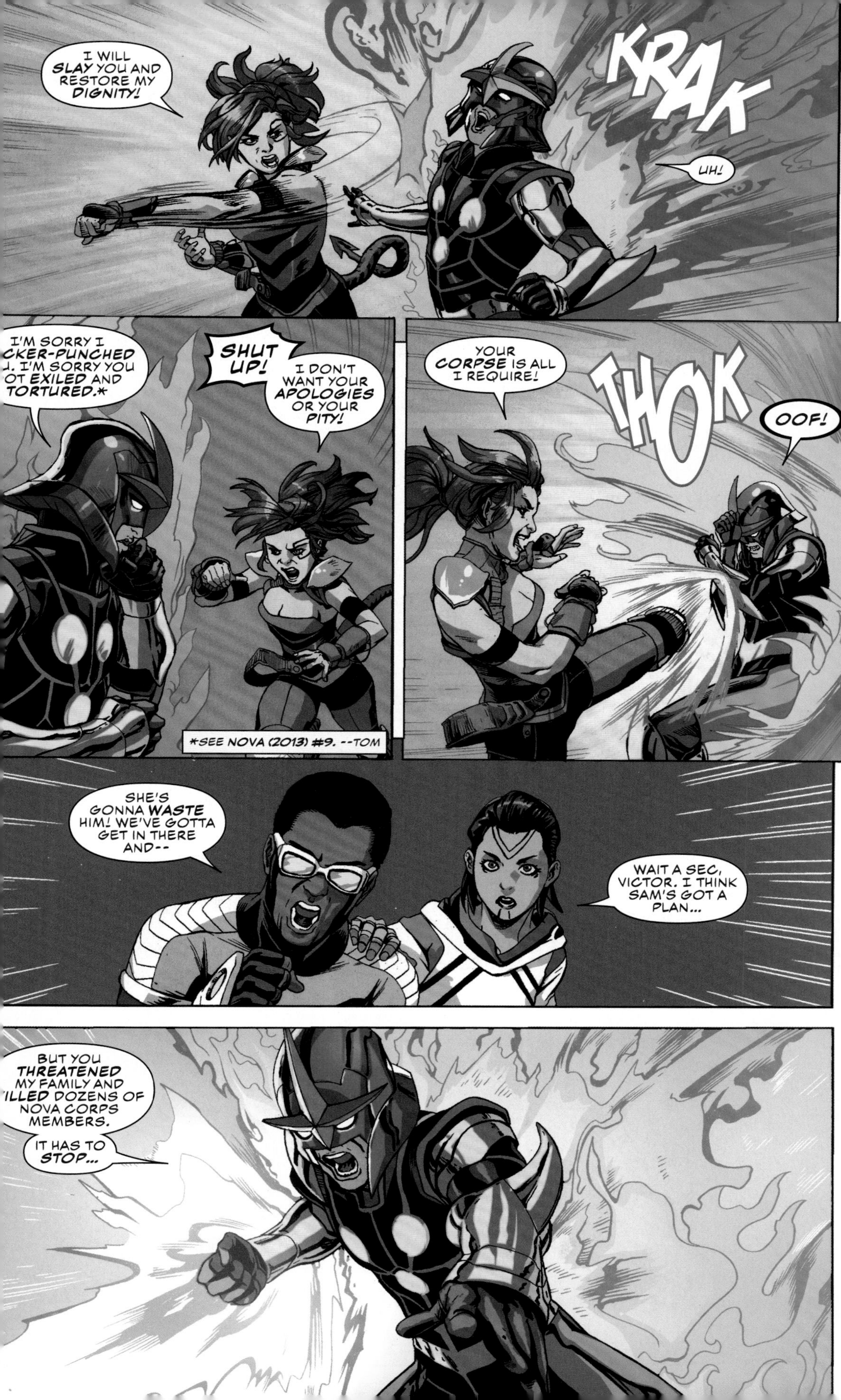
I WILL SLAY YOU AND RESTORE MY DIGNITY!
KRAK
UH!
I'M SORRY I CKER-PUNCHED U. I'M SORRY YOU OT EXILED AND TORTURED.*
SHUT UP!
I DON'T WANT YOUR APOLOGIES OR YOUR PITY!
*SEE NOVA (2013) #9. --TOM
YOUR CORPSE IS ALL I REQUIRE!
THOK
OOF!
SHE'S GONNA WASTE HIM! WE'VE GOTTA GET IN THERE AND--
WAIT A SEC, VICTOR. I THINK SAM'S GOT A PLAN...
BUT YOU THREATENED MY FAMILY AND ILLED DOZENS OF NOVA CORPS MEMBERS.
IT HAS TO STOP...

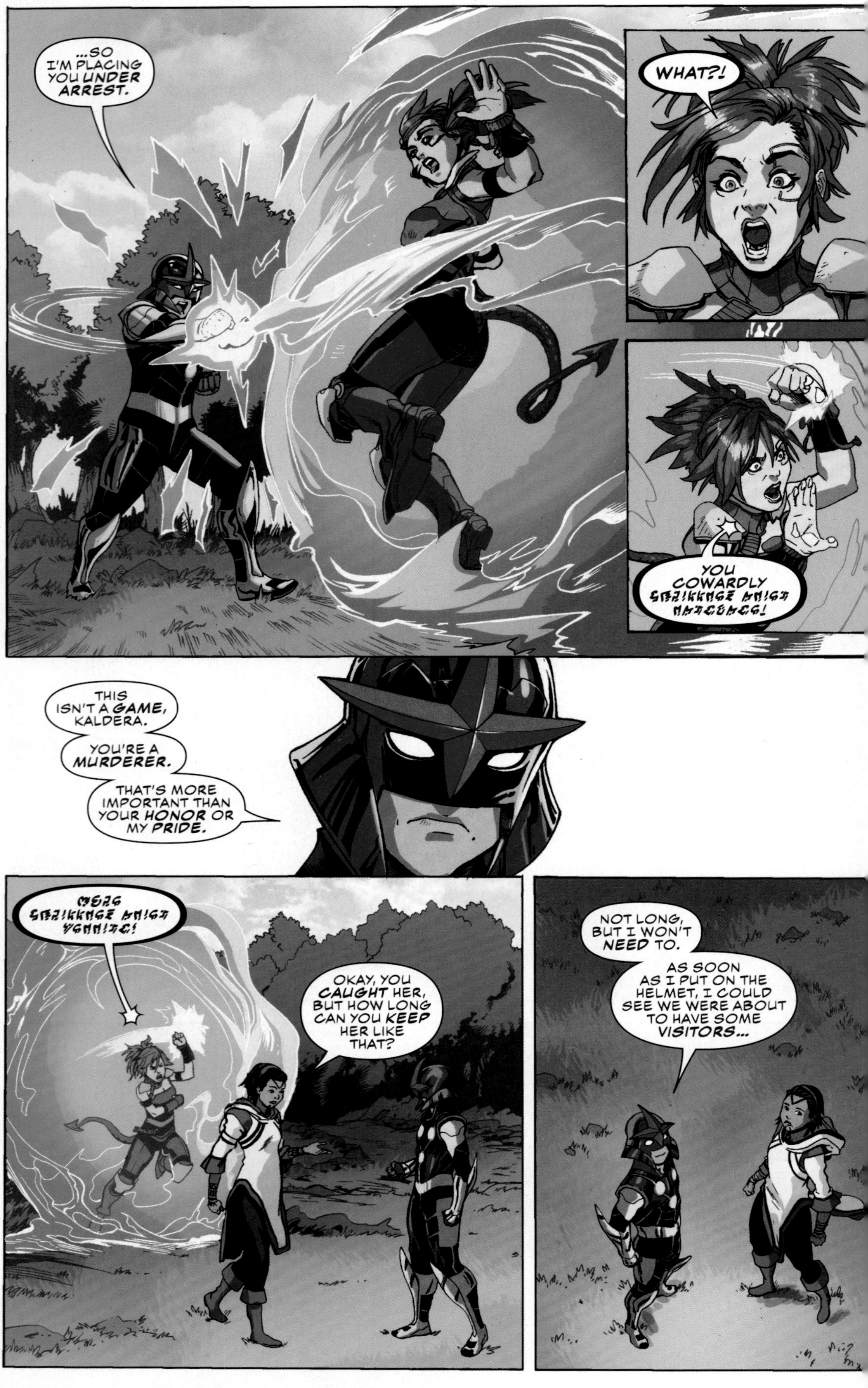

...SO I'M PLACING YOU UNDER ARREST.
WHAT?!
YOU COWARDLY
THIS ISN'T A GAME, KALDERA.
YOU'RE A MURDERER.
THAT'S MORE IMPORTANT THAN YOUR HONOR OR MY PRIDE.
OKAY, YOU CAUGHT HER, BUT HOW LONG CAN YOU KEEP HER LIKE THAT?
NOT LONG, BUT I WON'T NEED TO.
AS SOON AS I PUT ON THE HELMET, I COULD SEE WE WERE ABOUT TO HAVE SOME VISITORS...

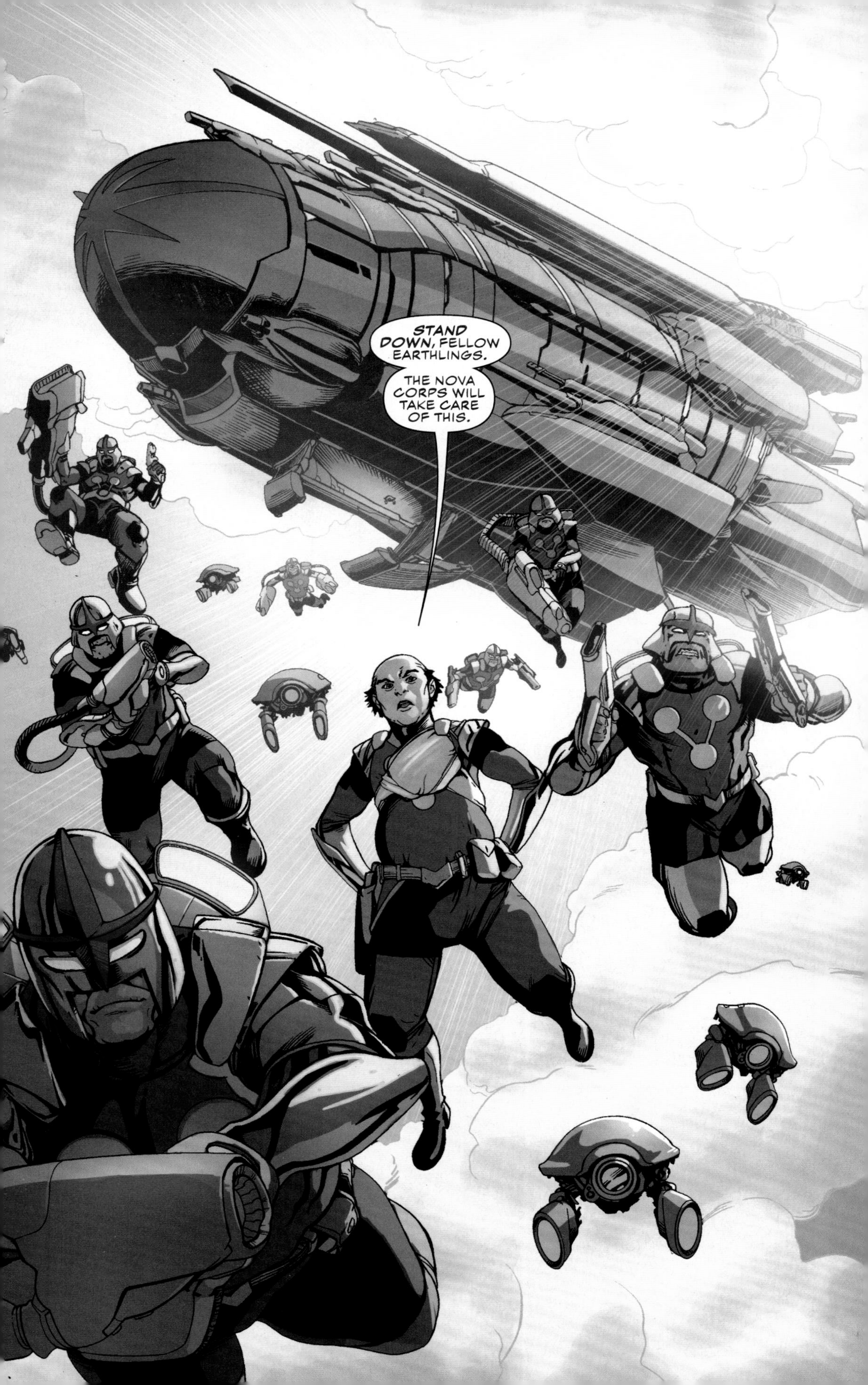
STAND DOWN, FELLOW EARTHLINGS.
THE NOVA CORPS WILL TAKE CARE OF THIS.

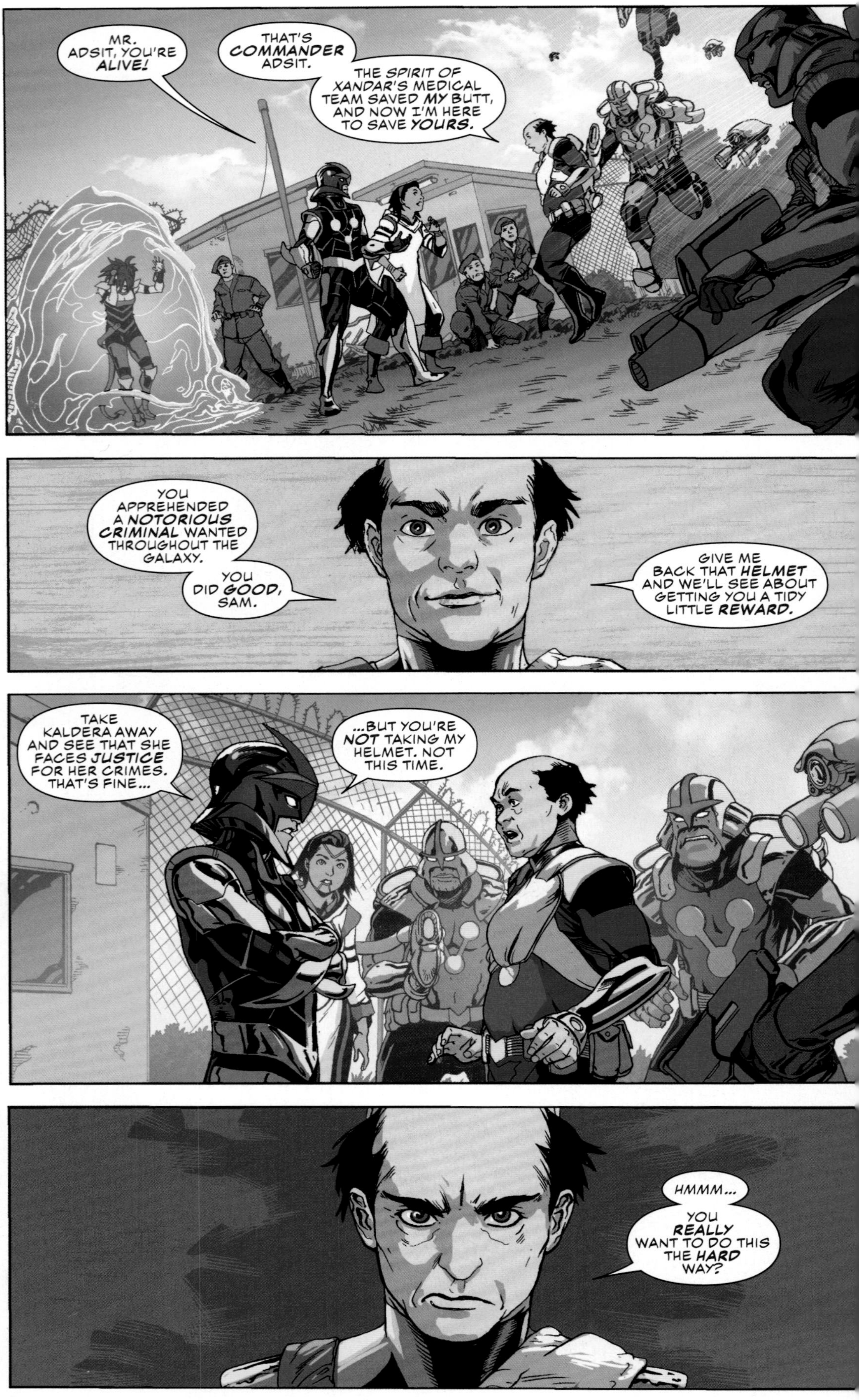
MR. ADSIT, YOU'RE ALIVE!
THAT'S COMMANDER ADSIT.
THE SPIRIT OF XANDAR'S MEDICAL TEAM SAVED MY BUTT, AND NOW I'M HERE TO SAVE YOURS.
YOU APPREHENDED A NOTORIOUS CRIMINAL WANTED THROUGHOUT THE GALAXY.
YOU DID GOOD, SAM.
GIVE ME BACK THAT HELMET AND WE'LL SEE ABOUT GETTING YOU A TIDY LITTLE REWARD.
TAKE KALDERA AWAY AND SEE THAT SHE FACES JUSTICE FOR HER CRIMES. THAT'S FINE...
...BUT YOU'RE NOT TAKING MY HELMET. NOT THIS TIME.
HMMM...
YOU REALLY WANT TO DO THIS THE HARD WAY?

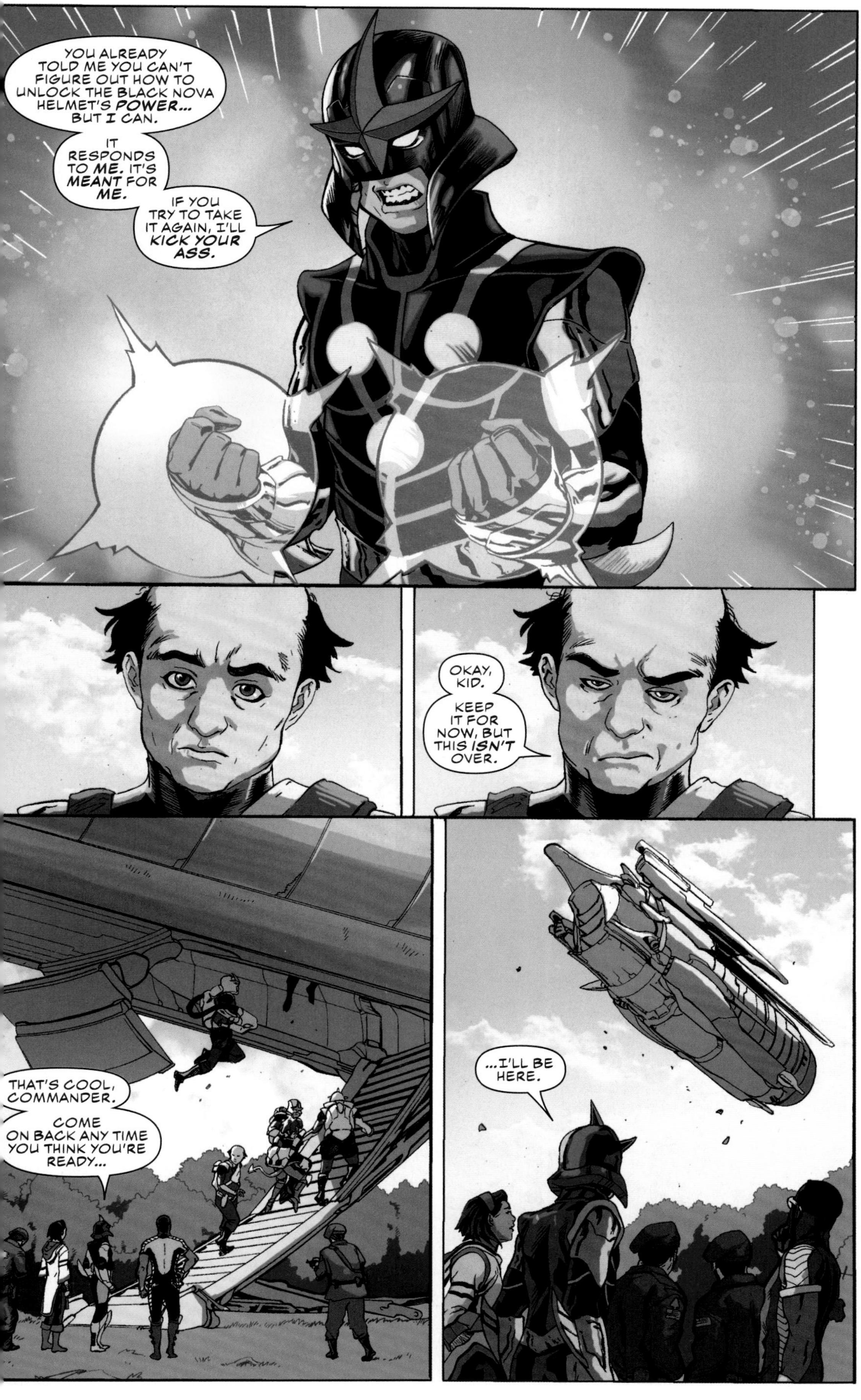
YOU ALREADY TOLD ME YOU CAN'T FIGURE OUT HOW TO UNLOCK THE BLACK NOVA HELMET'S POWER... BUT I CAN.
IT RESPONDS TO ME. IT'S MEANT FOR ME.
IF YOU TRY TO TAKE IT AGAIN, I'LL KICK YOUR ASS.
OKAY, KID.
KEEP IT FOR NOW, BUT THIS ISN'T OVER.
THAT'S COOL, COMMANDER.
COME ON BACK ANY TIME YOU THINK YOU'RE READY...
...I'LL BE HERE.

"I'LL BE HERE."

DAAAAMN. THAT WAS ICE COLD, SAMMY!

HEH.

WHEN'D YOU GET STONES LIKE THAT?!

ENOUGH WITH THE MACHO GARBAGE, BOTH OF YOU.

SAM, YOU TOOK A HUGE RISK HEADING OUT INTO SPACE WITH KALDERA. IT WAS SELFISH AND STUPID.

I KNOW.

WE'RE A TEAM. WE NEED TO WORK TOGETHER.

ANOTHER GRAND VICTORY FOR THE LOCUST AND HER ALLIES!

THIS FACILITY IS CLASSIFIED. NONE OF YOU SHOULD EVEN BE HERE!

FEAR NOT, MILITARY M THIS CAN AL SORTED IN NAME OF D PROCES

CHAMPS, ARE YOU THERE?

RIRI?

I NEED YOU TO HEAD TO THE CHAMPIONS MOBILE BUNKER AS SOON AS YOU CAN!

WHY? WHAT'S GOING ON?!

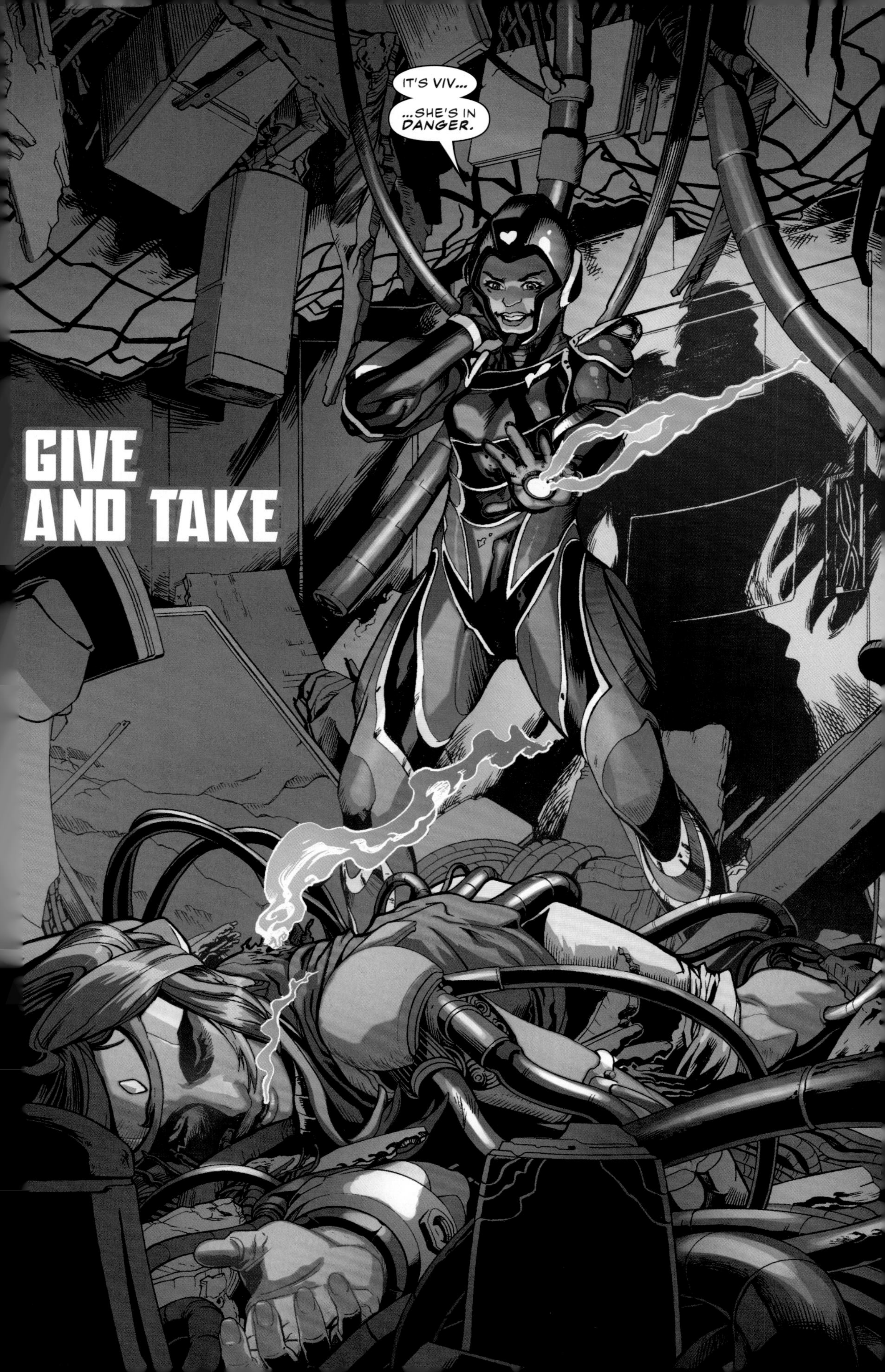
IT'S VIV...
...SHE'S IN DANGER.
GIVE AND TAKE

9

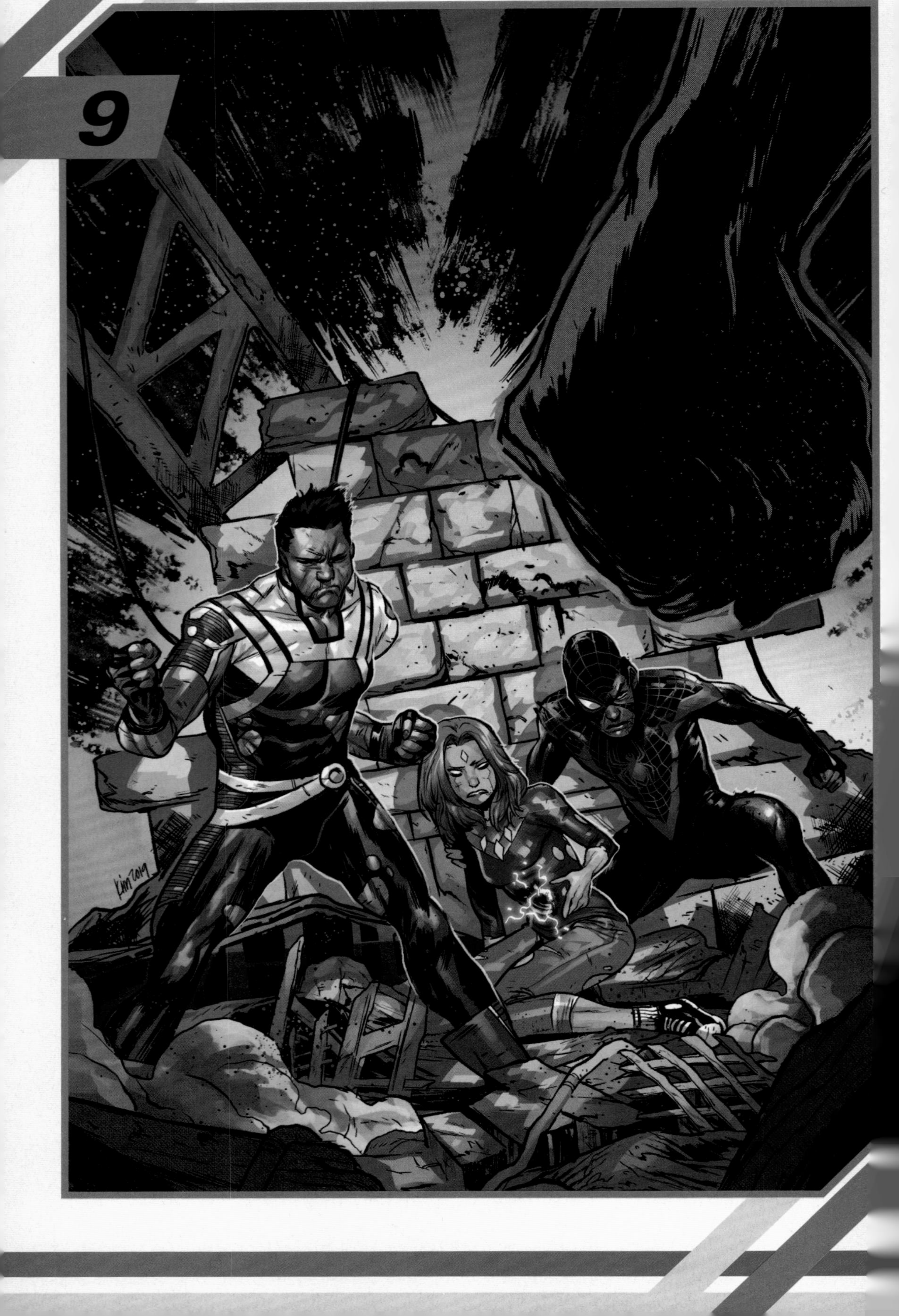

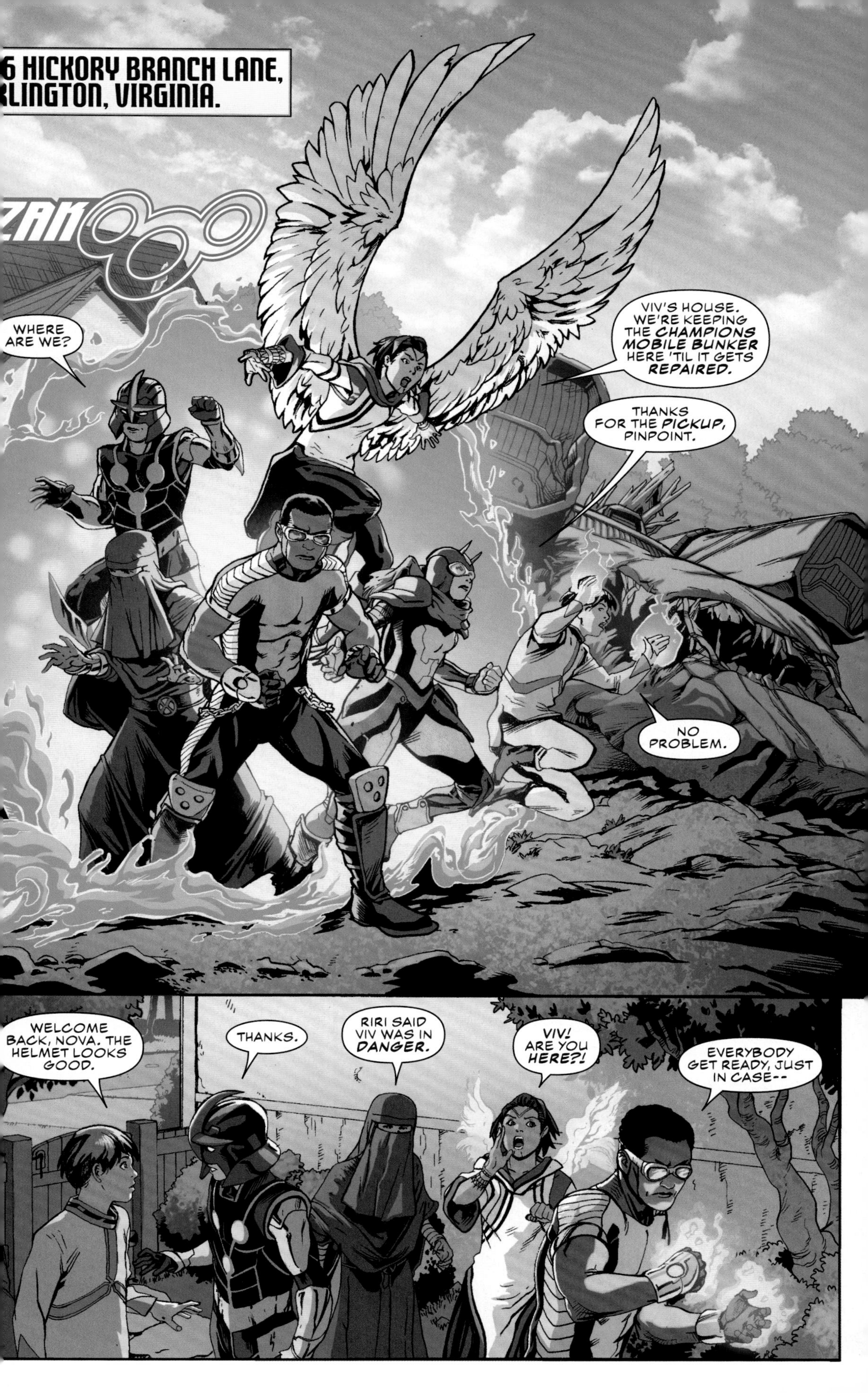
6 HICKORY BRANCH LANE,
LINGTON, VIRGINIA.
ZAK
WHERE ARE WE?
VIV'S HOUSE. WE'RE KEEPING THE CHAMPIONS MOBILE BUNKER HERE 'TIL IT GETS REPAIRED.
THANKS FOR THE PICKUP, PINPOINT.
NO PROBLEM.
WELCOME BACK, NOVA. THE HELMET LOOKS GOOD.
THANKS.
RIRI SAID VIV WAS IN DANGER.
VIV! ARE YOU HERE?!
EVERYBODY GET READY, JUST IN CASE--

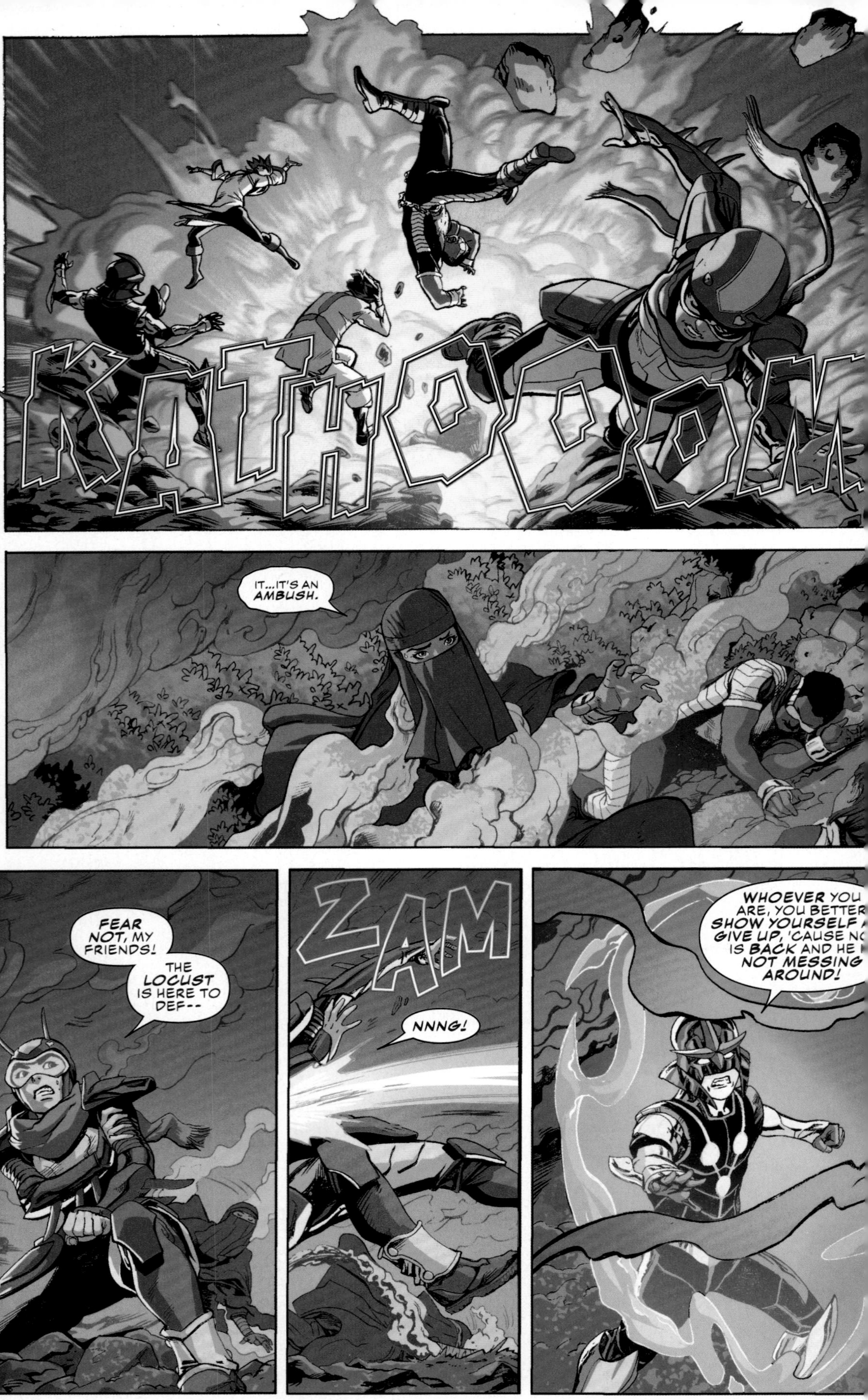
KATHOOOM
IT...IT'S AN AMBUSH.
FEAR NOT, MY FRIENDS!
THE LOCUST IS HERE TO DEF--
ZAM
NNNG!
WHOEVER YOU ARE, YOU BETTER SHOW YOURSELF A GIVE UP, 'CAUSE NO IS BACK AND HE NOT MESSING AROUND!

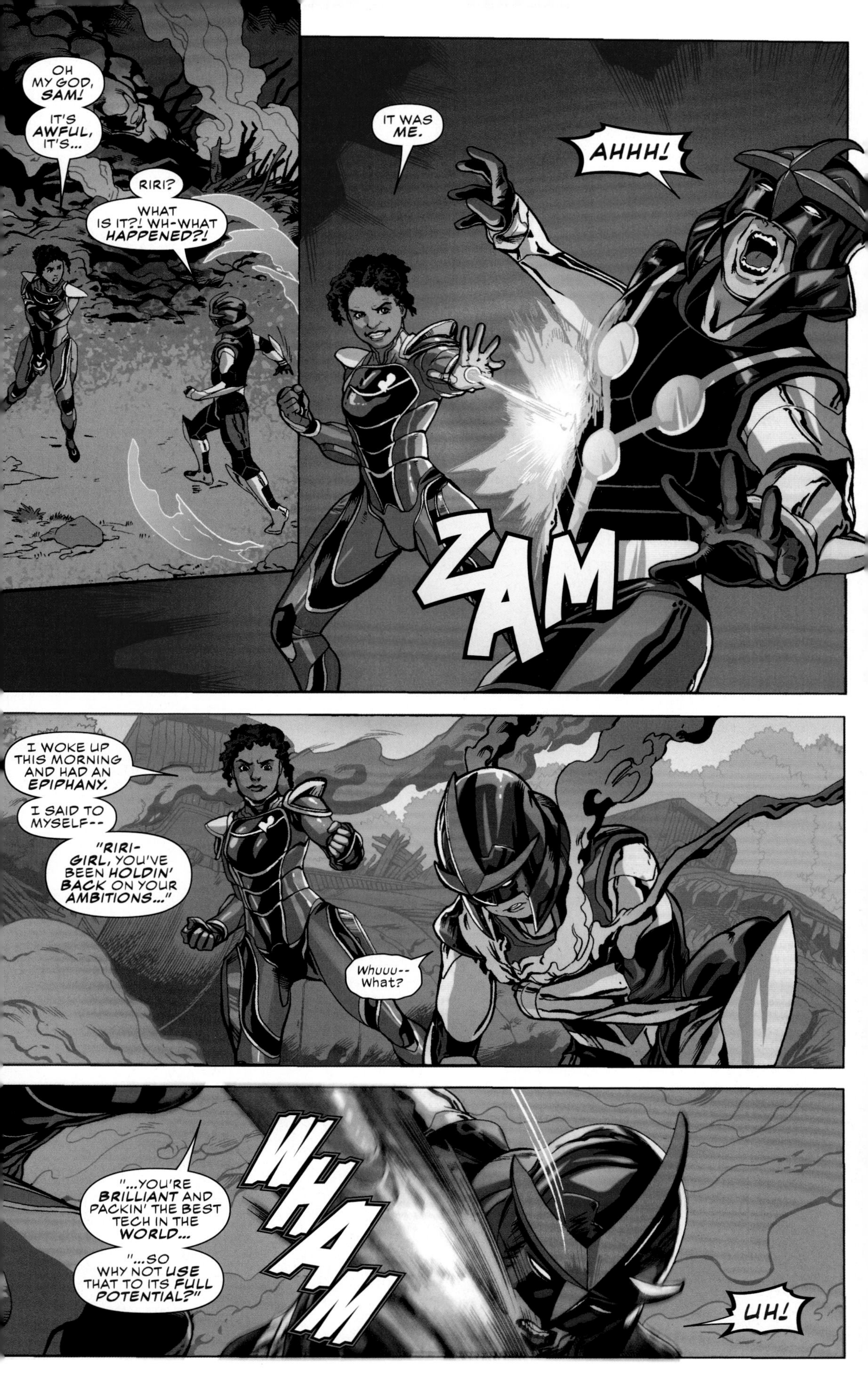
OH MY GOD, SAM!
IT'S AWFUL, IT'S...
RIRI?
WHAT IS IT?! WH-WHAT HAPPENED?!
IT WAS ME.
AHHH!
ZAM
I WOKE UP THIS MORNING AND HAD AN EPIPHANY.
I SAID TO MYSELF--
"RIRI-GIRL, YOU'VE BEEN HOLDIN' BACK ON YOUR AMBITIONS..."
Whuuu-- What?
"...YOU'RE BRILLIANT AND PACKIN' THE BEST TECH IN THE WORLD..."
"...SO WHY NOT USE THAT TO ITS FULL POTENTIAL?"
WHAM
UH!

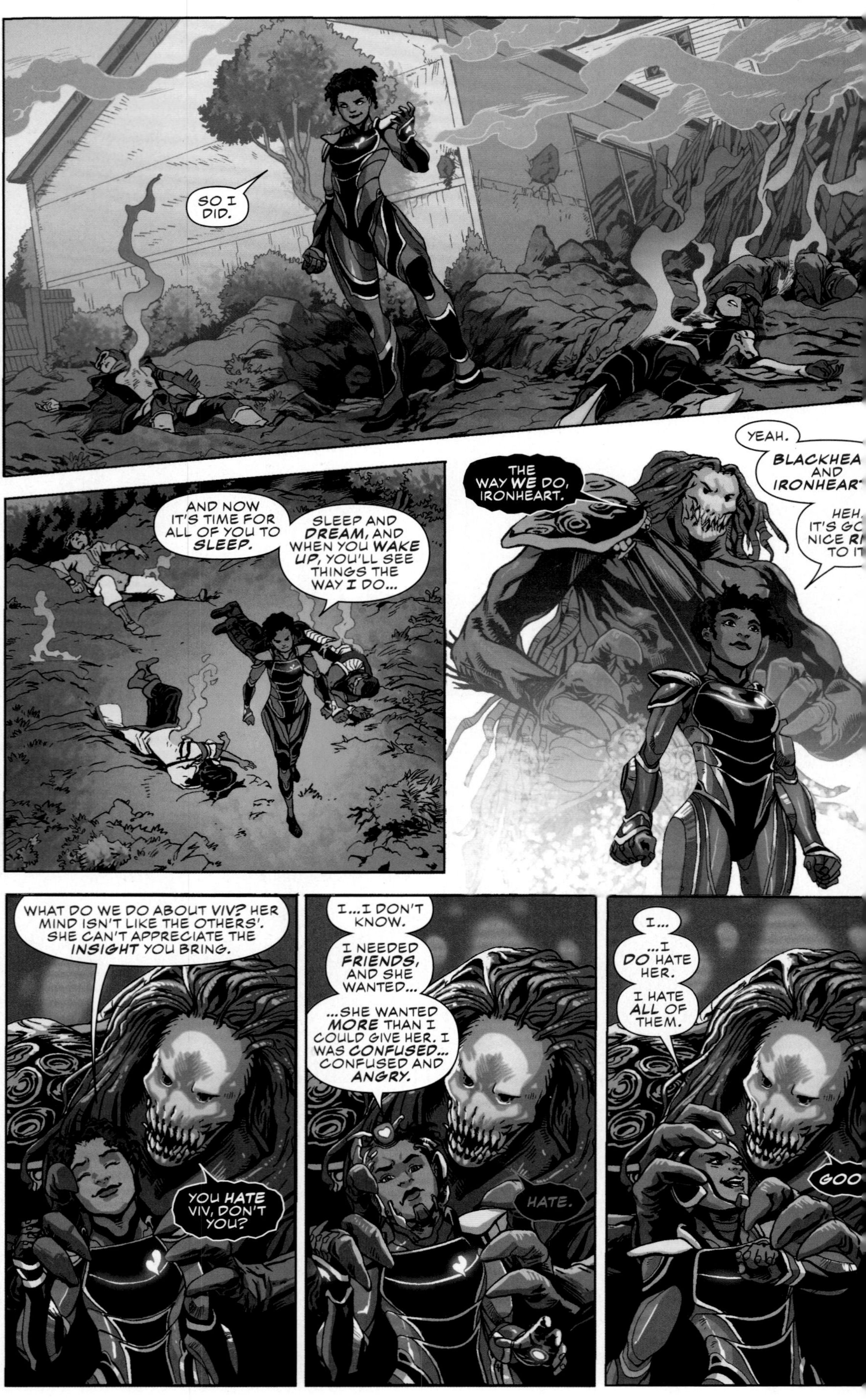
SO I DID.
AND NOW IT'S TIME FOR ALL OF YOU TO SLEEP.
SLEEP AND DREAM, AND WHEN YOU WAKE UP, YOU'LL SEE THINGS THE WAY I DO...
THE WAY WE DO, IRONHEART.
YEAH.
WHAT DO WE DO ABOUT VIV? HER MIND ISN'T LIKE THE OTHERS'. SHE CAN'T APPRECIATE THE INSIGHT YOU BRING.
YOU HATE VIV, DON'T YOU?
I...I DON'T KNOW.
I NEEDED FRIENDS, AND SHE WANTED...
...SHE WANTED MORE THAN I COULD GIVE HER. I WAS CONFUSED... CONFUSED AND ANGRY.
HATE.
I...
...I DO HATE HER.
I HATE ALL OF THEM.

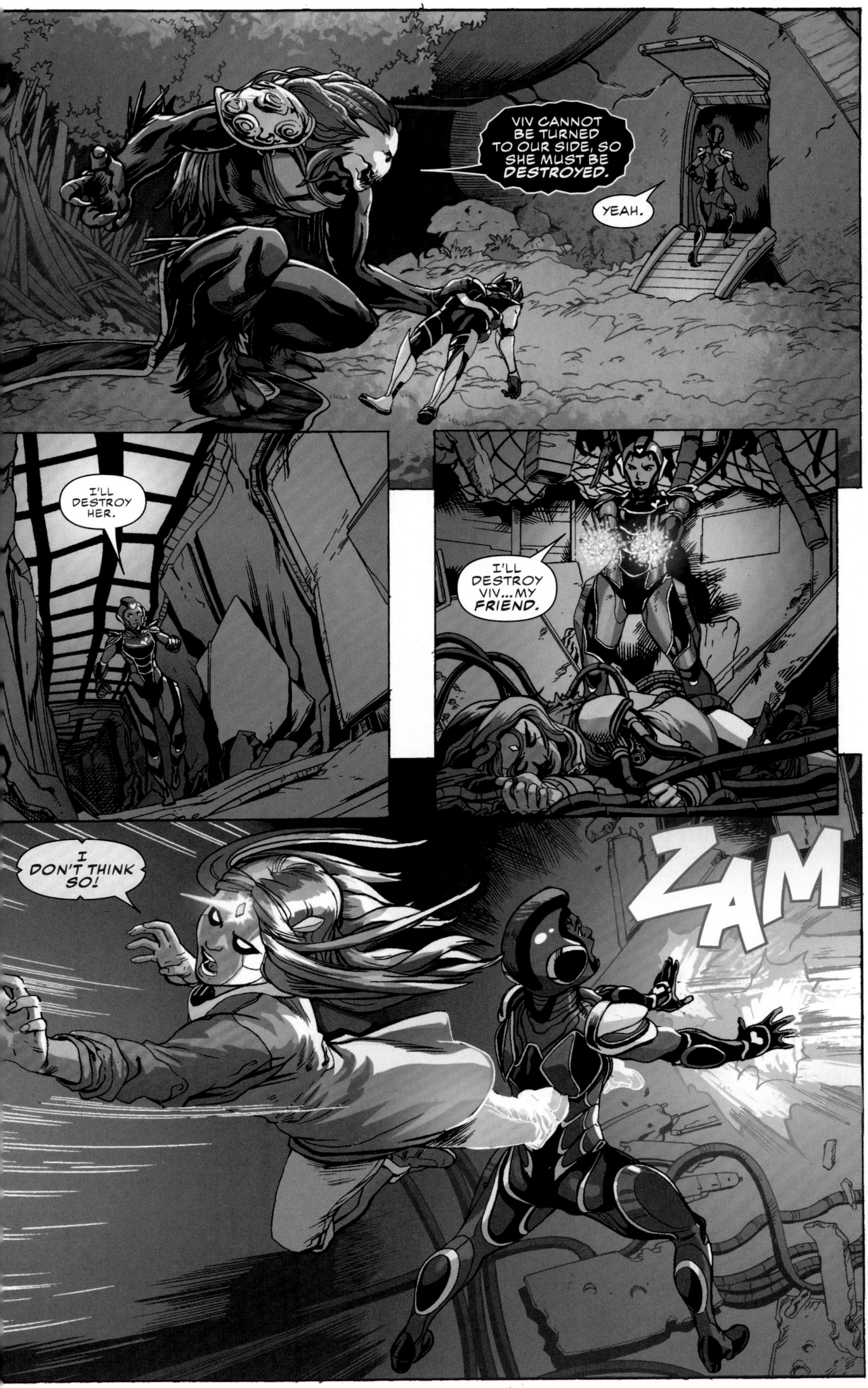
VIV CANNOT BE TURNED TO OUR SIDE, SO SHE MUST BE DESTROYED.
YEAH.
I'LL DESTROY HER.
I'LL DESTROY VIV... MY FRIEND.
I DON'T THINK SO!
ZAM

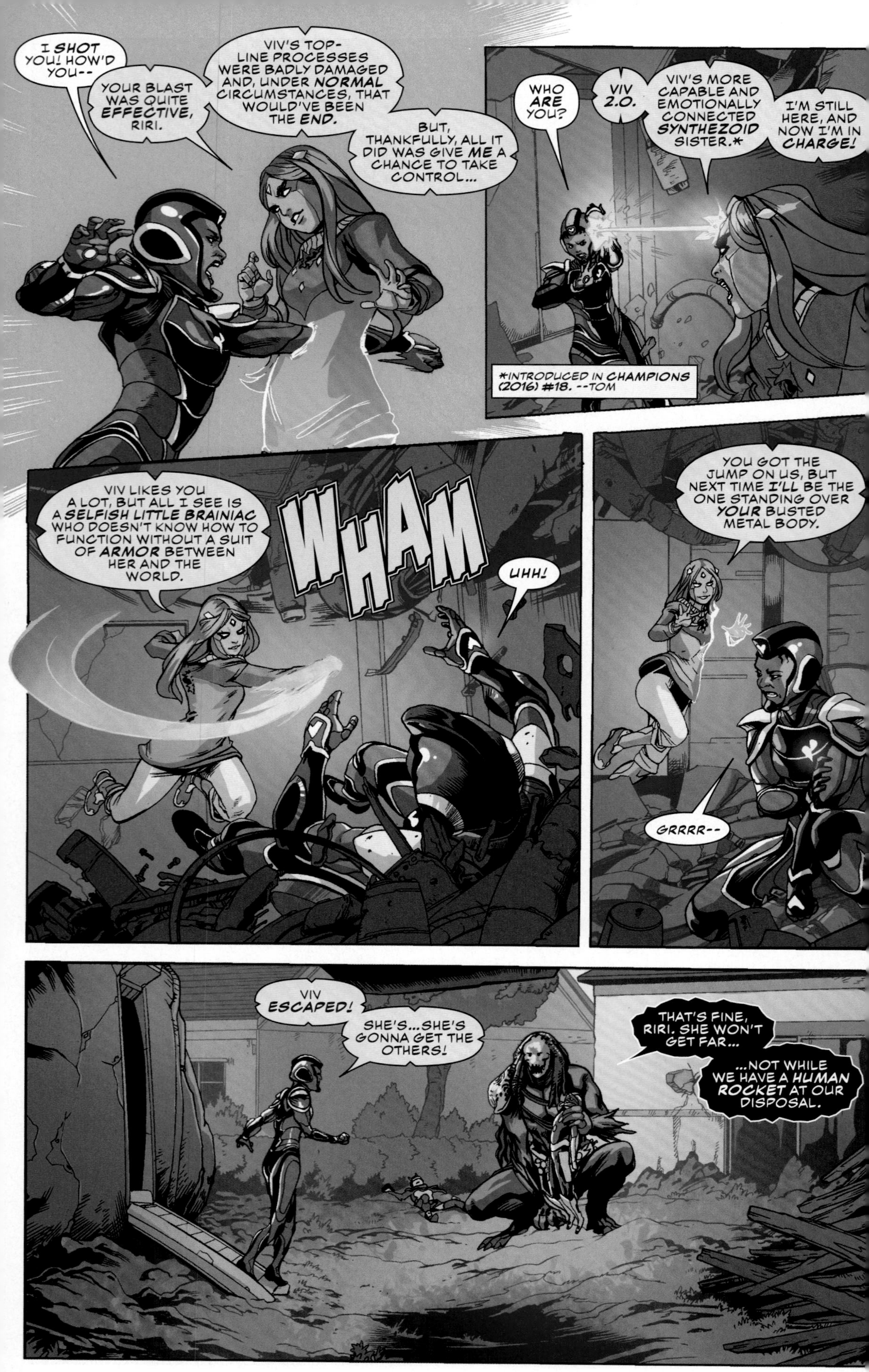
I SHOT YOU! HOW'D YOU--
YOUR BLAST WAS QUITE EFFECTIVE, RIRI.
VIV'S TOP-LINE PROCESSES WERE BADLY DAMAGED AND, UNDER NORMAL CIRCUMSTANCES, THAT WOULD'VE BEEN THE END.
BUT, THANKFULLY, ALL IT DID WAS GIVE ME A CHANCE TO TAKE CONTROL...
WHO ARE YOU?
VIV 2.0.
VIV'S MORE CAPABLE AND EMOTIONALLY CONNECTED SYNTHEZOID SISTER.*
I'M STILL HERE, AND NOW I'M IN CHARGE!
*INTRODUCED IN CHAMPIONS (2016) #18. --TOM
VIV LIKES YOU A LOT, BUT ALL I SEE IS A SELFISH LITTLE BRAINIAC WHO DOESN'T KNOW HOW TO FUNCTION WITHOUT A SUIT OF ARMOR BETWEEN HER AND THE WORLD.
WHAM
UHH!
YOU GOT THE JUMP ON US, BUT NEXT TIME I'LL BE THE ONE STANDING OVER YOUR BUSTED METAL BODY.
GRRRR--
VIV ESCAPED!
SHE'S...SHE'S GONNA GET THE OTHERS!
THAT'S FINE, RIRI. SHE WON'T GET FAR...
...NOT WHILE WE HAVE A HUMAN ROCKET AT OUR DISPOSAL.

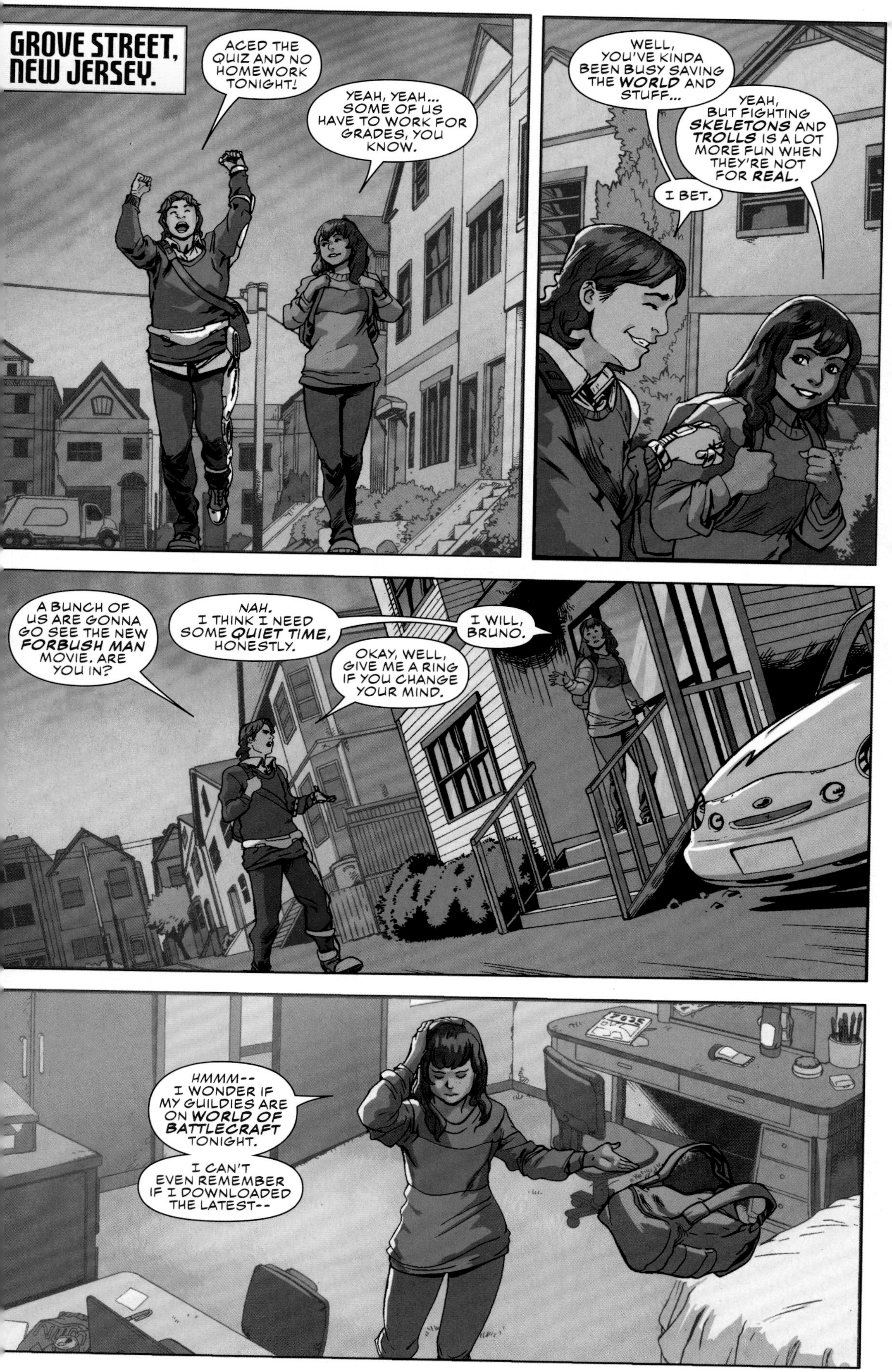
GROVE STREET, NEW JERSEY.
ACED THE QUIZ AND NO HOMEWORK TONIGHT!
YEAH, YEAH... SOME OF US HAVE TO WORK FOR GRADES, YOU KNOW.
WELL, YOU'VE KINDA BEEN BUSY SAVING THE WORLD AND STUFF...
YEAH, BUT FIGHTING SKELETONS AND TROLLS IS A LOT MORE FUN WHEN THEY'RE NOT FOR REAL.
I BET.
A BUNCH OF US ARE GONNA GO SEE THE NEW FORBUSH MAN MOVIE. ARE YOU IN?
NAH. I THINK I NEED SOME QUIET TIME, HONESTLY.
OKAY, WELL, GIVE ME A RING IF YOU CHANGE YOUR MIND.
I WILL, BRUNO.
HMMM-- I WONDER IF MY GUILDIES ARE ON WORLD OF BATTLECRAFT TONIGHT.
I CAN'T EVEN REMEMBER IF I DOWNLOADED THE LATEST--

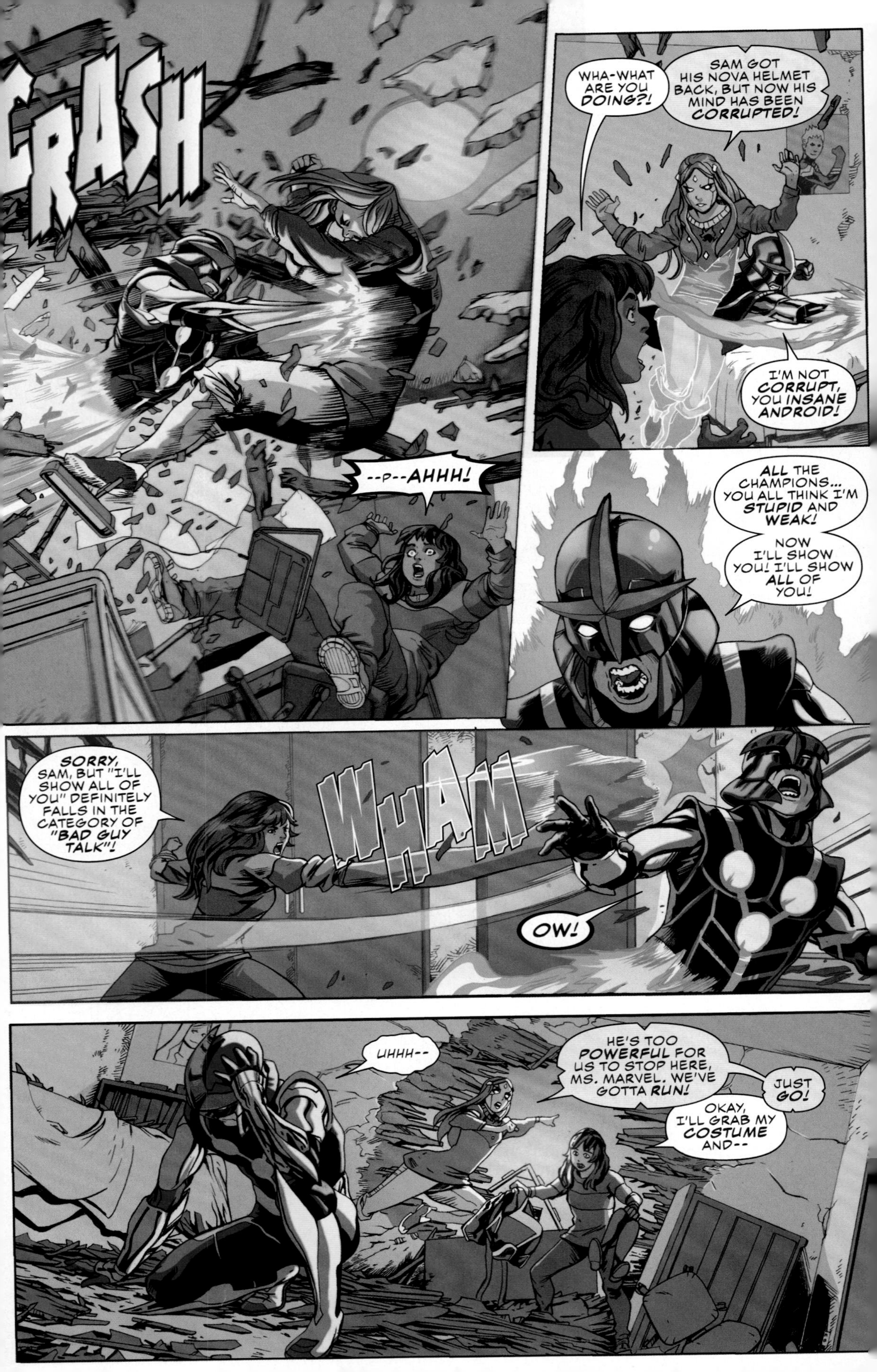
CRASH
WHA-WHAT ARE YOU DOING?!
SAM GOT HIS NOVA HELMET BACK, BUT NOW HIS MIND HAS BEEN CORRUPTED!
I'M NOT CORRUPT, YOU INSANE ANDROID!
--P--AHHH!
ALL THE CHAMPIONS... YOU ALL THINK I'M STUPID AND WEAK!
NOW I'LL SHOW YOU! I'LL SHOW ALL OF YOU!
SORRY, SAM, BUT "I'LL SHOW ALL OF YOU" DEFINITELY FALLS IN THE CATEGORY OF "BAD GUY TALK"!
WHAM
OW!
UHHH--
HE'S TOO POWERFUL FOR US TO STOP HERE, MS. MARVEL. WE'VE GOTTA RUN!
JUST GO!
OKAY, I'LL GRAB MY COSTUME AND--

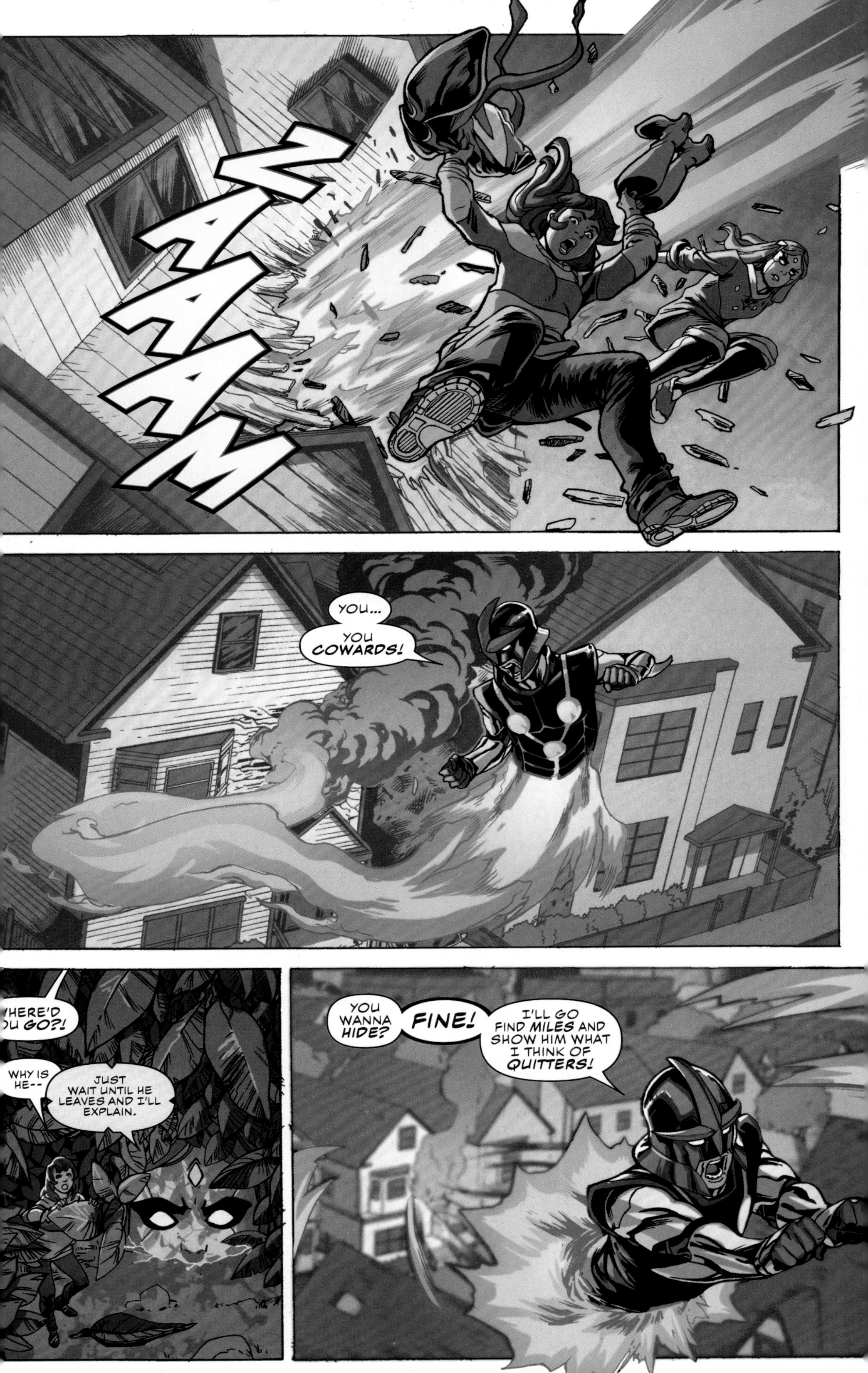

VAAAAM
YOU...
YOU COWARDS!
WHERE'D YOU GO?!
WHY IS HE--
JUST WAIT UNTIL HE LEAVES AND I'LL EXPLAIN.
YOU WANNA HIDE?
FINE!
I'LL GO FIND MILES AND SHOW HIM WHAT I THINK OF QUITTERS!

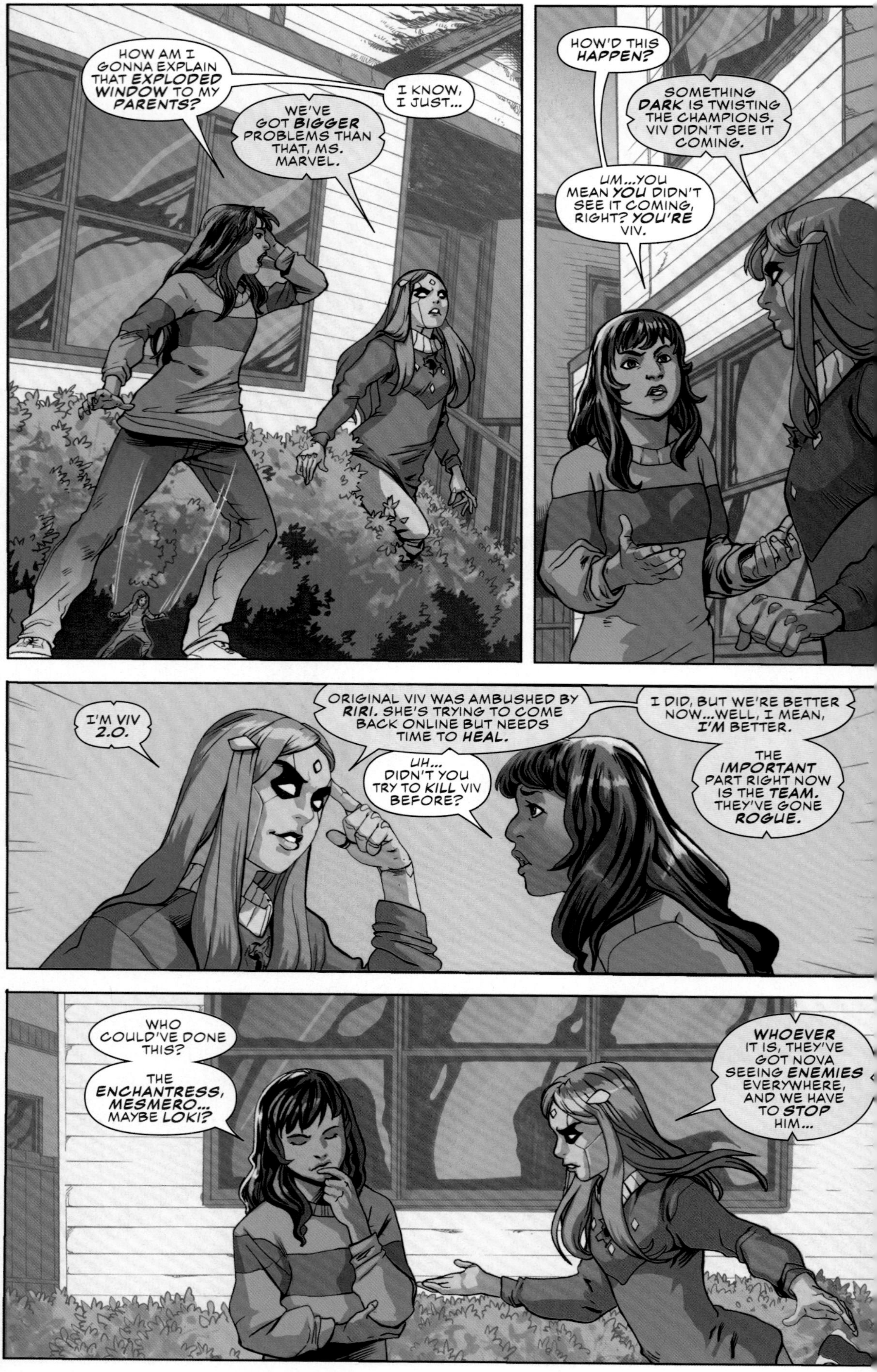
HOW AM I GONNA EXPLAIN THAT EXPLODED WINDOW TO MY PARENTS?
I KNOW, I JUST...
WE'VE GOT BIGGER PROBLEMS THAN THAT, MS. MARVEL.
HOW'D THIS HAPPEN?
SOMETHING DARK IS TWISTING THE CHAMPIONS. VIV DIDN'T SEE IT COMING.
UM...YOU MEAN YOU DIDN'T SEE IT COMING, RIGHT? YOU'RE VIV.
I'M VIV 2.0.
ORIGINAL VIV WAS AMBUSHED BY RIRI. SHE'S TRYING TO COME BACK ONLINE BUT NEEDS TIME TO HEAL.
UH... DIDN'T YOU TRY TO KILL VIV BEFORE?
I DID, BUT WE'RE BETTER NOW...WELL, I MEAN, I'M BETTER.
THE IMPORTANT PART RIGHT NOW IS THE TEAM. THEY'VE GONE ROGUE.
WHO COULD'VE DONE THIS?
THE ENCHANTRESS, MESMERO... MAYBE LOKI?
WHOEVER IT IS, THEY'VE GOT NOVA SEEING ENEMIES EVERYWHERE, AND WE HAVE TO STOP HIM...

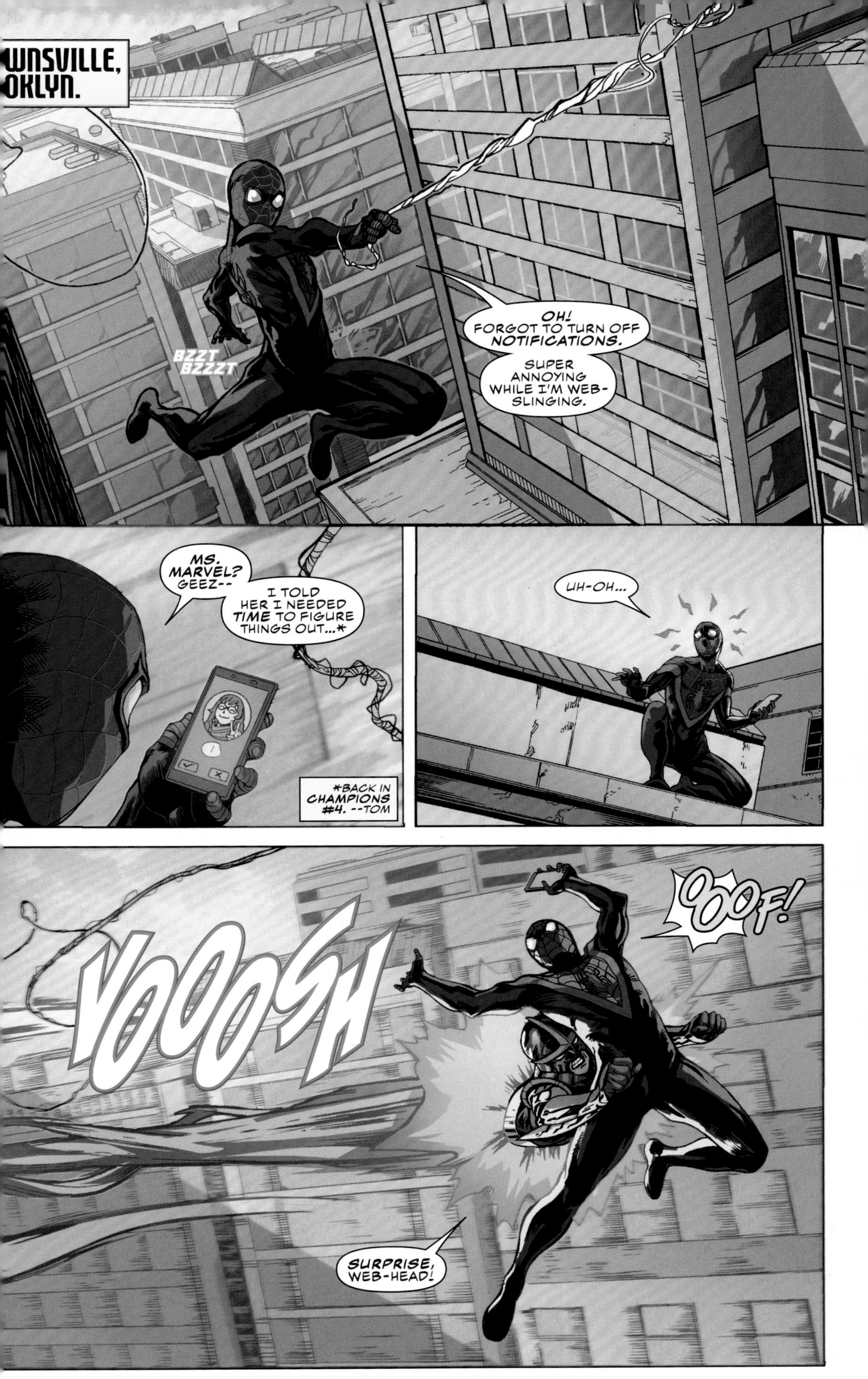
WNSVILLE,
OKLYN.
BZZT BZZZT
OH! FORGOT TO TURN OFF NOTIFICATIONS.
SUPER ANNOYING WHILE I'M WEB-SLINGING.
MS. MARVEL? GEEZ--
I TOLD HER I NEEDED TIME TO FIGURE THINGS OUT...*
*BACK IN CHAMPIONS #4. --TOM
UH-OH...
VOOOSH
OOOF!
SURPRISE, WEB-HEAD!

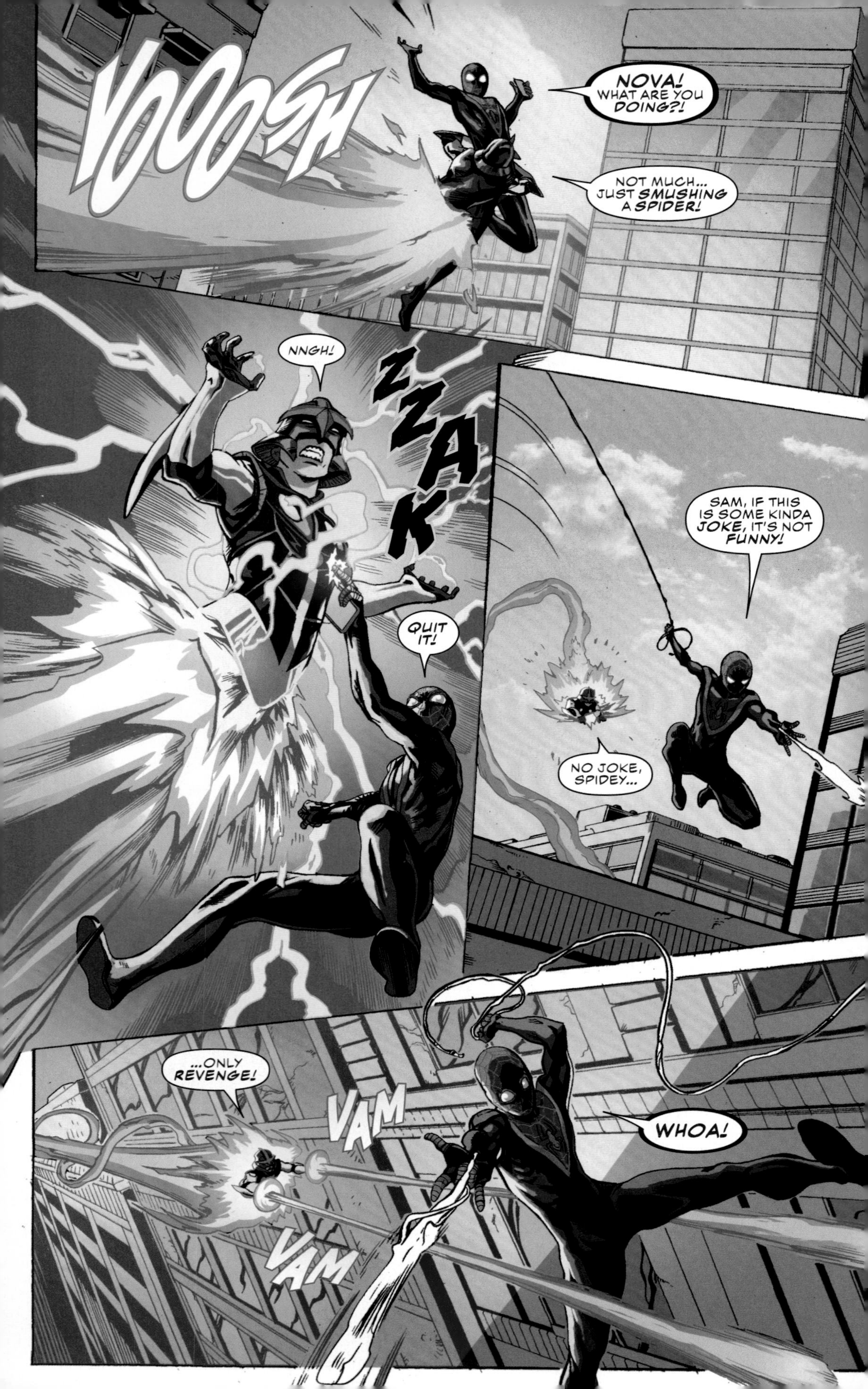
VOOOSH
NOVA! WHAT ARE YOU DOING?!
NOT MUCH... JUST SMUSHING A SPIDER!
NNGH!
ZZAK
QUIT IT!
SAM, IF THIS IS SOME KINDA JOKE, IT'S NOT FUNNY!
NO JOKE, SPIDEY...
...ONLY REVENGE!
VAM
VAM
WHOA!

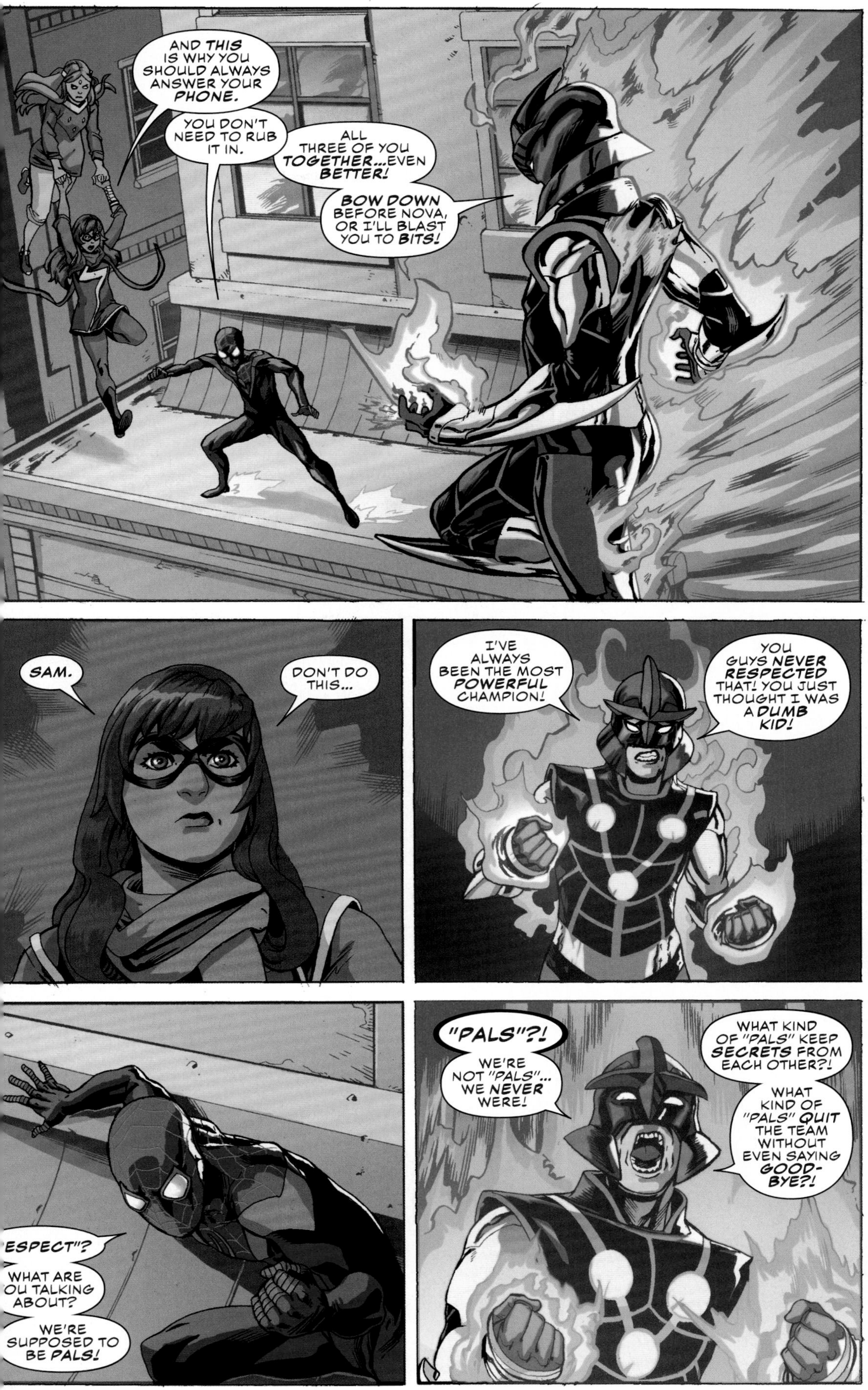
AND THIS IS WHY YOU SHOULD ALWAYS ANSWER YOUR PHONE.
YOU DON'T NEED TO RUB IT IN.
ALL THREE OF YOU TOGETHER...EVEN BETTER!
BOW DOWN BEFORE NOVA, OR I'LL BLAST YOU TO BITS!
SAM.
DON'T DO THIS...
I'VE ALWAYS BEEN THE MOST POWERFUL CHAMPION!
YOU GUYS NEVER RESPECTED THAT! YOU JUST THOUGHT I WAS A DUMB KID!
ESPECT"?
WHAT ARE OU TALKING ABOUT?
WE'RE SUPPOSED TO BE PALS!
"PALS"?!
WE'RE NOT "PALS"... WE NEVER WERE!
WHAT KIND OF "PALS" KEEP SECRETS FROM EACH OTHER?!
WHAT KIND OF "PALS" QUIT THE TEAM WITHOUT EVEN SAYING GOOD-BYE?!

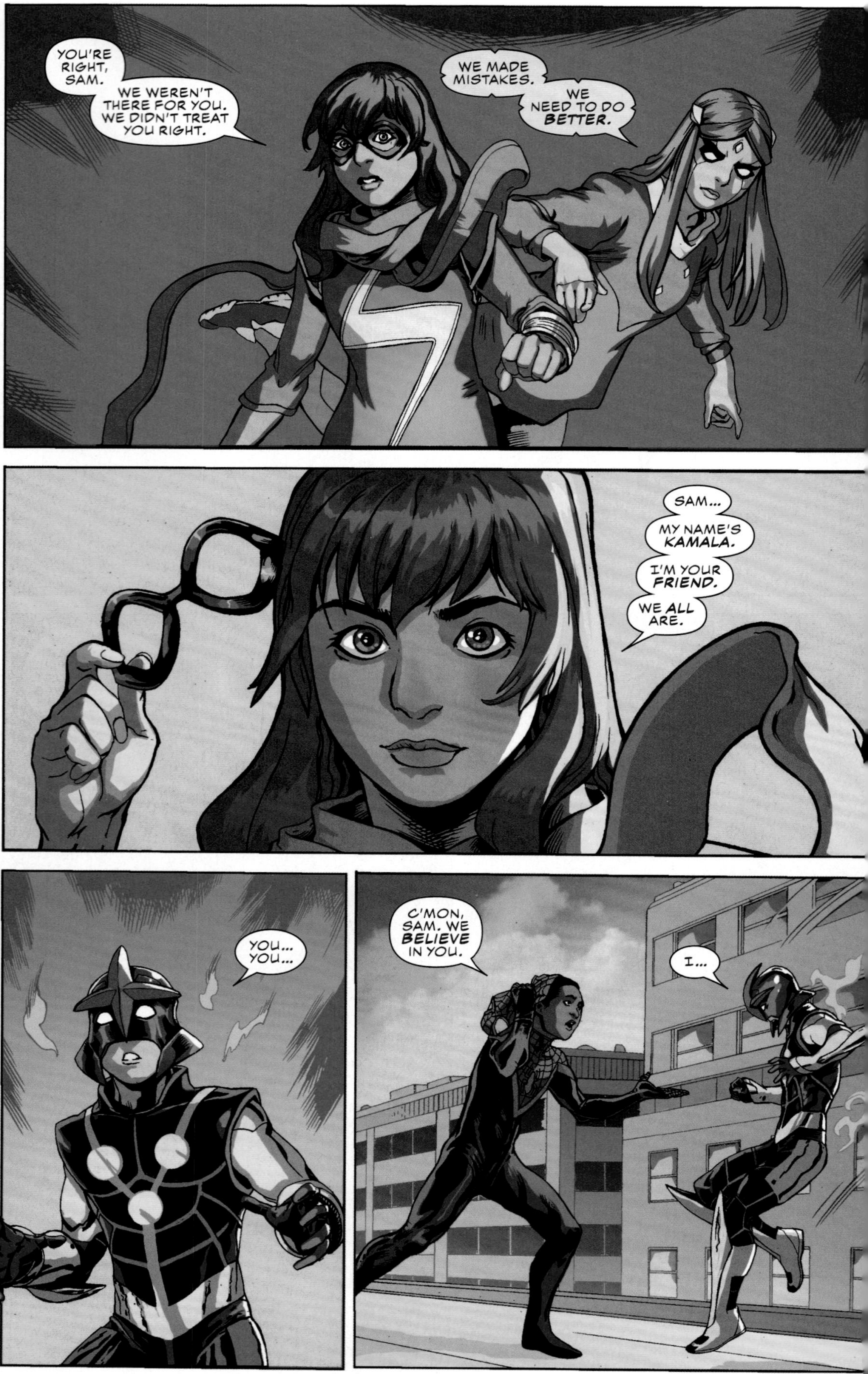
YOU'RE RIGHT, SAM.
WE WEREN'T THERE FOR YOU. WE DIDN'T TREAT YOU RIGHT.
WE MADE MISTAKES.
WE NEED TO DO BETTER.
SAM...
MY NAME'S KAMALA.
I'M YOUR FRIEND.
WE ALL ARE.
YOU... YOU...
C'MON, SAM. WE BELIEVE IN YOU.
I...

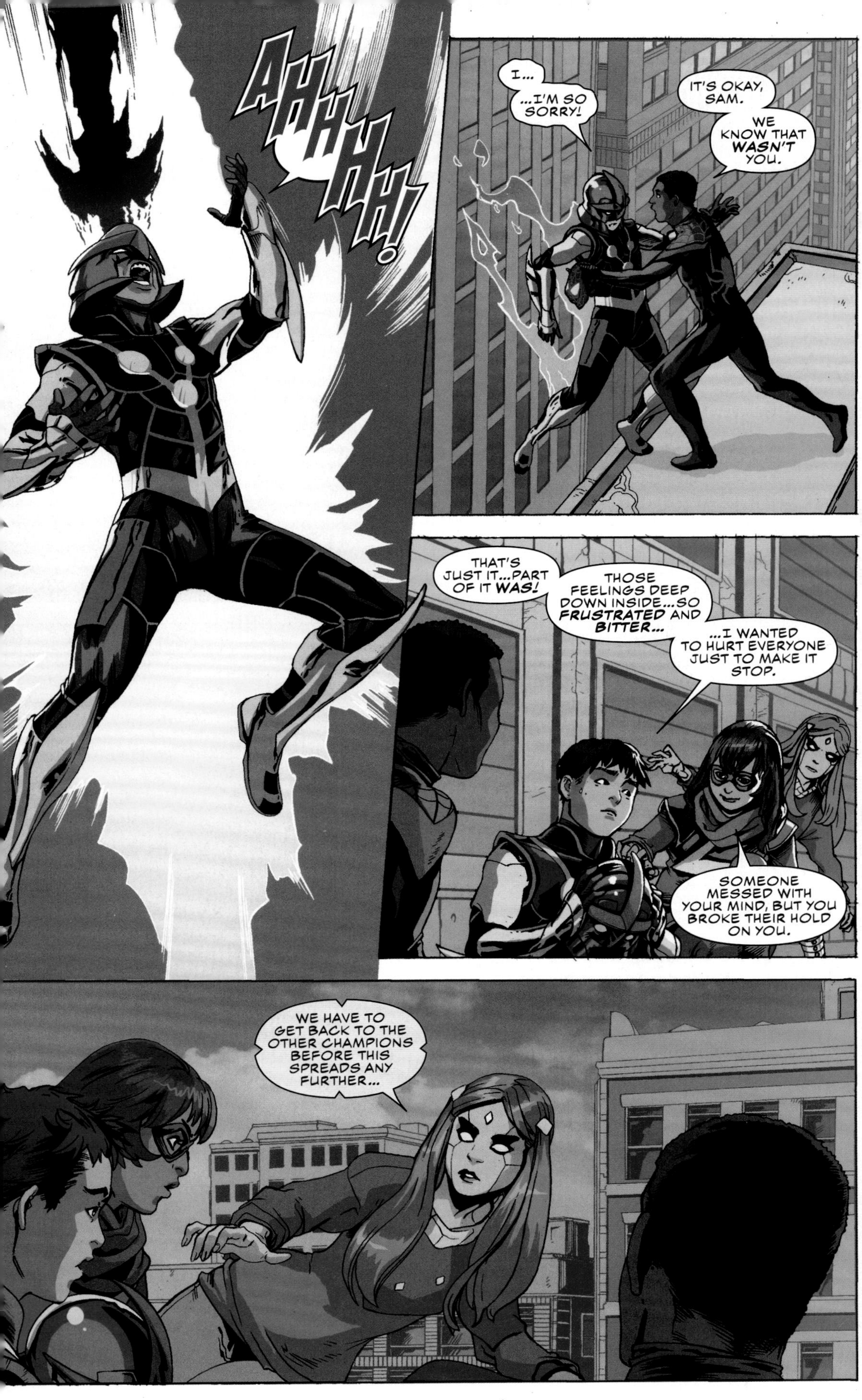
AHHHHH!
I... ...I'M SO SORRY!
IT'S OKAY, SAM.
WE KNOW THAT WASN'T YOU.
THAT'S JUST IT...PART OF IT WAS!
THOSE FEELINGS DEEP DOWN INSIDE...SO FRUSTRATED AND BITTER...
...I WANTED TO HURT EVERYONE JUST TO MAKE IT STOP.
SOMEONE MESSED WITH YOUR MIND, BUT YOU BROKE THEIR HOLD ON YOU.
WE HAVE TO GET BACK TO THE OTHER CHAMPIONS BEFORE THIS SPREADS ANY FURTHER...

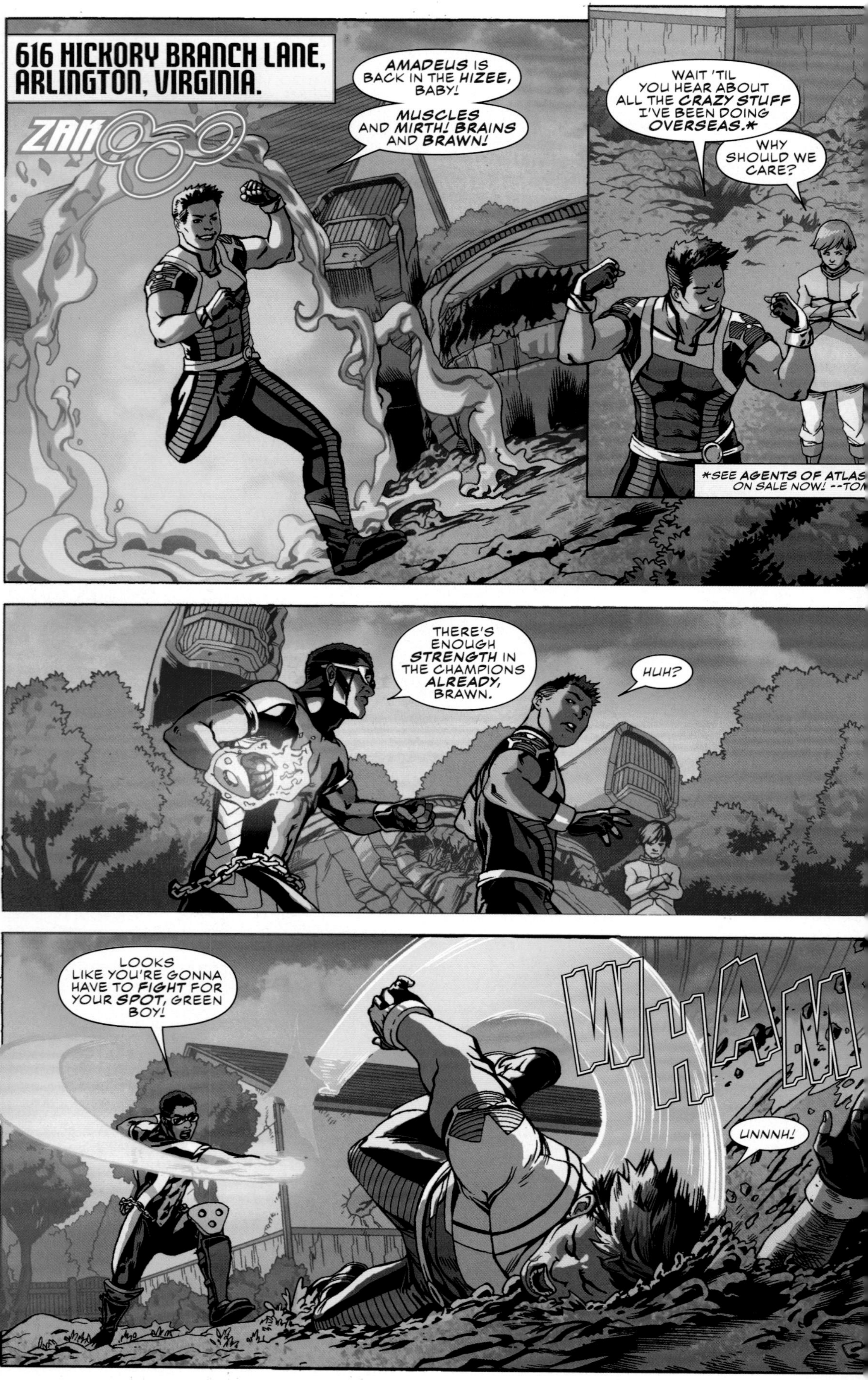
616 HICKORY BRANCH LANE, ARLINGTON, VIRGINIA.
ZAK
AMADEUS IS BACK IN THE HIZEE, BABY!
MUSCLES AND MIRTH! BRAINS AND BRAWN!
WAIT 'TIL YOU HEAR ABOUT ALL THE CRAZY STUFF I'VE BEEN DOING OVERSEAS.*
WHY SHOULD WE CARE?
*SEE AGENTS OF ATLAS ON SALE NOW! --TOM
THERE'S ENOUGH STRENGTH IN THE CHAMPIONS ALREADY, BRAWN.
HUH?
LOOKS LIKE YOU'RE GONNA HAVE TO FIGHT FOR YOUR SPOT, GREEN BOY!
WHAM
UNNNH!

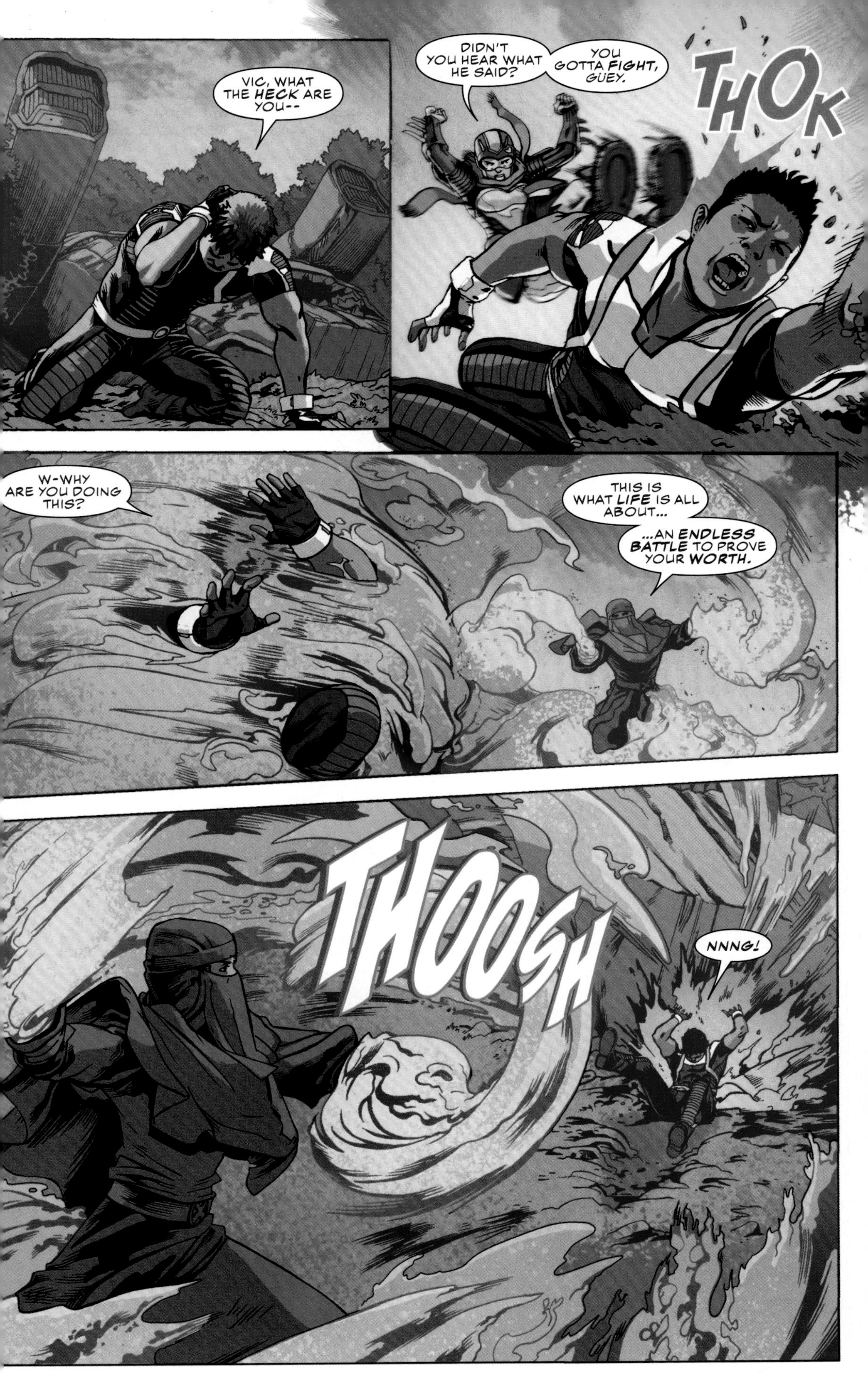
VIC, WHAT THE HECK ARE YOU--
DIDN'T YOU HEAR WHAT HE SAID?
YOU GOTTA FIGHT, GUEY.
THOK
W-WHY ARE YOU DOING THIS?
THIS IS WHAT LIFE IS ALL ABOUT...
...AN ENDLESS BATTLE TO PROVE YOUR WORTH.
THOOSH
NNNG!

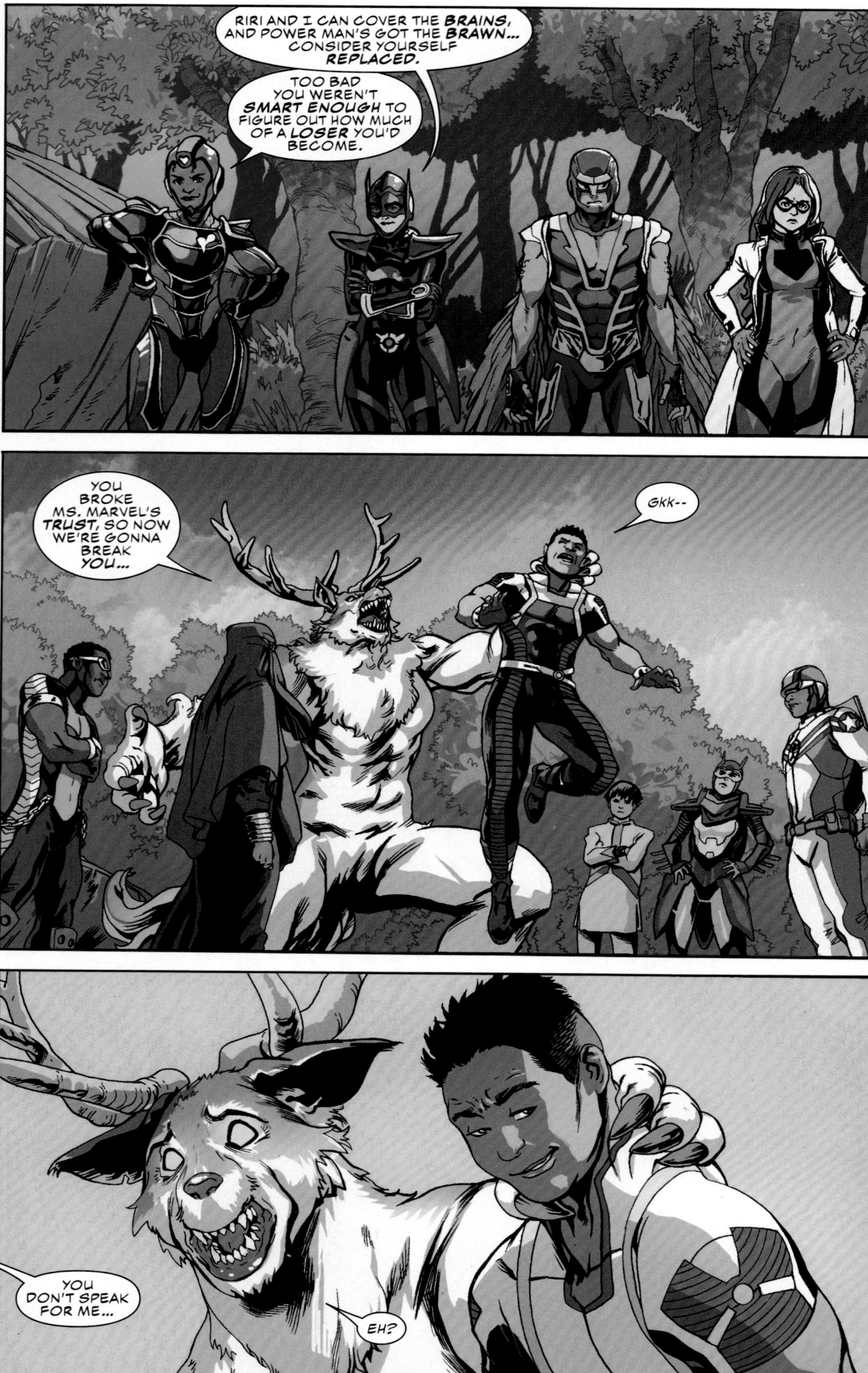
RIRI AND I CAN COVER THE **BRAINS**, AND POWER MAN'S GOT THE **BRAWN**... CONSIDER YOURSELF **REPLACED**.
TOO BAD YOU WEREN'T **SMART ENOUGH** TO FIGURE OUT HOW MUCH OF A **LOSER** YOU'D BECOME.
YOU BROKE MS. MARVEL'S **TRUST**, SO NOW WE'RE GONNA BREAK **YOU**...
GKK--
YOU DON'T SPEAK FOR ME...
EH?

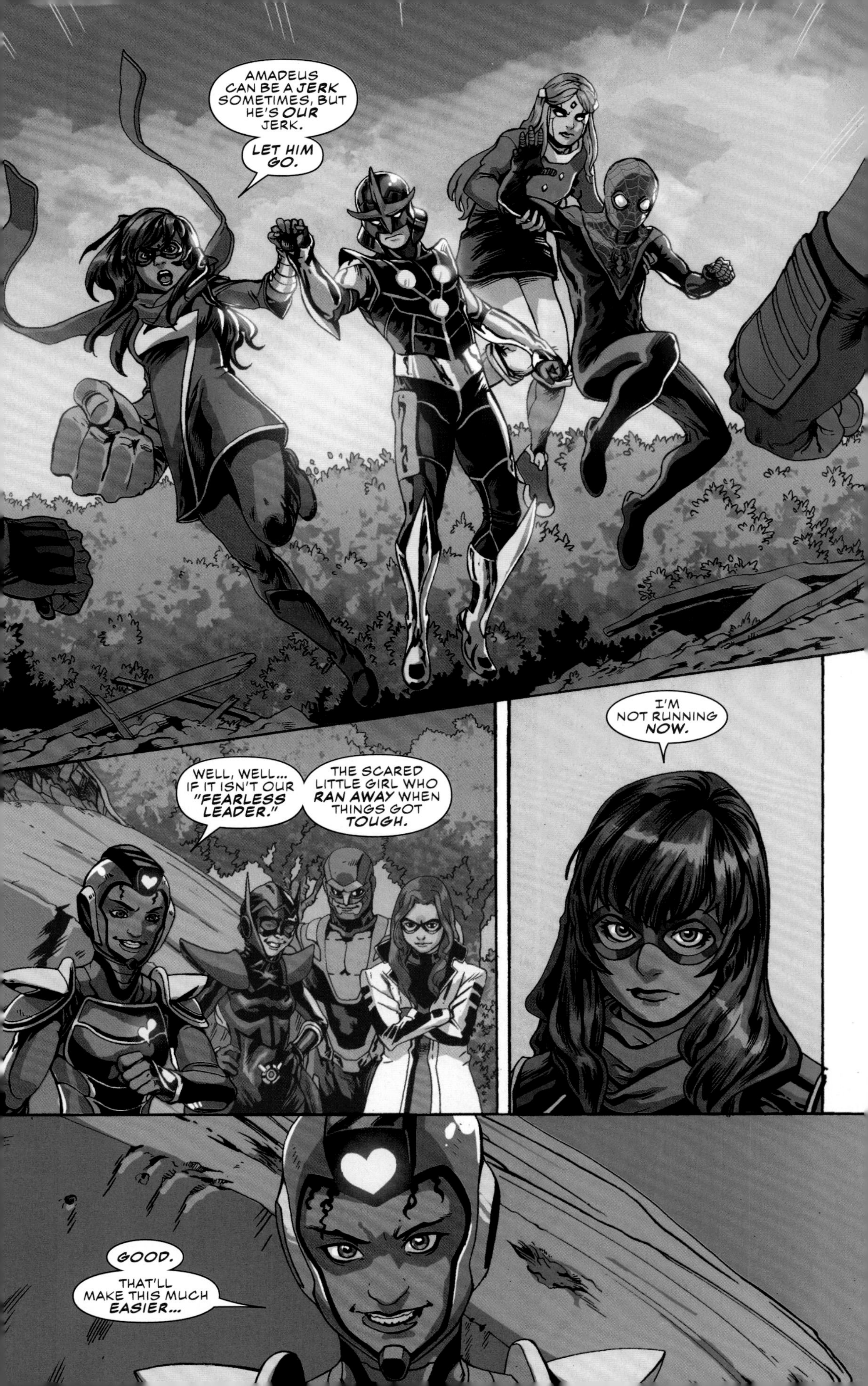
AMADEUS CAN BE A JERK SOMETIMES, BUT HE'S OUR JERK.
LET HIM GO.
WELL, WELL... IF IT ISN'T OUR "FEARLESS LEADER."
THE SCARED LITTLE GIRL WHO RAN AWAY WHEN THINGS GOT TOUGH.
I'M NOT RUNNING NOW.
GOOD.
THAT'LL MAKE THIS MUCH EASIER...

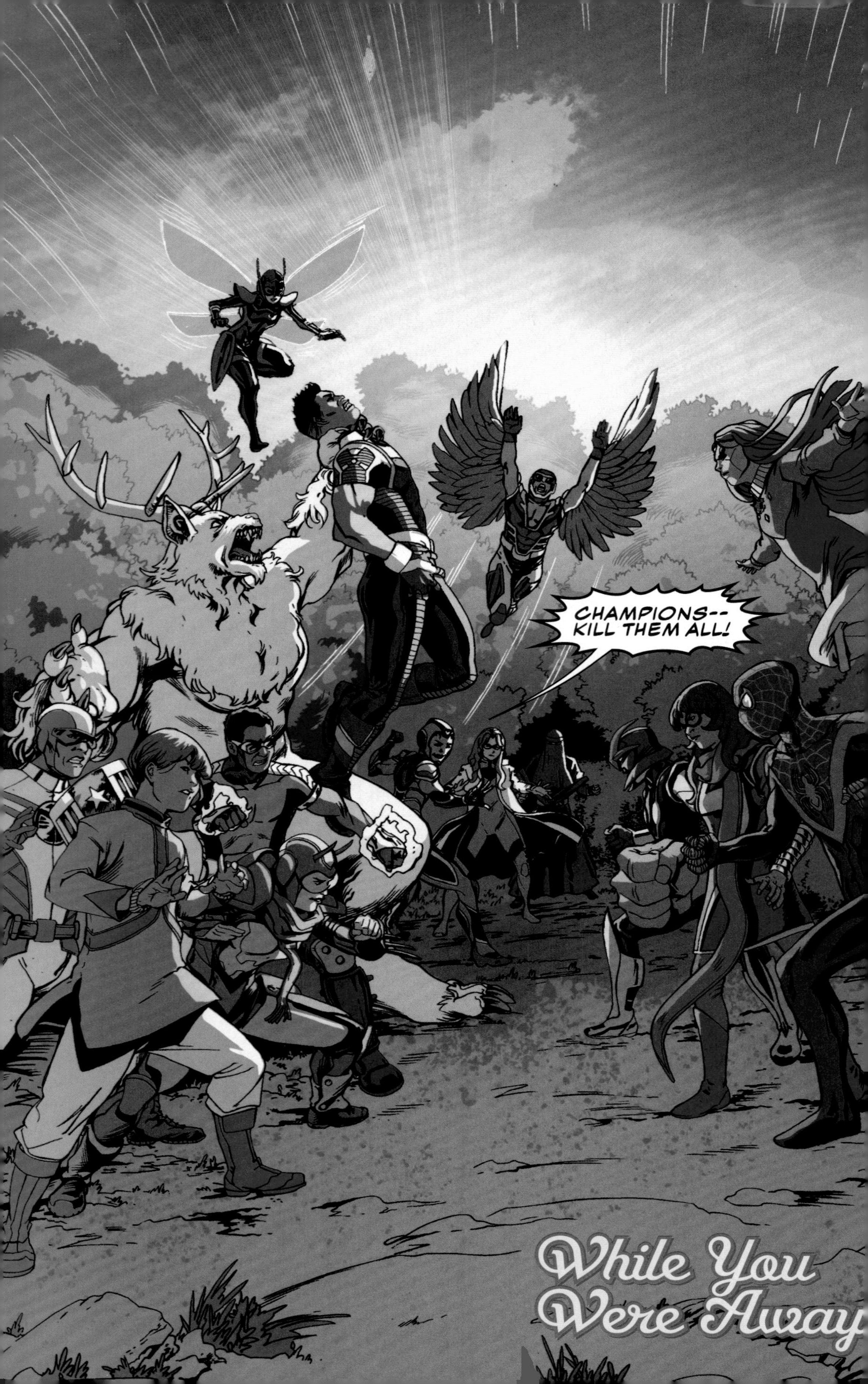
CHAMPIONS--
KILL THEM ALL!
While You
Were Away

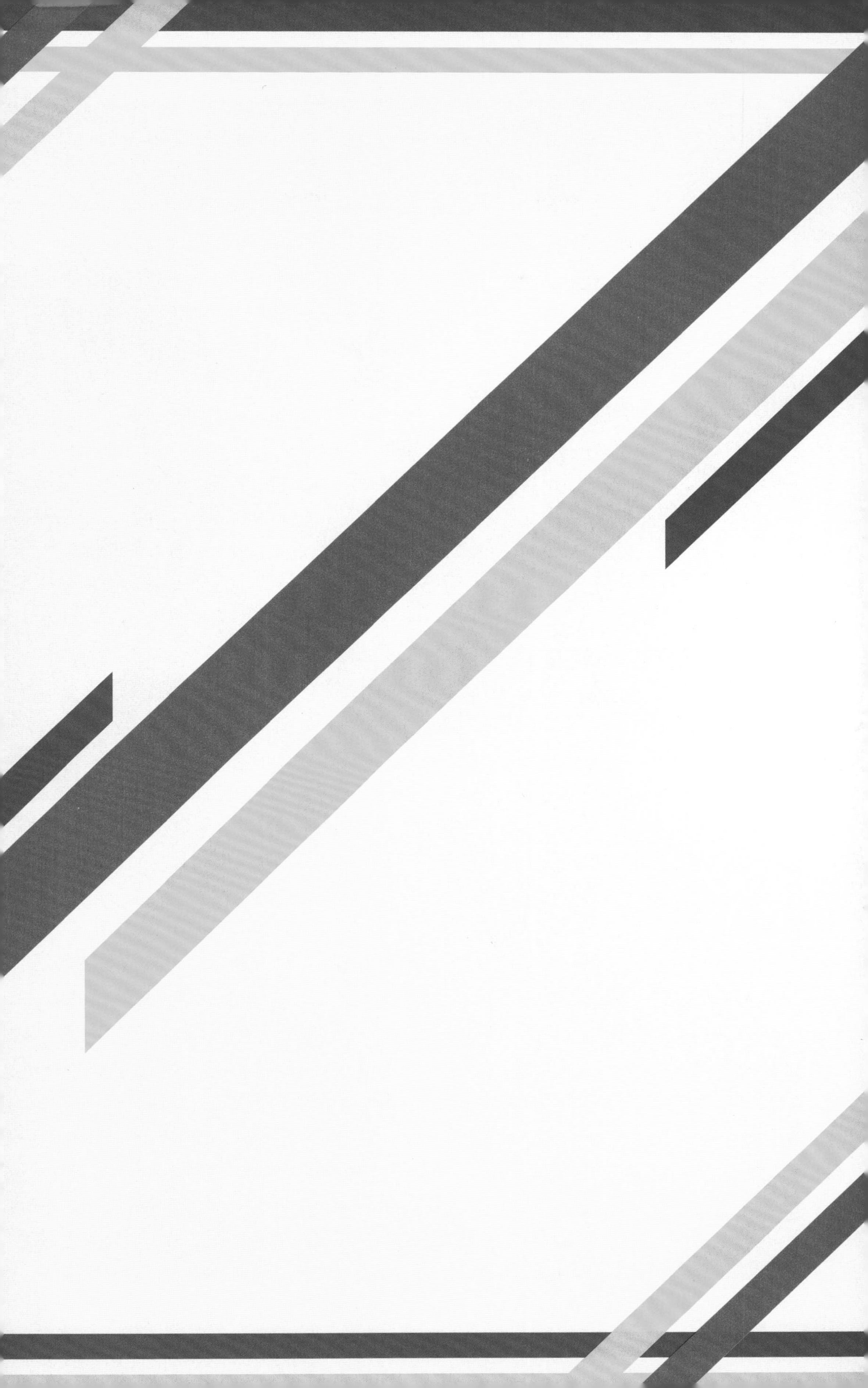

10

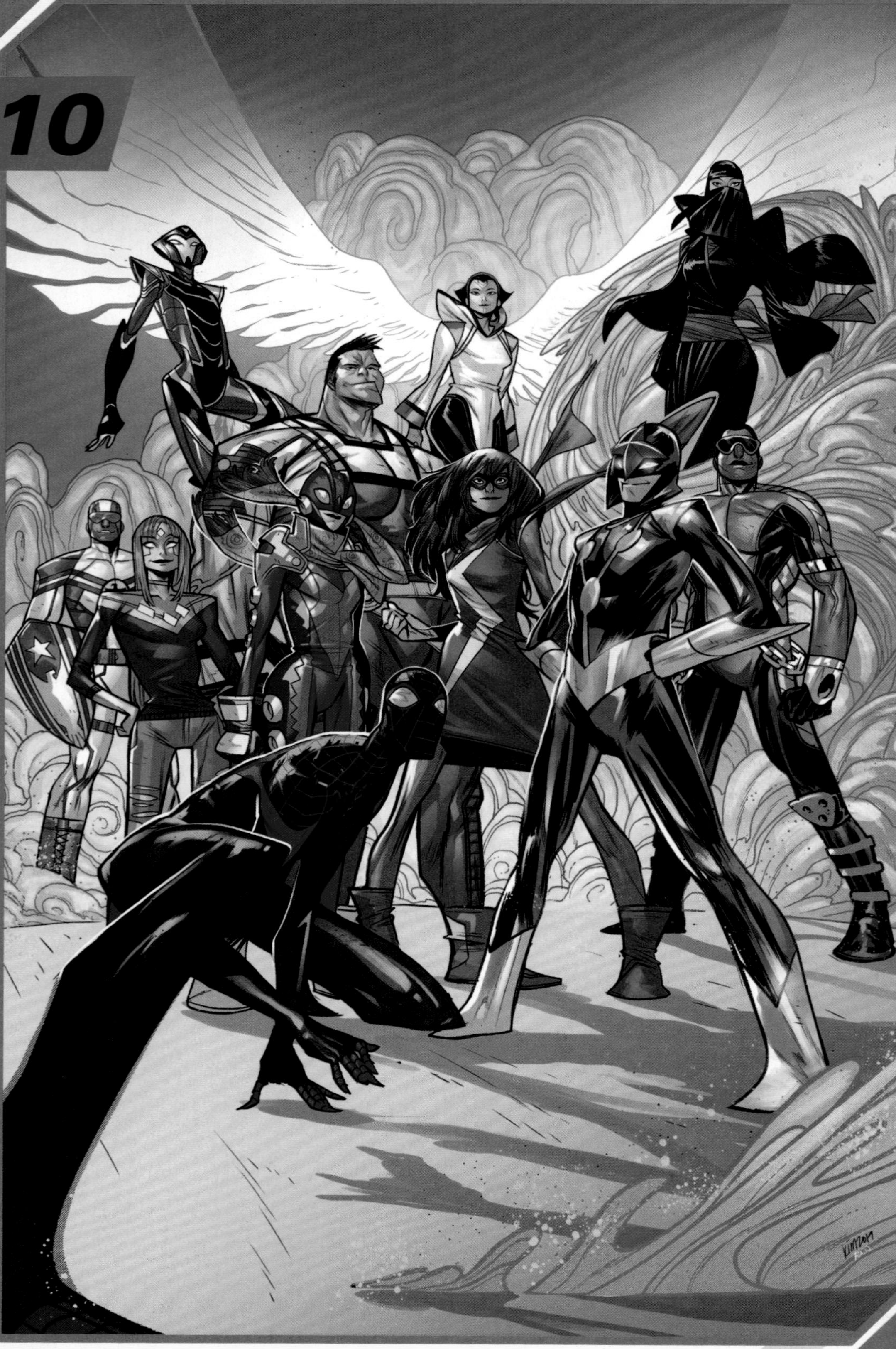

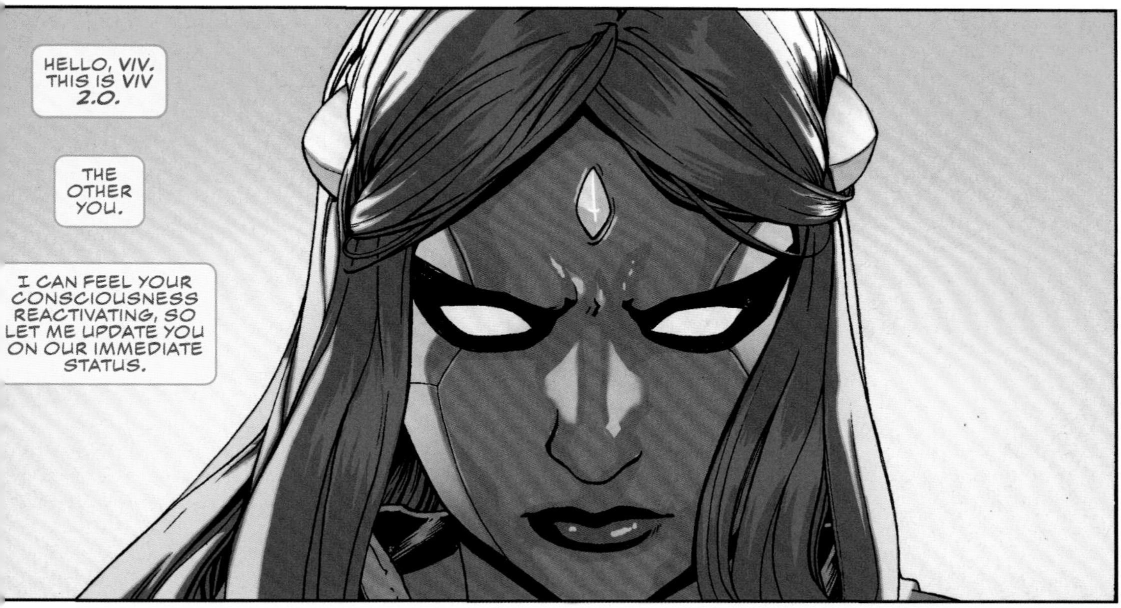
HELLO, VIV. THIS IS VIV 2.0.
THE OTHER YOU.
I CAN FEEL YOUR CONSCIOUSNESS REACTIVATING, SO LET ME UPDATE YOU ON OUR IMMEDIATE STATUS.

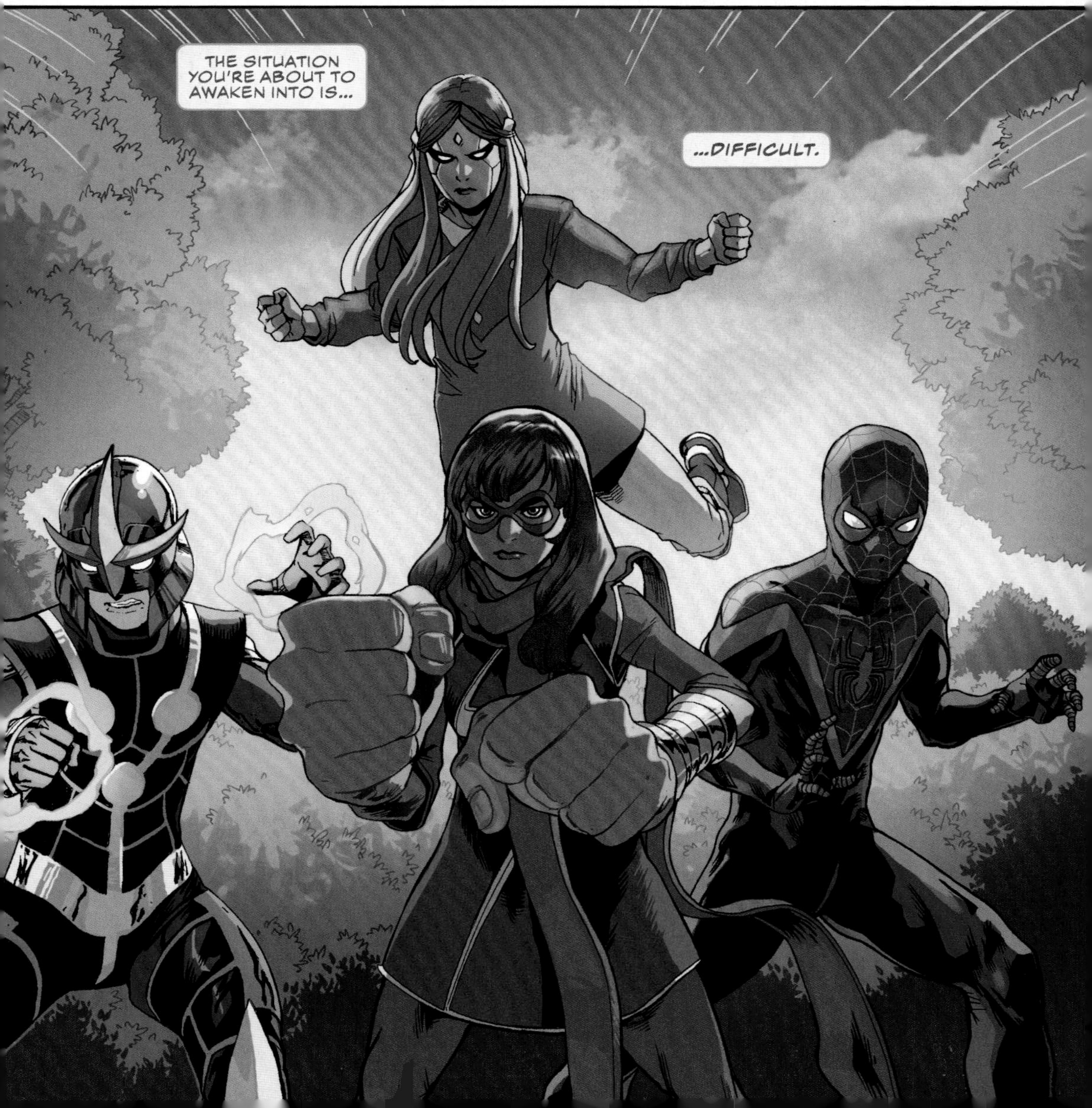
THE SITUATION YOU'RE ABOUT TO AWAKEN INTO IS...
...DIFFICULT.

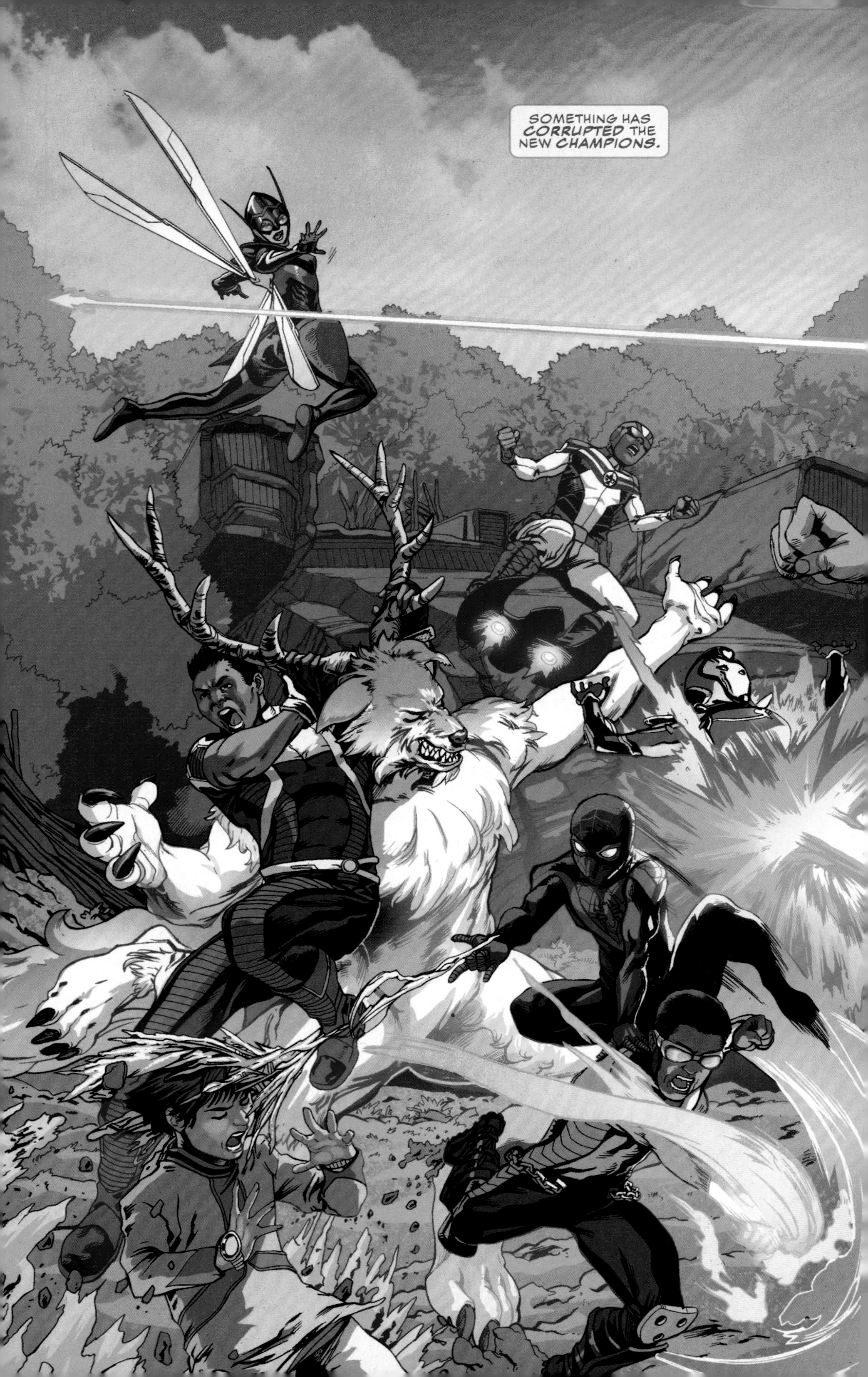
SOMETHING HAS CORRUPTED THE NEW CHAMPIONS.

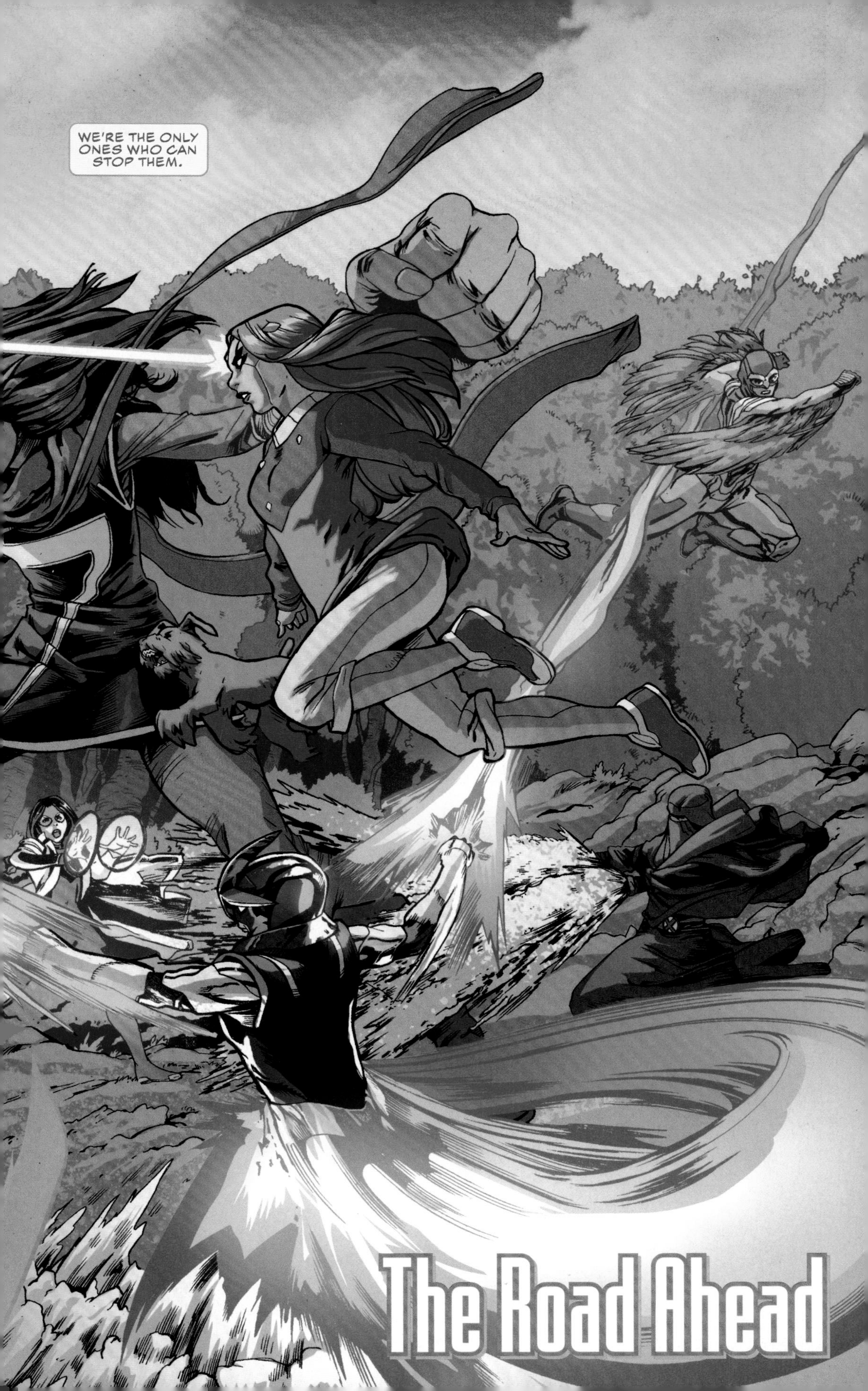
WE'RE THE ONLY ONES WHO CAN STOP THEM.
The Road Ahead

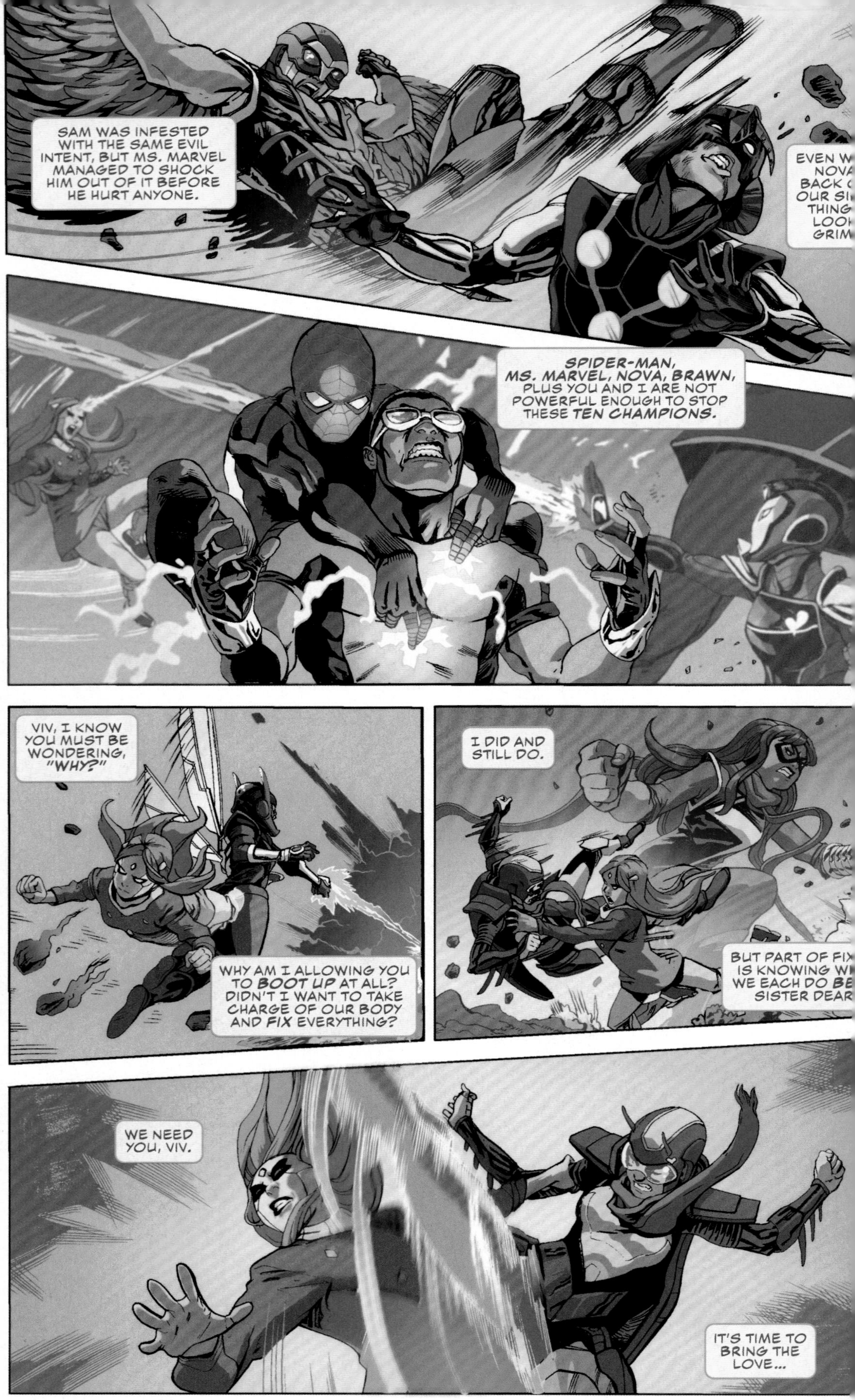
SAM WAS INFESTED WITH THE SAME EVIL INTENT, BUT MS. MARVEL MANAGED TO SHOCK HIM OUT OF IT BEFORE HE HURT ANYONE.
EVEN W NOVA BACK OUR S THING LOOK GRIM
SPIDER-MAN, MS. MARVEL, NOVA, BRAWN, PLUS YOU AND I ARE NOT POWERFUL ENOUGH TO STOP THESE TEN CHAMPIONS.
VIV, I KNOW YOU MUST BE WONDERING, "WHY?"
WHY AM I ALLOWING YOU TO BOOT UP AT ALL? DIDN'T I WANT TO TAKE CHARGE OF OUR BODY AND FIX EVERYTHING?
I DID AND STILL DO.
BUT PART OF FIX IS KNOWING W WE EACH DO BE SISTER DEAR
WE NEED YOU, VIV.
IT'S TIME TO BRING THE LOVE...

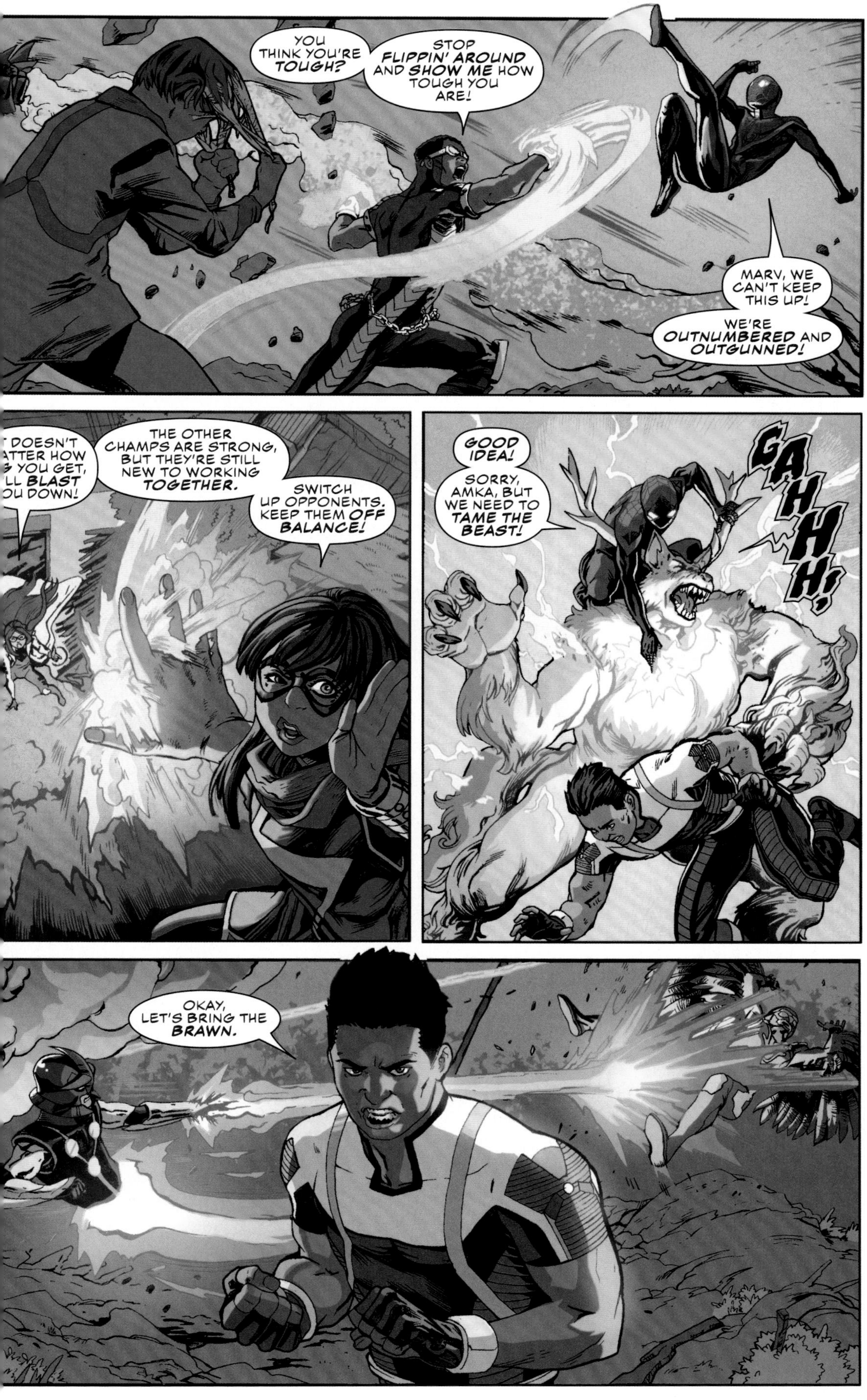
YOU THINK YOU'RE TOUGH?
STOP FLIPPIN' AROUND AND SHOW ME HOW TOUGH YOU ARE!
MARV, WE CAN'T KEEP THIS UP!
WE'RE OUTNUMBERED AND OUTGUNNED!
T DOESN'T ATTER HOW YOU GET, LL BLAST OU DOWN!
THE OTHER CHAMPS ARE STRONG, BUT THEY'RE STILL NEW TO WORKING TOGETHER.
SWITCH UP OPPONENTS. KEEP THEM OFF BALANCE!
GOOD IDEA!
SORRY, AMKA, BUT WE NEED TO TAME THE BEAST!
GAHHH!
OKAY, LET'S BRING THE BRAWN.

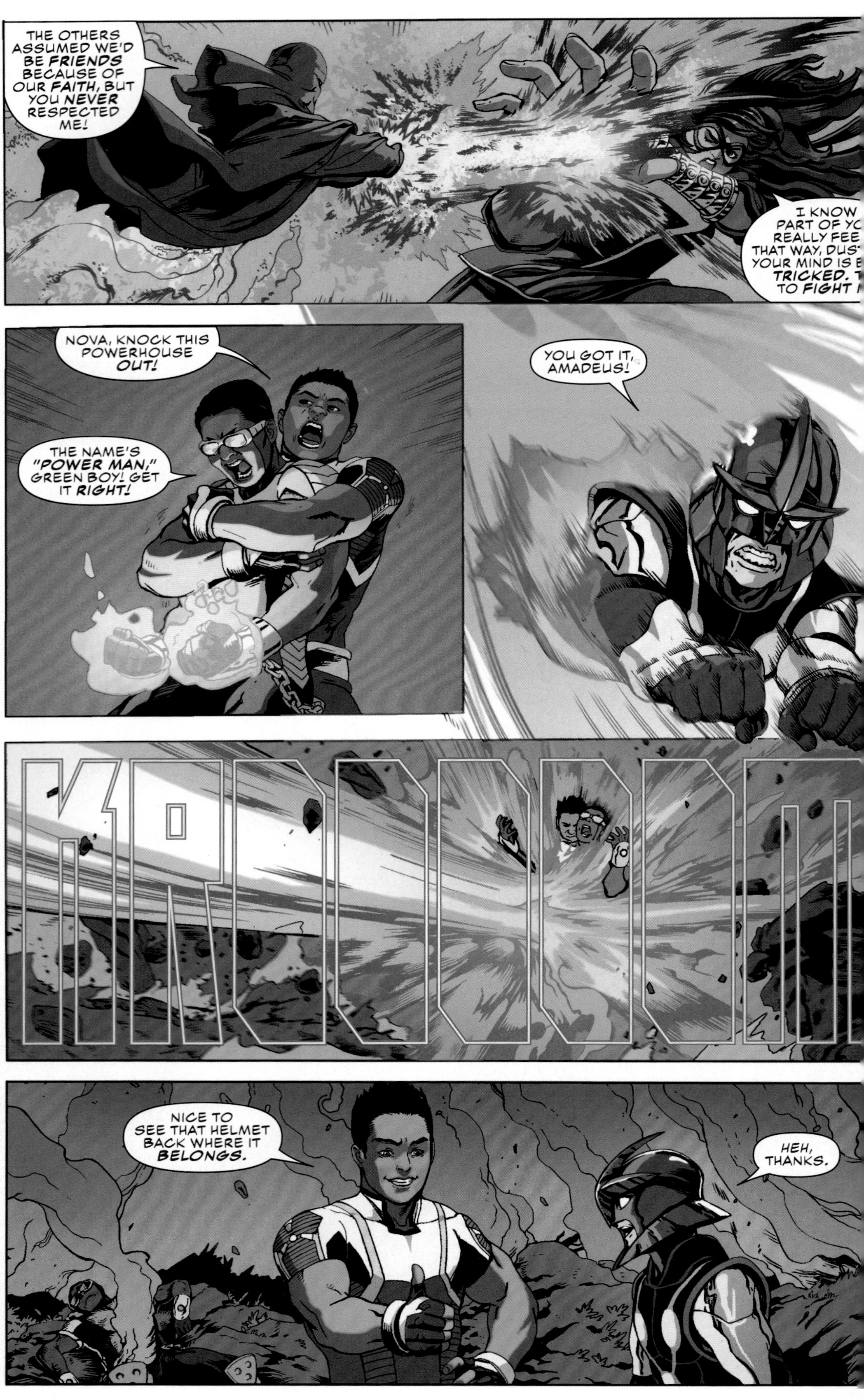
THE OTHERS ASSUMED WE'D BE FRIENDS BECAUSE OF OUR FAITH, BUT YOU NEVER RESPECTED ME!
I KNOW PART OF YO REALLY FEE THAT WAY, DUST YOUR MIND IS B TRICKED. T TO FIGHT I
NOVA, KNOCK THIS POWERHOUSE OUT!
THE NAME'S "POWER MAN," GREEN BOY! GET IT RIGHT!
YOU GOT IT, AMADEUS!
NICE TO SEE THAT HELMET BACK WHERE IT BELONGS.
HEH, THANKS.

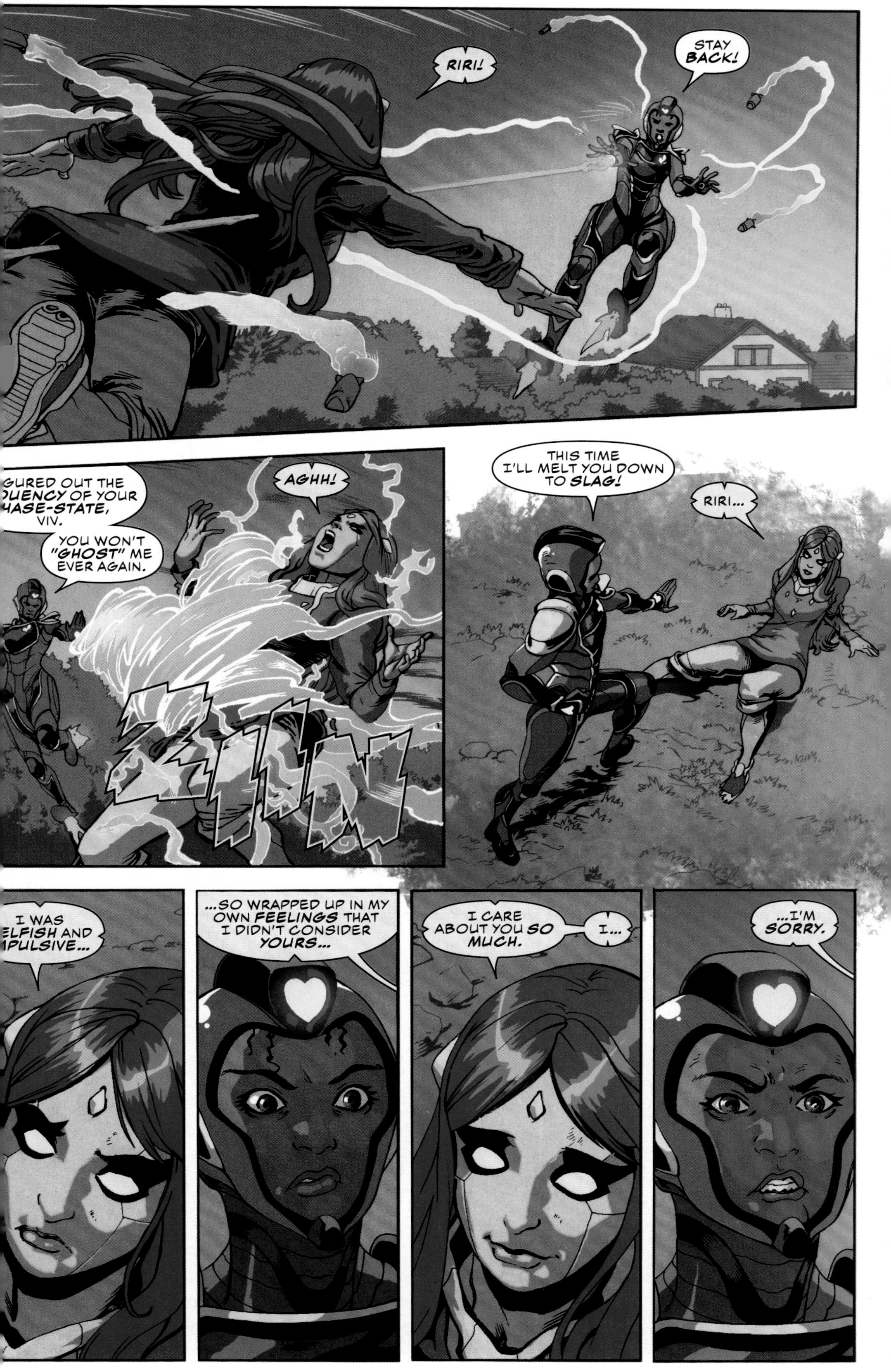

RIRI!
STAY BACK!
GURED OUT THE
QUENCY OF YOUR
HASE-STATE, VIV.
AGHH!
YOU WON'T "GHOST" ME EVER AGAIN.
ZMMM
THIS TIME I'LL MELT YOU DOWN TO SLAG!
RIRI...
I WAS
ELFISH AND
MPULSIVE...
...SO WRAPPED UP IN MY OWN FEELINGS THAT I DIDN'T CONSIDER YOURS...
I CARE ABOUT YOU SO MUCH.
I...
...I'M SORRY.

RAAAAAH!

VIV! IT WAS HORRIFYING... COULDN'T STOP THAT ANGER...

IT'S OKAY, RIRI. I KNOW.

I WISH WE COULD TALK IT THROUGH NOW, BUT THE OTHER ARE STILL BEING CONTROLLED.

ROGER THAT.

I BUILT THE IRONHEART 3.0 ARMOR WITH A TON OF NONLETHAL CONFRONTATION OPTIONS, SO LET'S PUT 'EM TO THE TEST.

COVER YOU! OCULARS, VIV...

...BIG FLASH COMING UP!

AND NOW A QUICK BURST OF ULTRASONICS TO CALM THINGS DOWN.

REEEEEEEEEEEEEEEEE

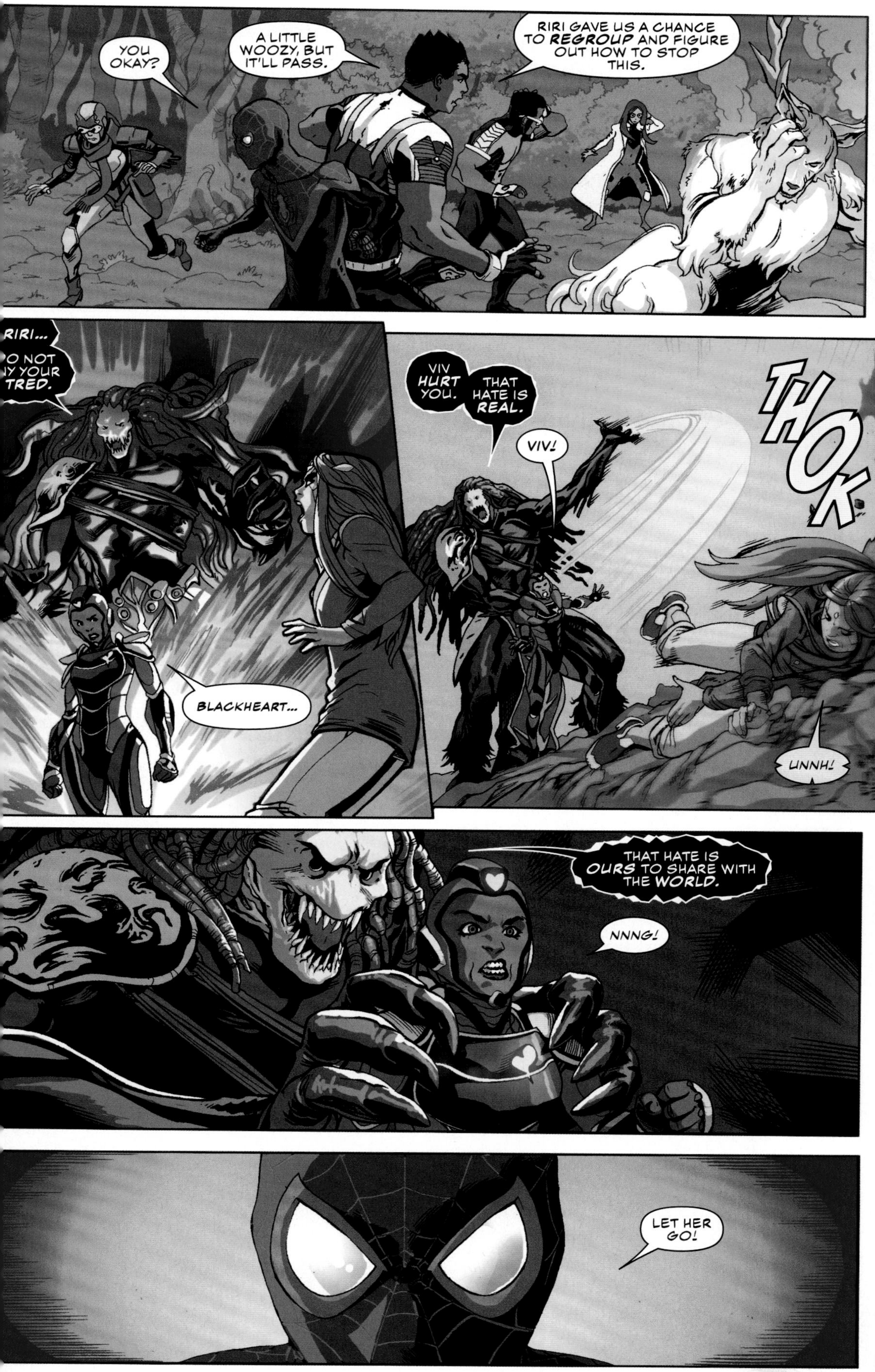
YOU OKAY?
A LITTLE WOOZY, BUT IT'LL PASS.
RIRI GAVE US A CHANCE TO REGROUP AND FIGURE OUT HOW TO STOP THIS.
RIRI...
O NOT NY YOUR TRED.
BLACKHEART...
VIV HURT YOU.
THAT HATE IS REAL.
VIV!
THOK
UNNH!
THAT HATE IS OURS TO SHARE WITH THE WORLD.
NNNG!
LET HER GO!

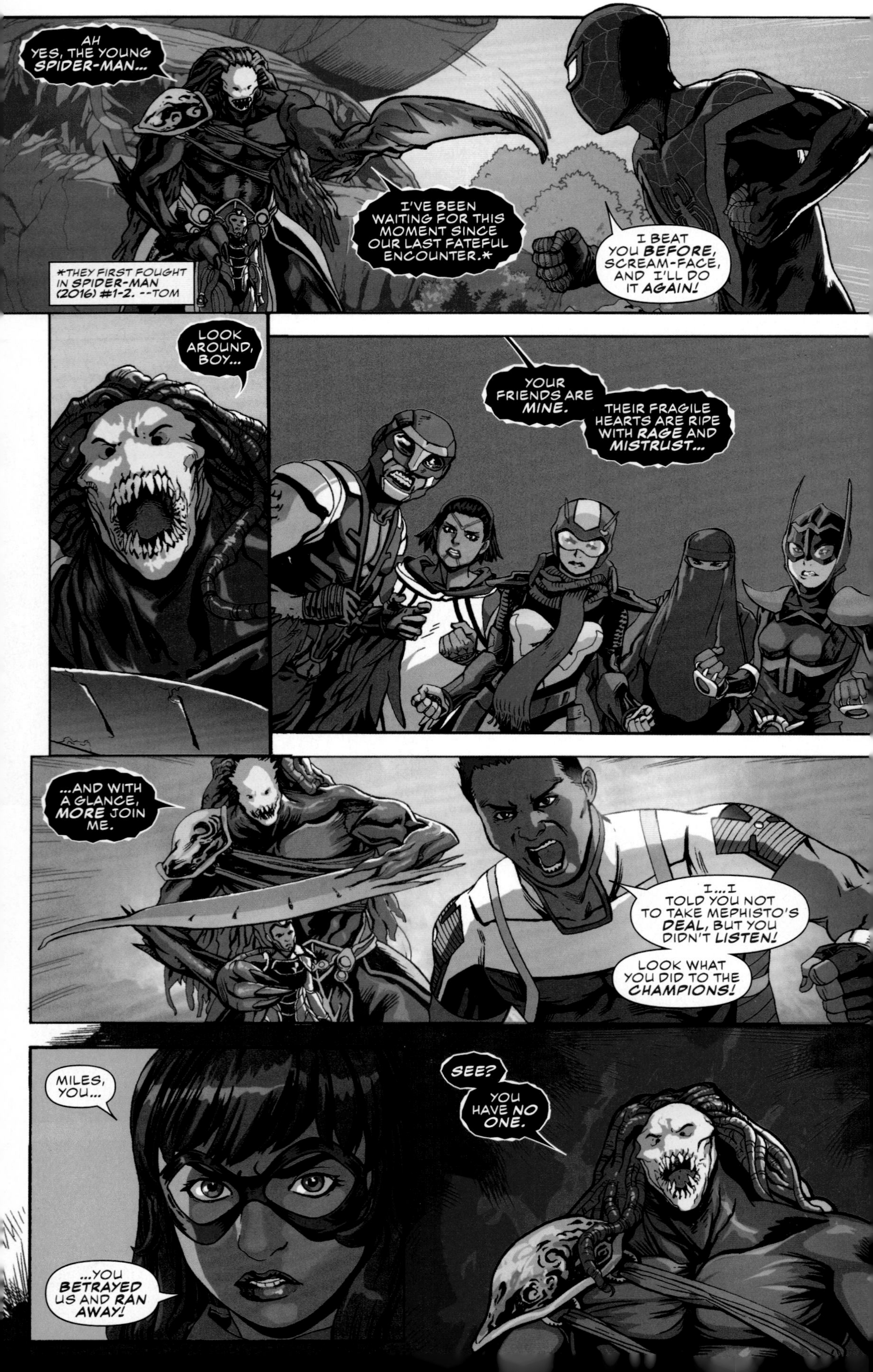
AH YES, THE YOUNG SPIDER-MAN...
I'VE BEEN WAITING FOR THIS MOMENT SINCE OUR LAST FATEFUL ENCOUNTER.*
*THEY FIRST FOUGHT IN SPIDER-MAN (2016) #1-2. --TOM
I BEAT YOU BEFORE, SCREAM-FACE, AND I'LL DO IT AGAIN!
LOOK AROUND, BOY...
YOUR FRIENDS ARE MINE.
THEIR FRAGILE HEARTS ARE RIPE WITH RAGE AND MISTRUST...
...AND WITH A GLANCE, MORE JOIN ME.
I...I TOLD YOU NOT TO TAKE MEPHISTO'S DEAL, BUT YOU DIDN'T LISTEN!
LOOK WHAT YOU DID TO THE CHAMPIONS!
MILES, YOU...
SEE?
YOU HAVE NO ONE.
...YOU BETRAYED US AND RAN AWAY!

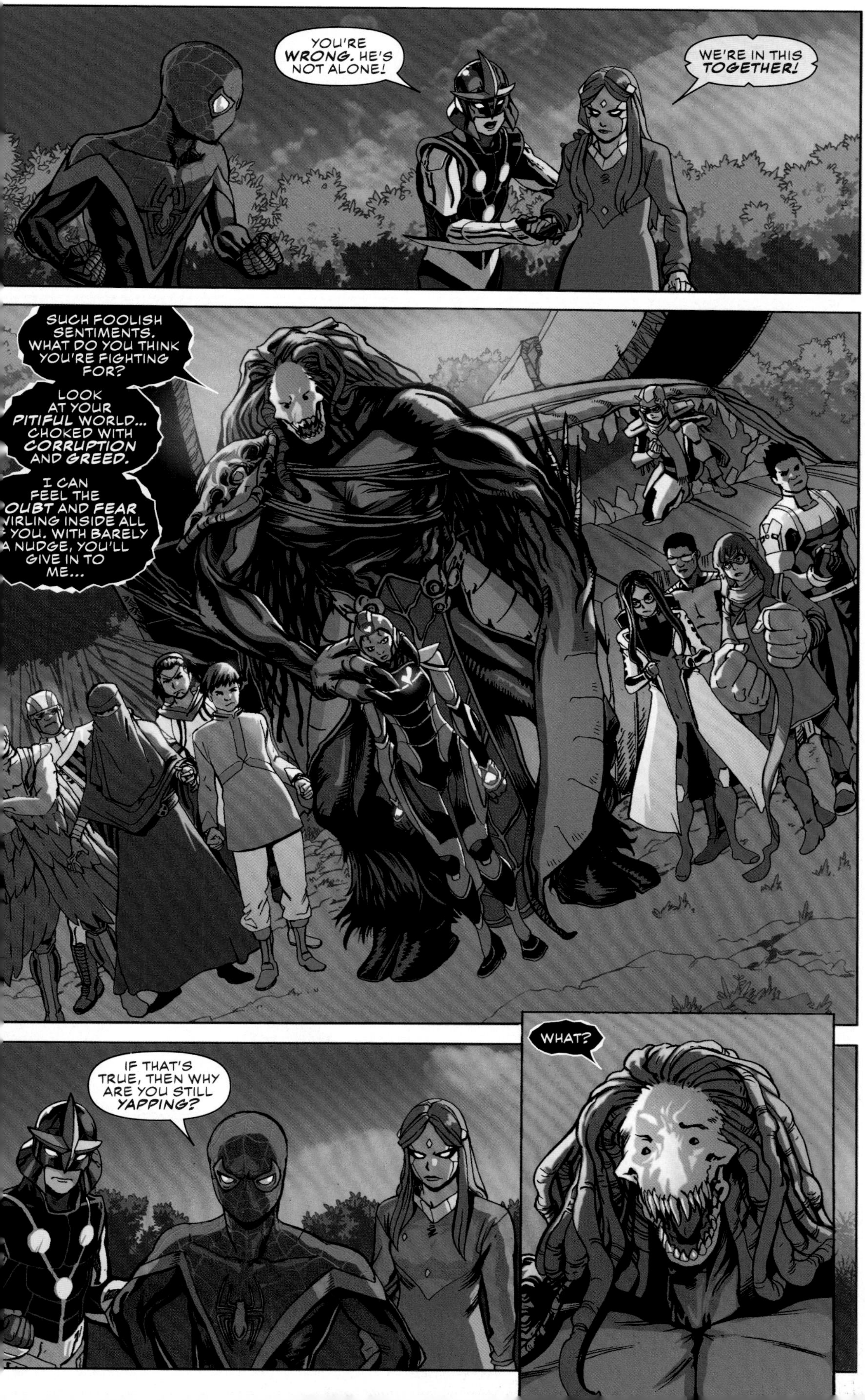
YOU'RE WRONG. HE'S NOT ALONE!
WE'RE IN THIS TOGETHER!
SUCH FOOLISH SENTIMENTS. WHAT DO YOU THINK YOU'RE FIGHTING FOR?
LOOK AT YOUR PITIFUL WORLD... CHOKED WITH CORRUPTION AND GREED.
I CAN FEEL THE OUBT AND FEAR VIRLING INSIDE ALL YOU. WITH BARELY A NUDGE, YOU'LL GIVE IN TO ME...
IF THAT'S TRUE, THEN WHY ARE YOU STILL YAPPING?
WHAT?

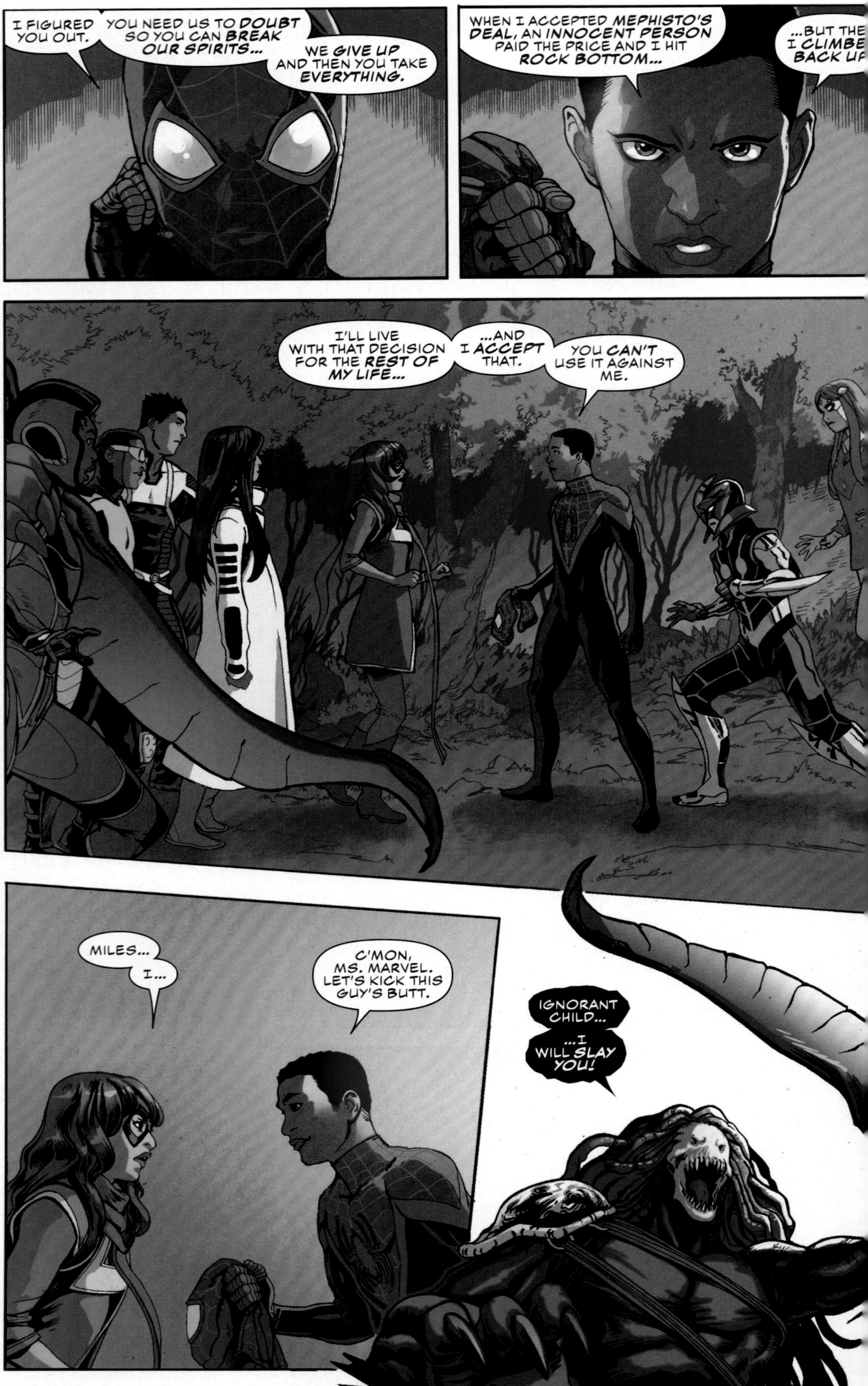
I FIGURED YOU OUT.
YOU NEED US TO DOUBT SO YOU CAN BREAK OUR SPIRITS...
WE GIVE UP AND THEN YOU TAKE EVERYTHING.
WHEN I ACCEPTED MEPHISTO'S DEAL, AN INNOCENT PERSON PAID THE PRICE AND I HIT ROCK BOTTOM...
...BUT THE I CLIMBE BACK UP
I'LL LIVE WITH THAT DECISION FOR THE REST OF MY LIFE...
...AND I ACCEPT THAT.
YOU CAN'T USE IT AGAINST ME.
MILES...
I...
C'MON, MS. MARVEL. LET'S KICK THIS GUY'S BUTT.
IGNORANT CHILD...
...I WILL SLAY YOU!

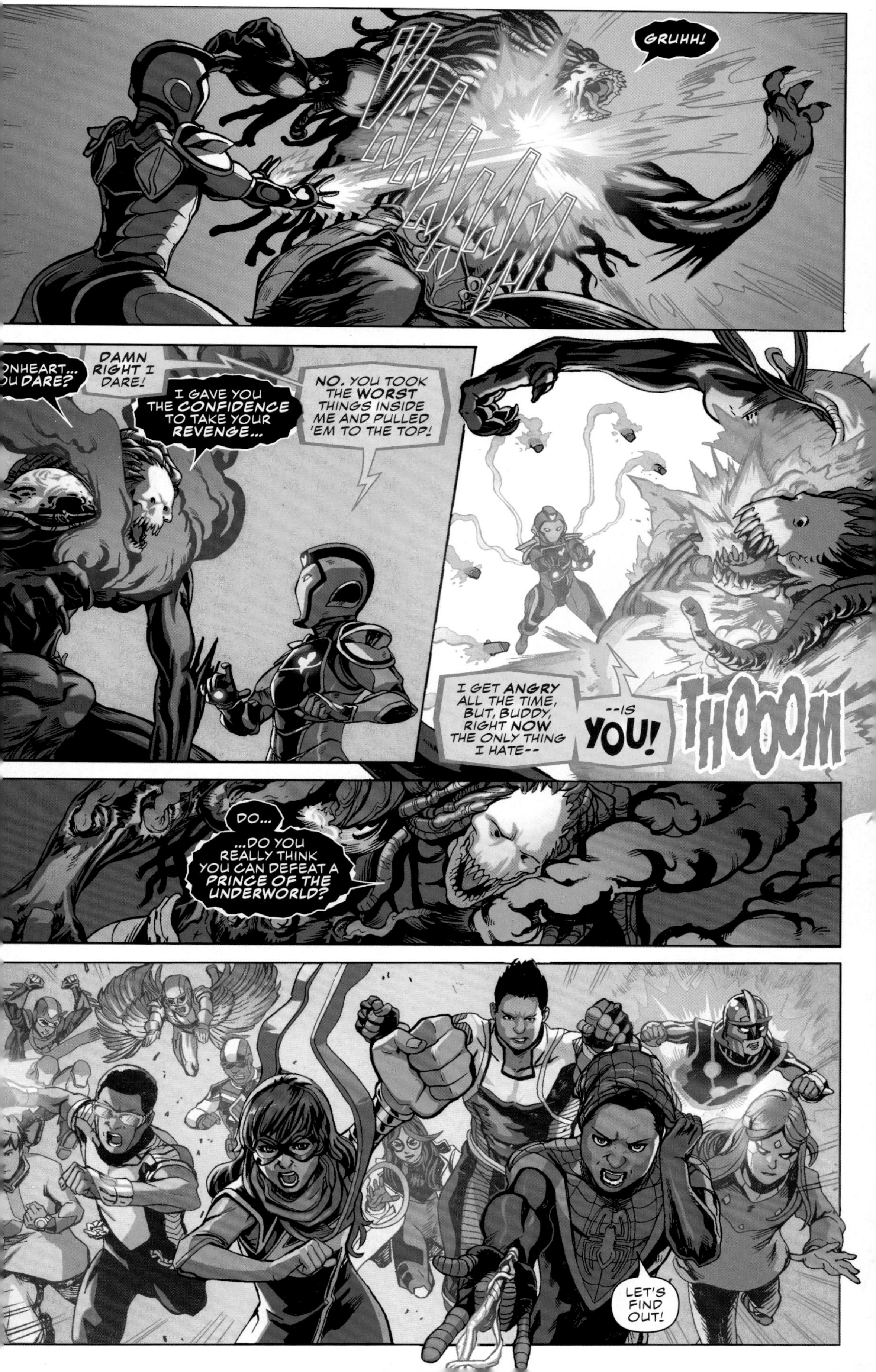
GRUHH!
ONHEART... OU DARE?
DAMN RIGHT I DARE!
I GAVE YOU THE CONFIDENCE TO TAKE YOUR REVENGE...
NO. YOU TOOK THE WORST THINGS INSIDE ME AND PULLED 'EM TO THE TOP!
I GET ANGRY ALL THE TIME, BUT, BUDDY, RIGHT NOW THE ONLY THING I HATE--
--IS YOU!
THOOOM
DO...
...DO YOU REALLY THINK YOU CAN DEFEAT A PRINCE OF THE UNDERWORLD?
LET'S FIND OUT!

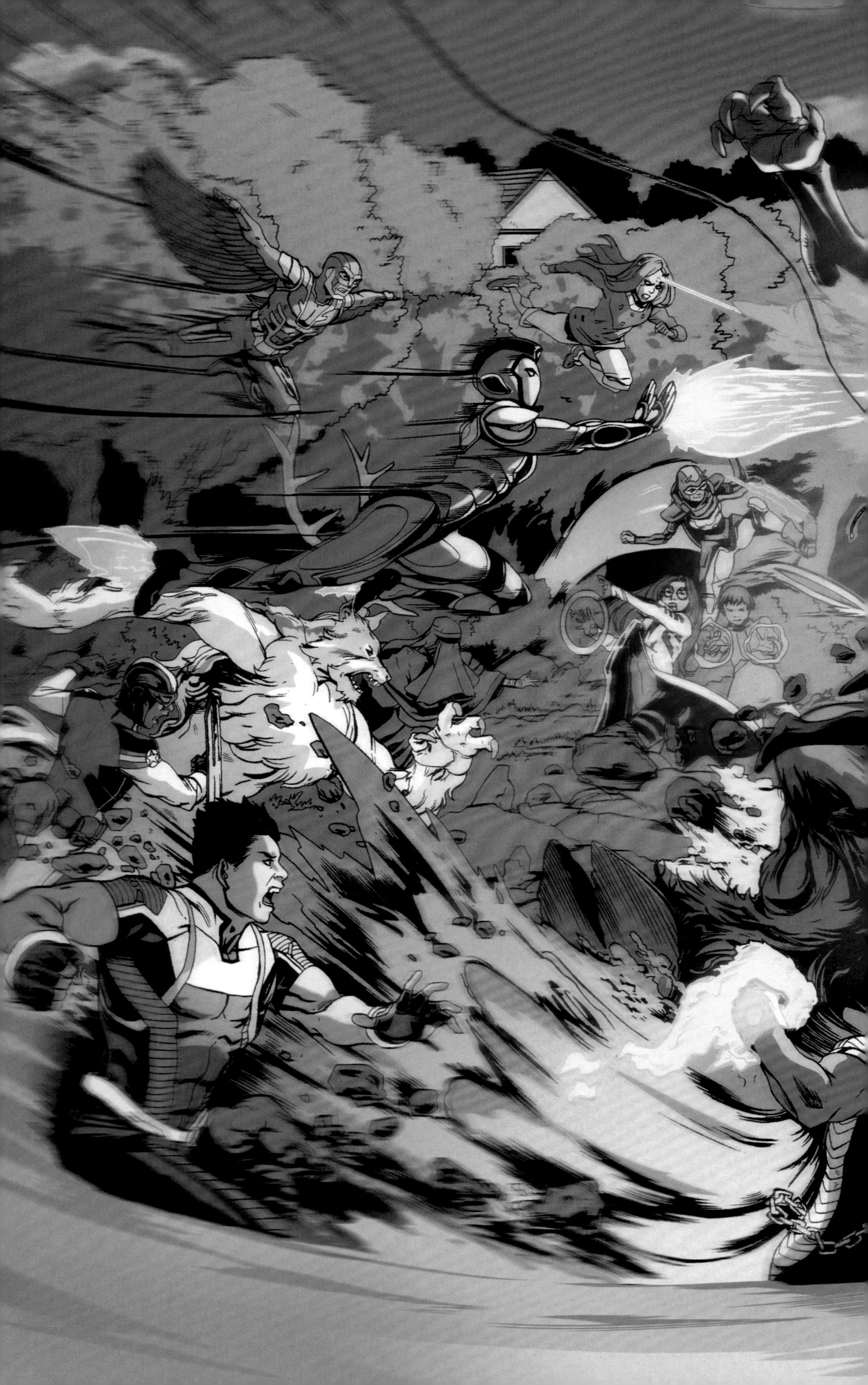

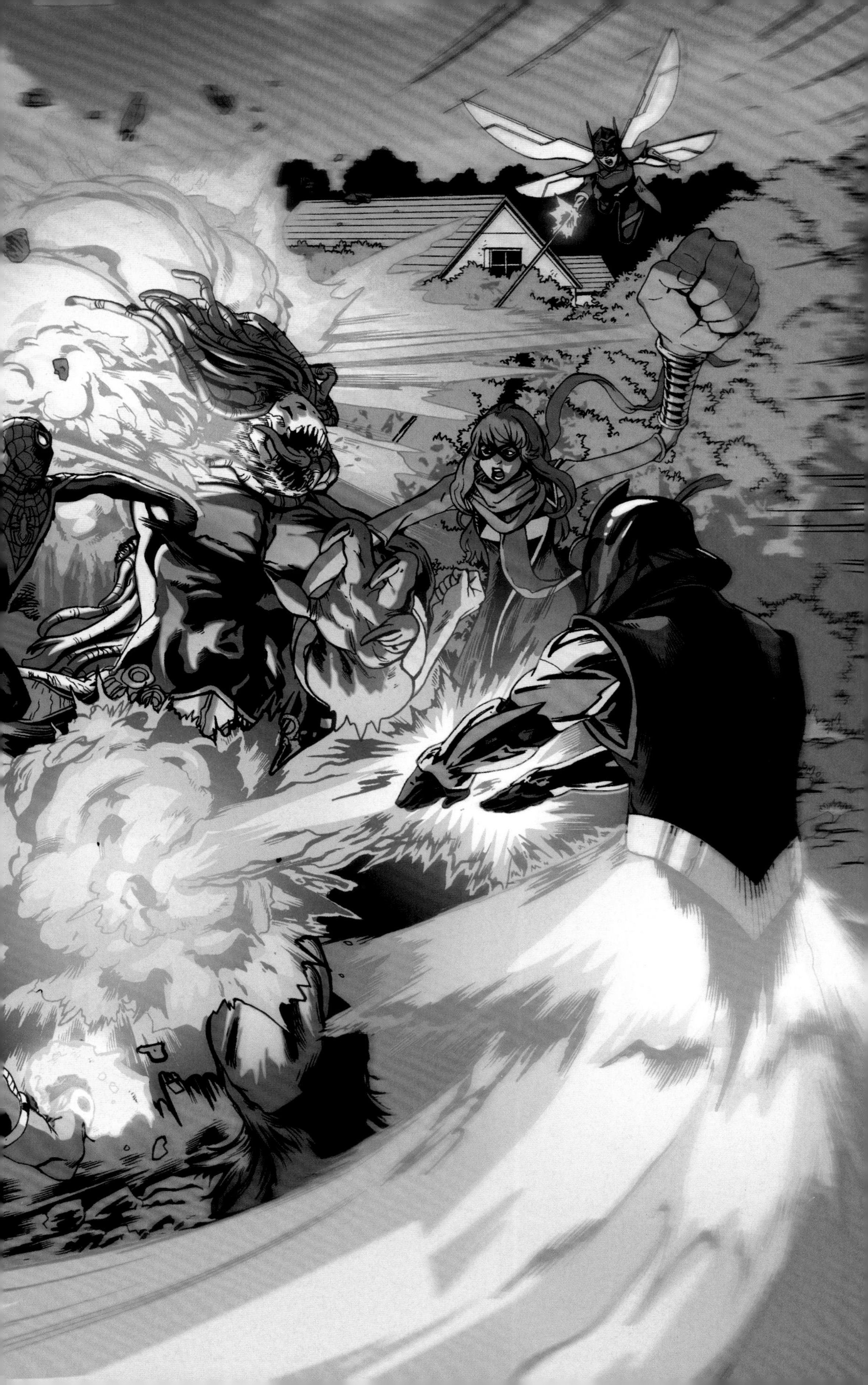

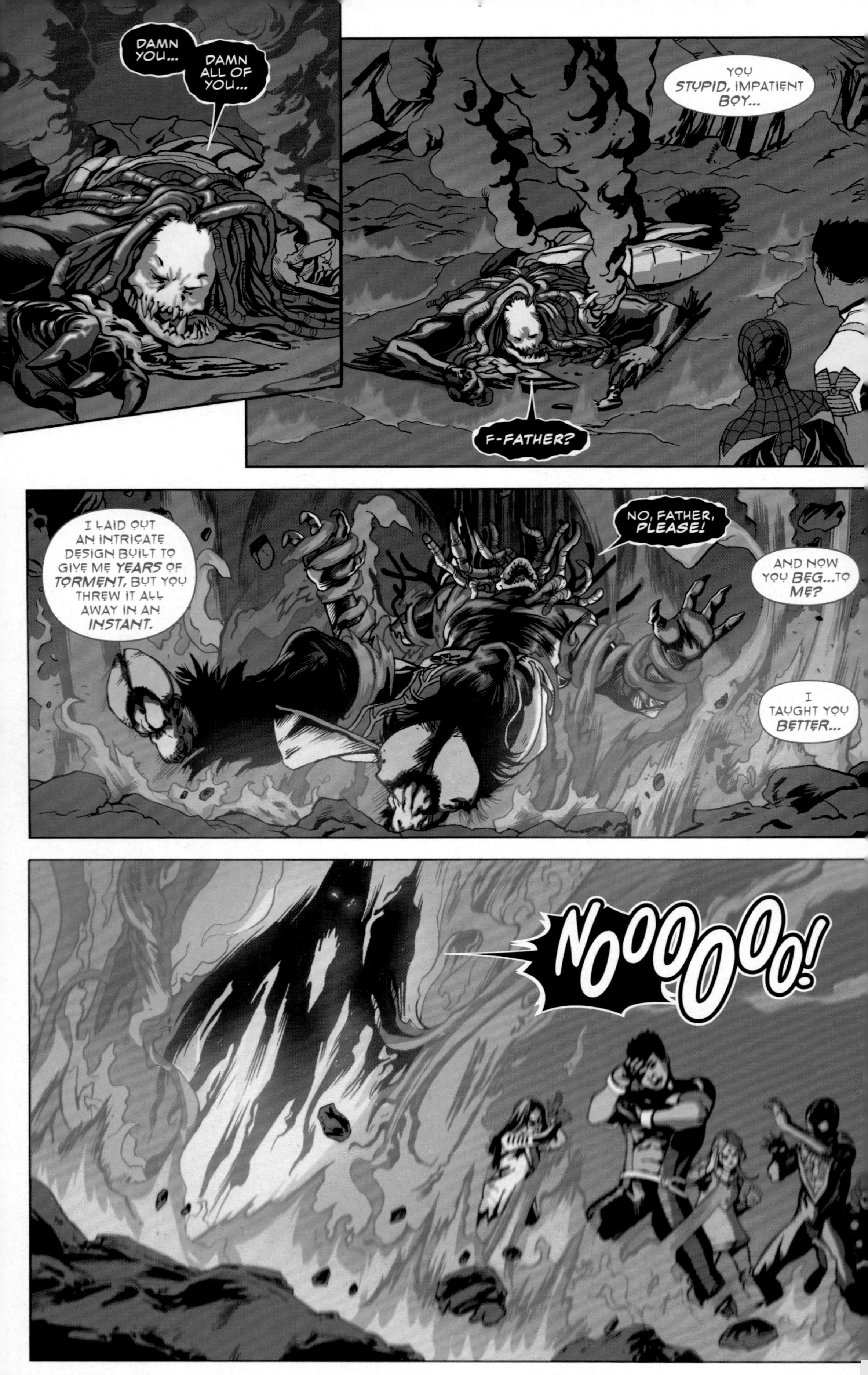
DAMN YOU...
DAMN ALL OF YOU...
YOU STUPID, IMPATIENT BOY...
F-FATHER?
I LAID OUT AN INTRICATE DESIGN BUILT TO GIVE ME YEARS OF TORMENT, BUT YOU THREW IT ALL AWAY IN AN INSTANT.
NO, FATHER, PLEASE!
AND NOW YOU BEG...TO ME?
I TAUGHT YOU BETTER...
NOOOOOO!

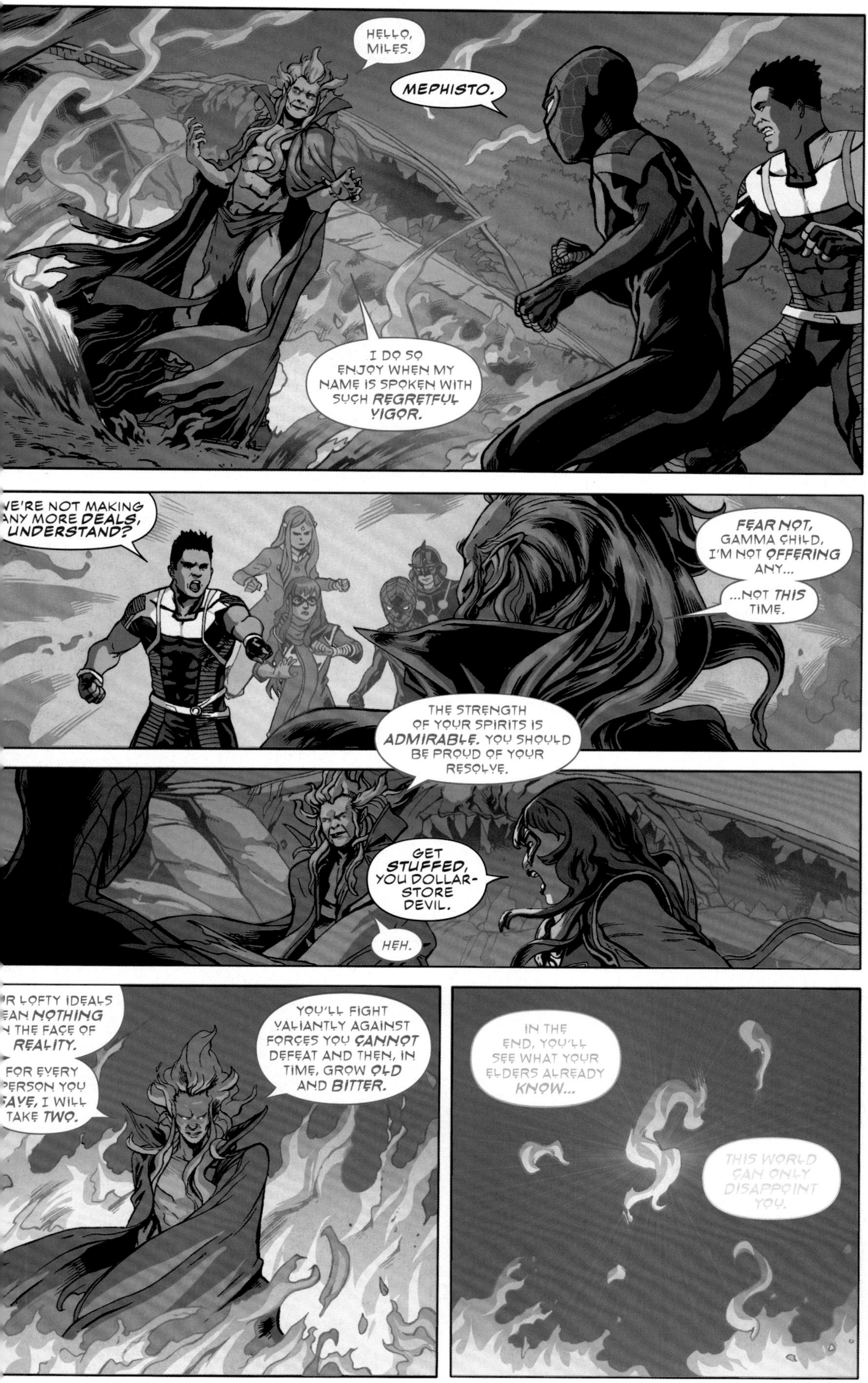
HELLO, MILES.
MEPHISTO.
I DO SO ENJOY WHEN MY NAME IS SPOKEN WITH SUCH REGRETFUL VIGOR.
WE'RE NOT MAKING ANY MORE DEALS, UNDERSTAND?
FEAR NOT, GAMMA CHILD, I'M NOT OFFERING ANY...
...NOT THIS TIME.
THE STRENGTH OF YOUR SPIRITS IS ADMIRABLE. YOU SHOULD BE PROUD OF YOUR RESOLVE.
GET STUFFED, YOU DOLLAR-STORE DEVIL.
HEH.
R LOFTY IDEALS EAN NOTHING N THE FACE OF REALITY.
FOR EVERY PERSON YOU SAVE, I WILL TAKE TWO.
YOU'LL FIGHT VALIANTLY AGAINST FORCES YOU CANNOT DEFEAT AND THEN, IN TIME, GROW OLD AND BITTER.
IN THE END, YOU'LL SEE WHAT YOUR ELDERS ALREADY KNOW...
THIS WORLD CAN ONLY DISAPPOINT YOU.

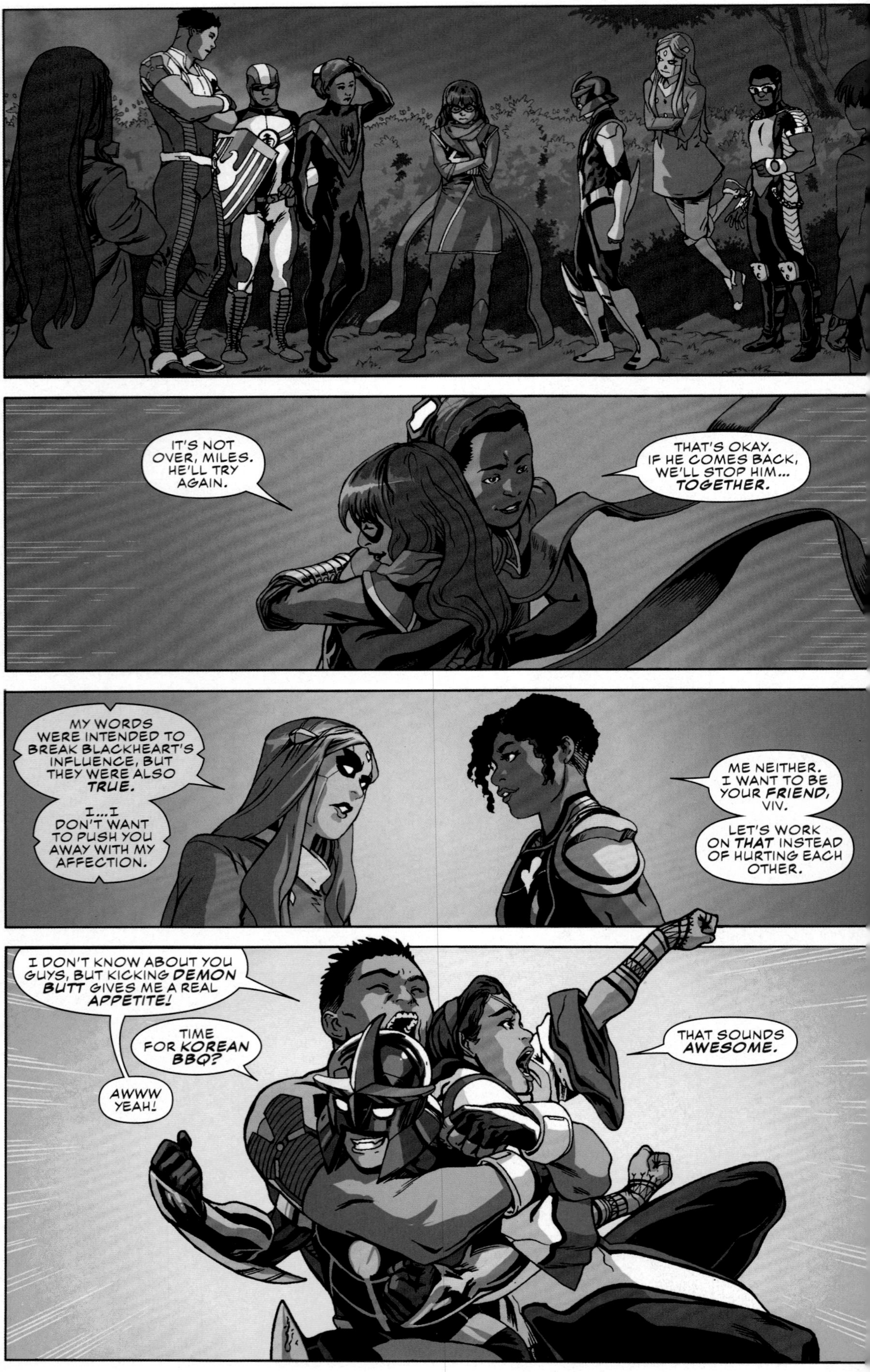

IT'S NOT OVER, MILES. HE'LL TRY AGAIN.
THAT'S OKAY. IF HE COMES BACK, WE'LL STOP HIM... TOGETHER.
MY WORDS WERE INTENDED TO BREAK BLACKHEART'S INFLUENCE, BUT THEY WERE ALSO TRUE.
I...I DON'T WANT TO PUSH YOU AWAY WITH MY AFFECTION.
ME NEITHER. I WANT TO BE YOUR FRIEND, VIV.
LET'S WORK ON THAT INSTEAD OF HURTING EACH OTHER.
I DON'T KNOW ABOUT YOU GUYS, BUT KICKING DEMON BUTT GIVES ME A REAL APPETITE!
TIME FOR KOREAN BBQ?
AWWW YEAH!
THAT SOUNDS AWESOME.

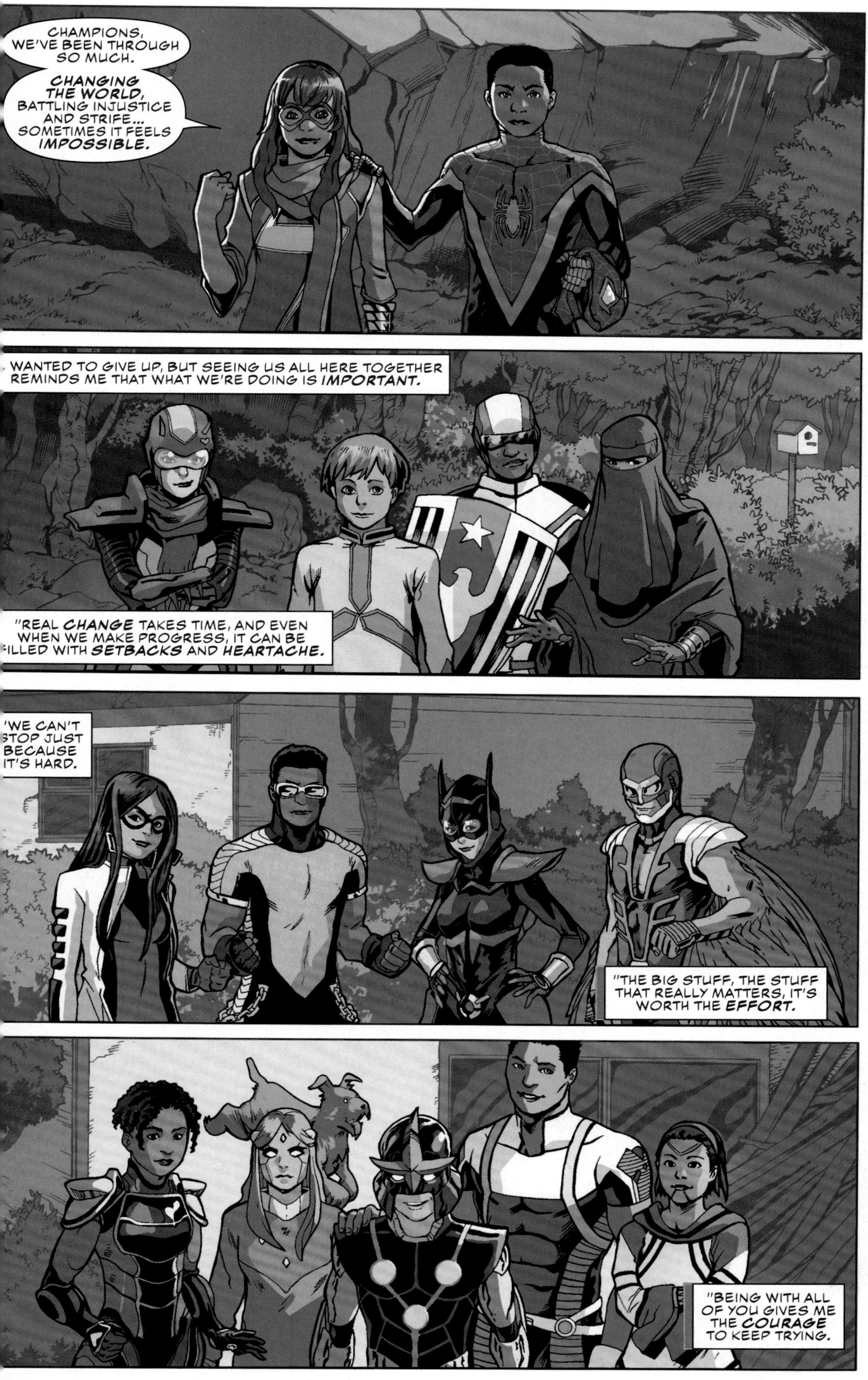
CHAMPIONS, WE'VE BEEN THROUGH SO MUCH.
CHANGING THE WORLD, BATTLING INJUSTICE AND STRIFE... SOMETIMES IT FEELS IMPOSSIBLE.
WANTED TO GIVE UP, BUT SEEING US ALL HERE TOGETHER REMINDS ME THAT WHAT WE'RE DOING IS IMPORTANT.
"REAL CHANGE TAKES TIME, AND EVEN WHEN WE MAKE PROGRESS, IT CAN BE FILLED WITH SETBACKS AND HEARTACHE.
"WE CAN'T STOP JUST BECAUSE IT'S HARD.
"THE BIG STUFF, THE STUFF THAT REALLY MATTERS, IT'S WORTH THE EFFORT.
"BEING WITH ALL OF YOU GIVES ME THE COURAGE TO KEEP TRYING.

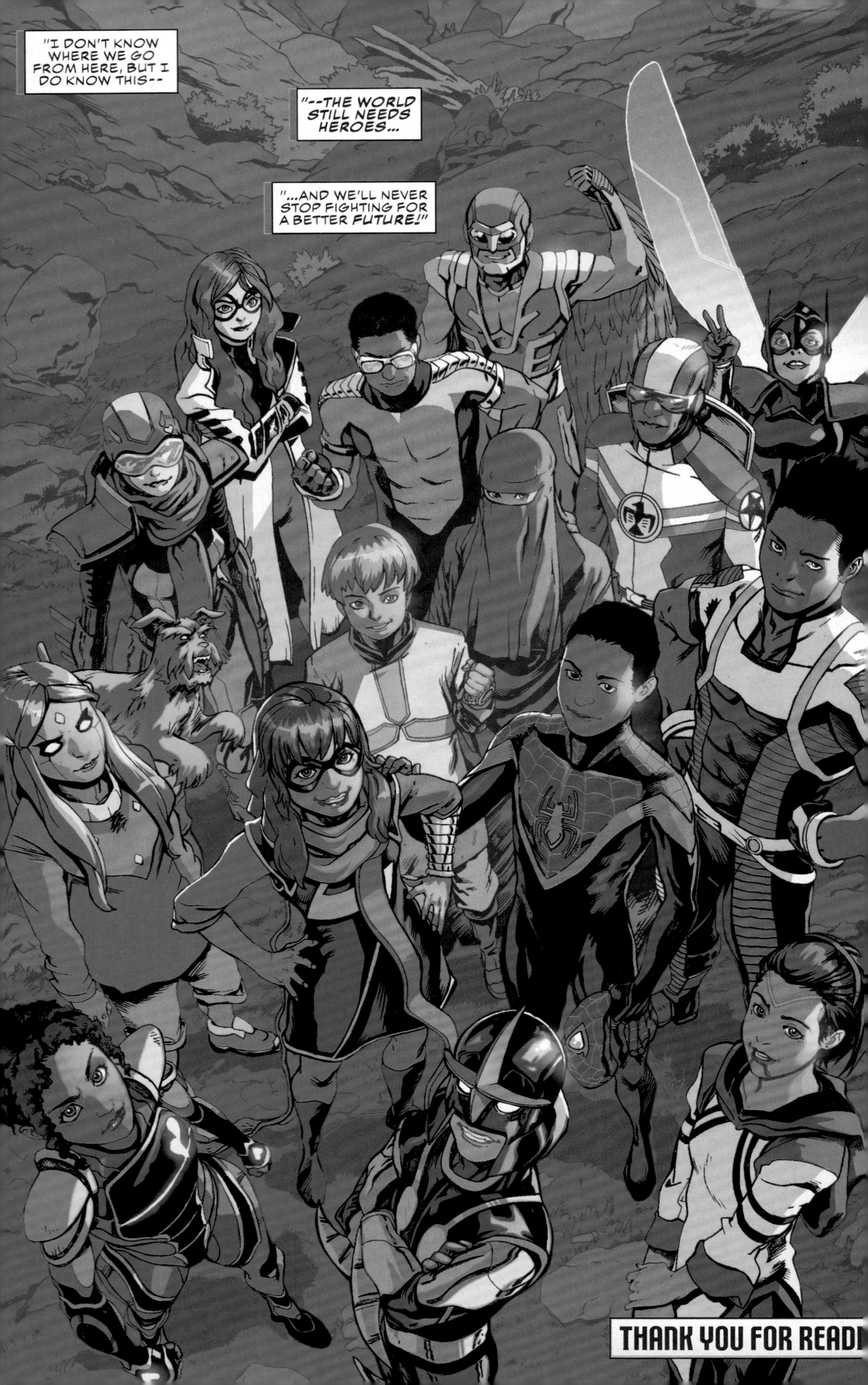
"I DON'T KNOW WHERE WE GO FROM HERE, BUT I DO KNOW THIS--
"--THE WORLD STILL NEEDS HEROES...
"...AND WE'LL NEVER STOP FIGHTING FOR A BETTER FUTURE!"
THANK YOU FOR READI

WE ARE THE CHAMPIONS

I built this new take on the team as a way to try to bridge classic teen superheroic drama with an eclectic cast of characters--old-school Marvel brought to the present with a new generation of heroes.

It was a risk and I knew that. In this case, the risk didn't pay off in sales the way we planned, but that's how the market goes sometimes. The only way to build new classic stories is to push out into the unknown and see what's possible.

Obviously I'm sad about it. Dressing that up any other way would be disingenuous. I wish it had worked out. I'm sorry if I let you down.

The readers and reviewers who keyed into what we were going for were incredible. Their excitement kept us going month after month.

Huge thanks to our whole creative team--Steven Cummings, Marcio Menyz, Clayton Cowles, Juanan Ramírez, Kim Jacinto and Rain Beredo. An even deeper thank you to editors C.B. Cebulski, Tom Brevoort, Alanna Smith and Shannon Andrews Ballesteros for letting me run with this wild idea in the first place.

If you're lamenting the future of your favorite young heroes, I can tell you that there are big plans for Marvel's teens in 2020. I've heard a bit about what comes next--it's exciting, vibrant and absolutely worthy of the House of Ideas. I'm a bit wistful that it's not mine to tell, but also hopeful for the future of these inspiring young heroes.

Thanks for the support,
Jim

When I was asked to join the team for the new version of CHAMPIONS, I was thrilled beyond words. The great cast of characters combined with Jim's wonderful words not only met my expectations for the series but more than surpassed them. The result was something in the vein of what made me fall in love with Marvel as a kid and I was honored to be a part of it.

All good things have to end though, and that includes this run of CHAMPIONS. It is sad to have to say goodbye to such a wonderful adventure and cast of characters, but I am grateful for the chance to draw this group. More than that I am grateful for all the readers who followed our tale. Thank you. Each and every one of you.

A giant thanks also to everyone on our creative team: Jim Zub, Marcio Menyz, Clayton Cowles, Juanan Ramírez, Kim Jacinto and Rain Beredo. You guys did great work and made our book look amazing!

An even bigger titan-sized thanks to everyone in Editorial who helped guide us: Tom Brevoort, Alanna Smith and Shannon Andrews Ballesteros. Thank you for waiting patiently and for helping with all the reference!

I can't wait to see what adventures you have in store for these characters!

Steven Cummings

I'm extremely grateful to have had the chance to take part in this whole Champions journey. It was a very important title for me, and I have a lot of affection for it. As for the creative team, I only have compliments--such talented and good people. Thanks for the run, guys! We did our best! And a special thanks for the great editorial team that we had!

It was a beautiful journey that made us feel like we're actually Champions!

Marcio Menyz

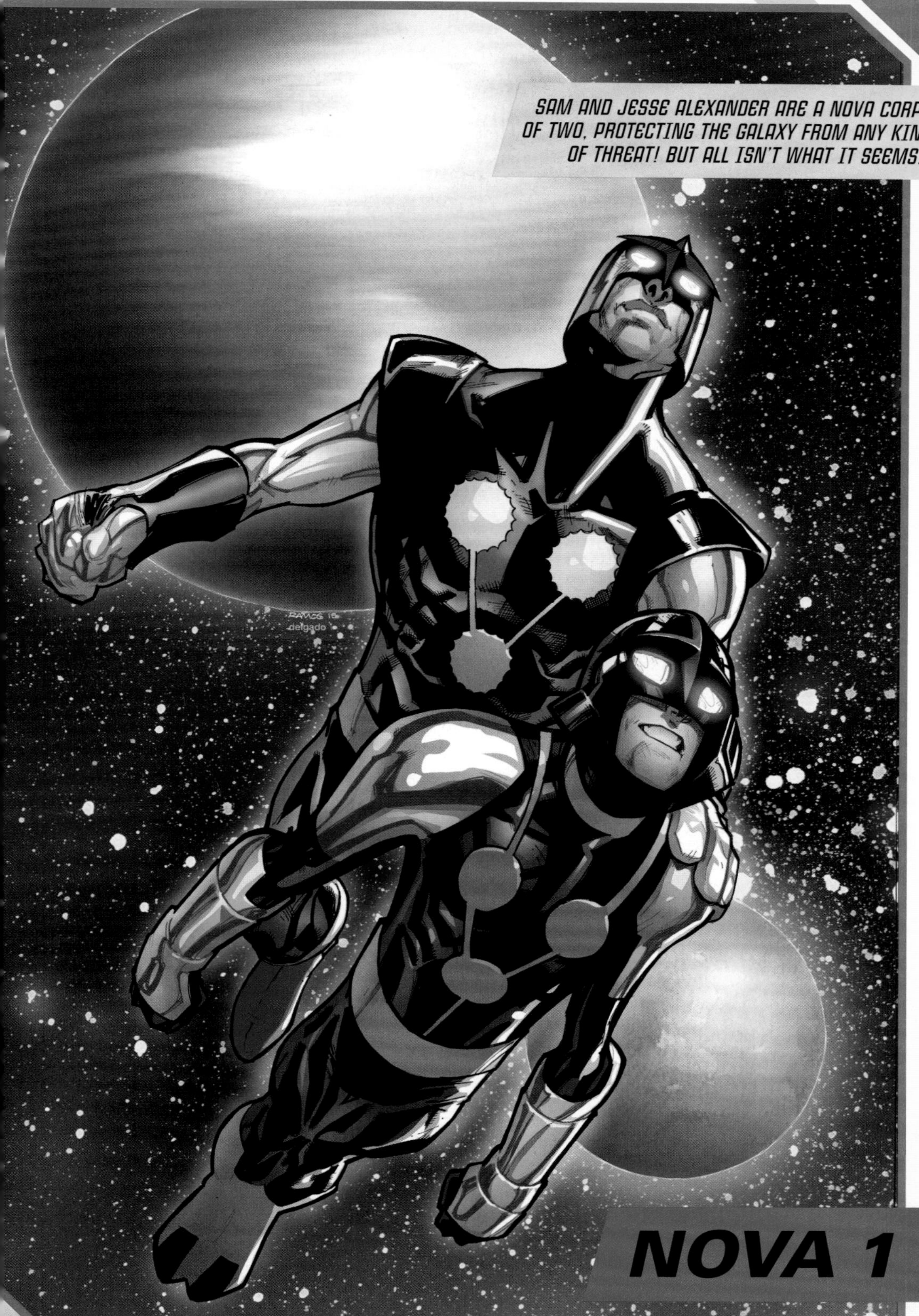
SAM AND JESSE ALEXANDER ARE A NOVA CORPS OF TWO, PROTECTING THE GALAXY FROM ANY KIND OF THREAT! BUT ALL ISN'T WHAT IT SEEMS...

NOVA 1

MARVEL COMICS PROUDLY PRESENTS

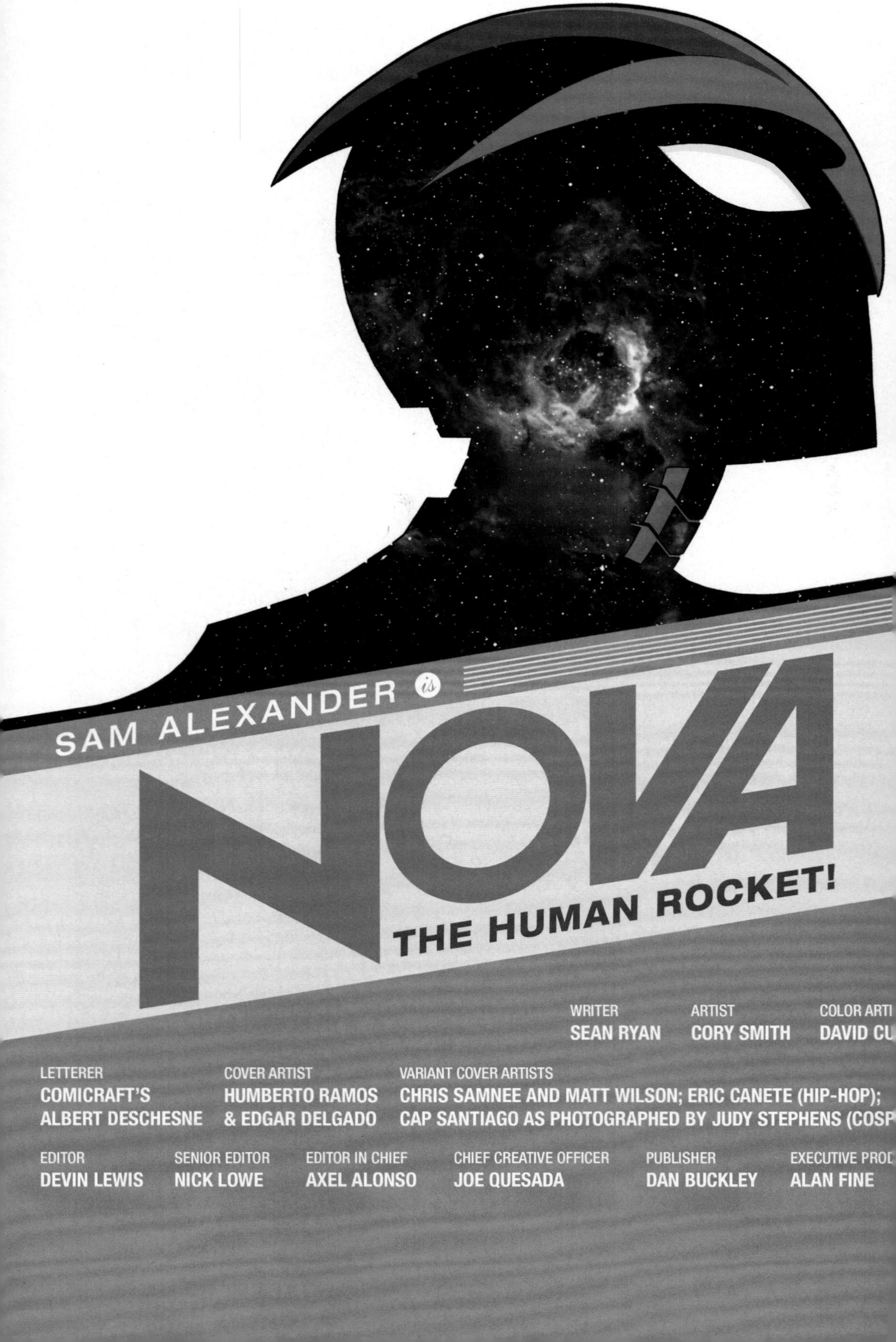

SAM ALEXANDER *is*

NOVA

THE HUMAN ROCKET!

WRITER
SEAN RYAN

ARTIST
CORY SMITH

COLOR ARTI
DAVID CU

LETTERER
COMICRAFT'S ALBERT DESCHESNE

COVER ARTIST
HUMBERTO RAMOS & EDGAR DELGADO

VARIANT COVER ARTISTS
CHRIS SAMNEE AND MATT WILSON; ERIC CANETE (HIP-HOP); CAP SANTIAGO AS PHOTOGRAPHED BY JUDY STEPHENS (COSP

EDITOR
DEVIN LEWIS

SENIOR EDITOR
NICK LOWE

EDITOR IN CHIEF
AXEL ALONSO

CHIEF CREATIVE OFFICER
JOE QUESADA

PUBLISHER
DAN BUCKLEY

EXECUTIVE PROD
ALAN FINE

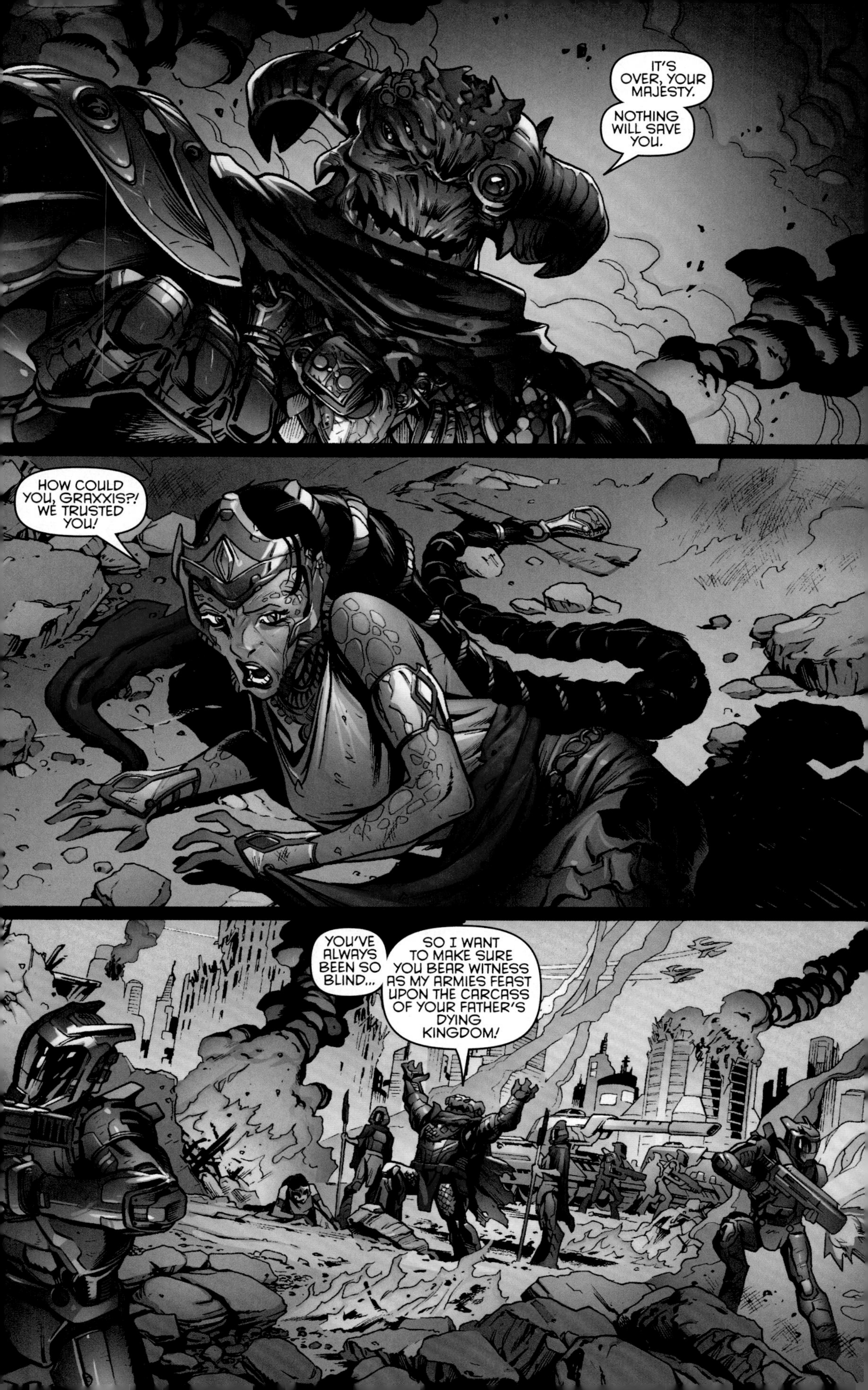
IT'S OVER, YOUR MAJESTY.
NOTHING WILL SAVE YOU.
HOW COULD YOU, GRAXXIS?! WE TRUSTED YOU!
YOU'VE ALWAYS BEEN SO BLIND...
SO I WANT TO MAKE SURE YOU BEAR WITNESS AS MY ARMIES FEAST UPON THE CARCASS OF YOUR FATHER'S DYING KINGDOM!

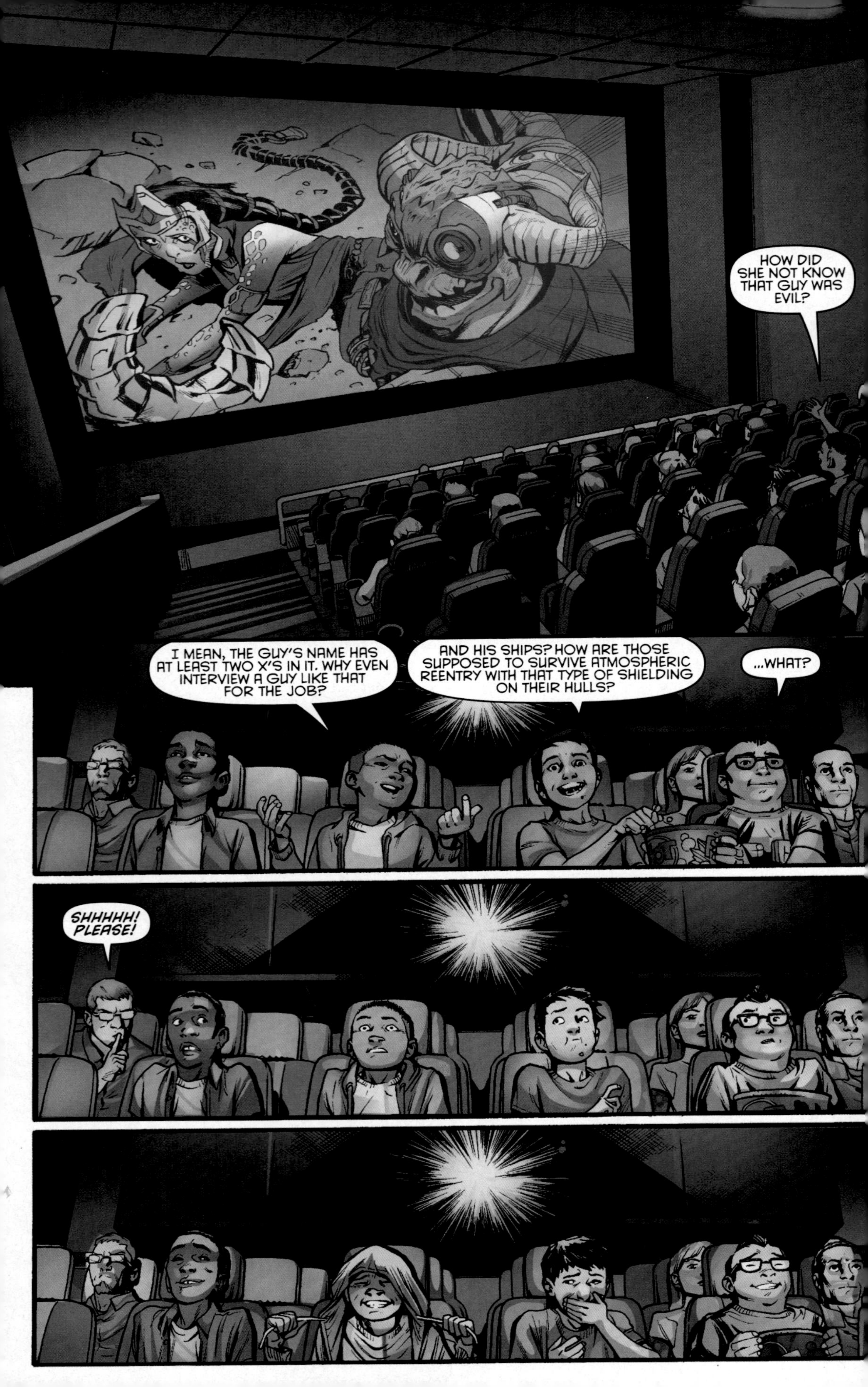
HOW DID SHE NOT KNOW THAT GUY WAS EVIL?
I MEAN, THE GUY'S NAME HAS AT LEAST TWO X'S IN IT. WHY EVEN INTERVIEW A GUY LIKE THAT FOR THE JOB?
AND HIS SHIPS? HOW ARE THOSE SUPPOSED TO SURVIVE ATMOSPHERIC REENTRY WITH THAT TYPE OF SHIELDING ON THEIR HULLS?
...WHAT?
SHHHHH! PLEASE!

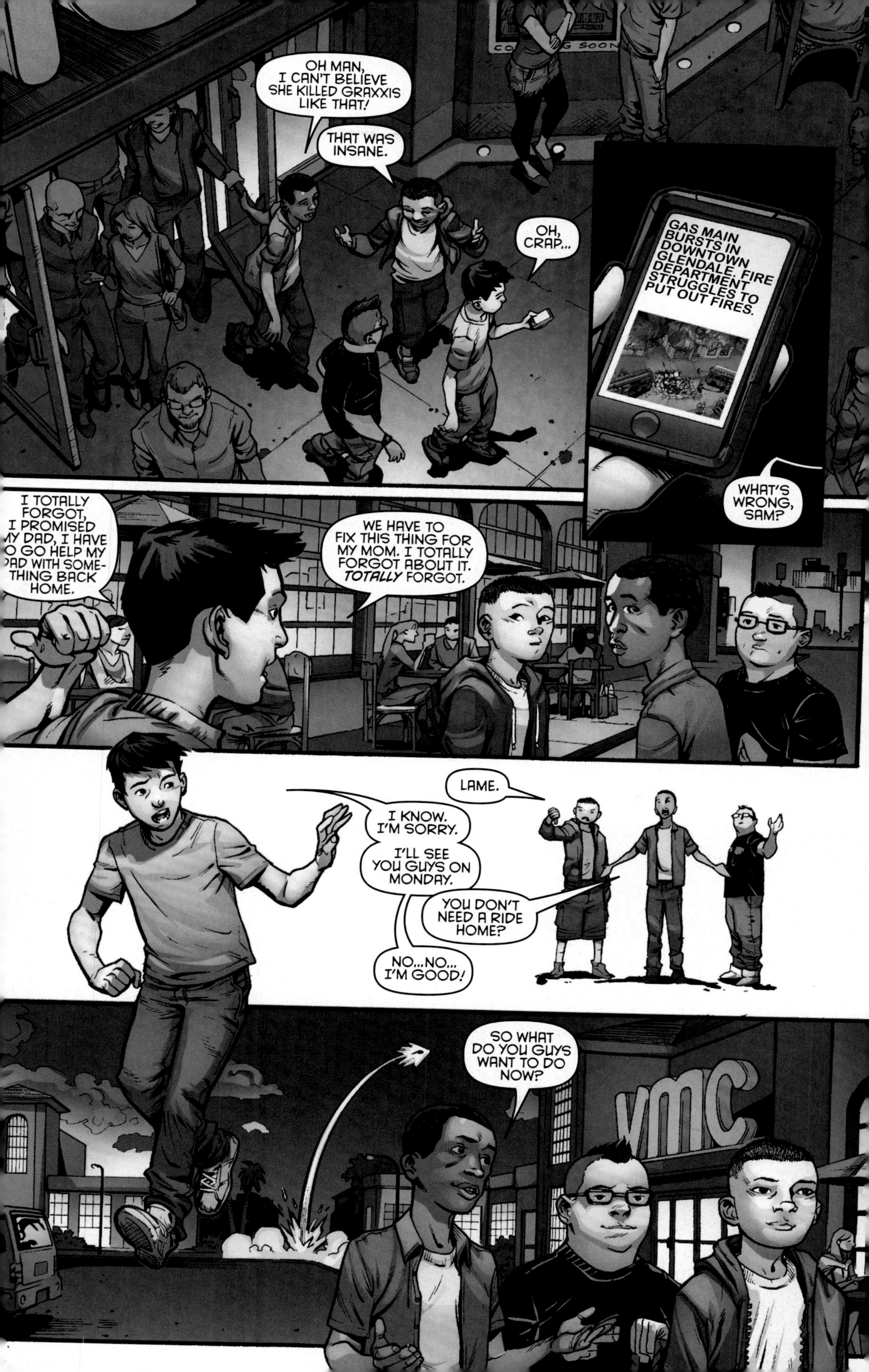
COMING SOON
OH MAN, I CAN'T BELIEVE SHE KILLED GRAXXIS LIKE THAT!
THAT WAS INSANE.
OH, CRAP...
GAS MAIN BURSTS IN DOWNTOWN GLENDALE. FIRE DEPARTMENT STRUGGLES TO PUT OUT FIRES.
WHAT'S WRONG, SAM?
I TOTALLY FORGOT, I PROMISED MY DAD, I HAVE TO GO HELP MY DAD WITH SOMETHING BACK HOME.
WE HAVE TO FIX THIS THING FOR MY MOM. I TOTALLY FORGOT ABOUT IT. *TOTALLY* FORGOT.
LAME.
I KNOW. I'M SORRY.
I'LL SEE YOU GUYS ON MONDAY.
YOU DON'T NEED A RIDE HOME?
NO...NO... I'M GOOD!
SO WHAT DO YOU GUYS WANT TO DO NOW?
VMC

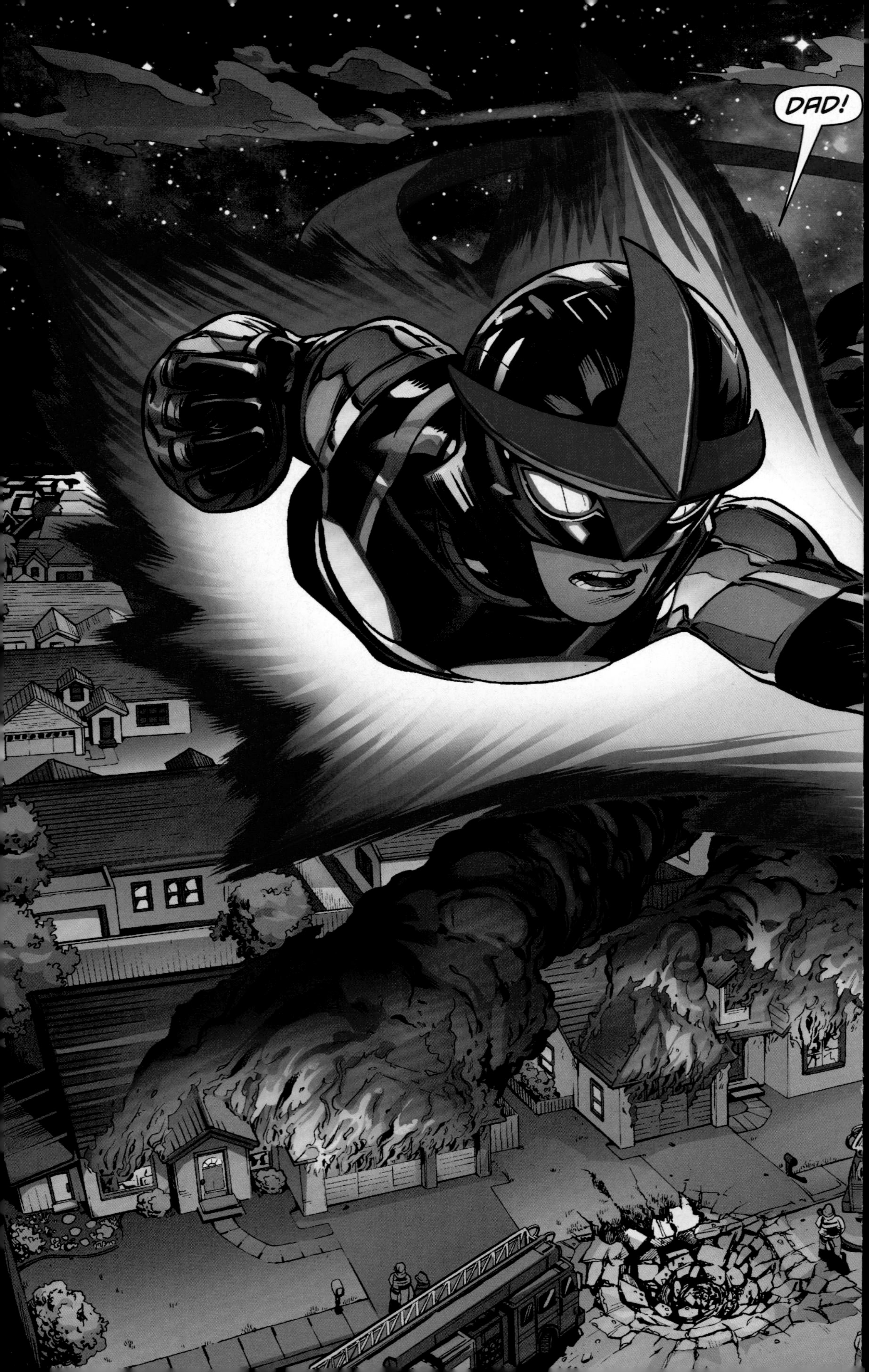
DAD!

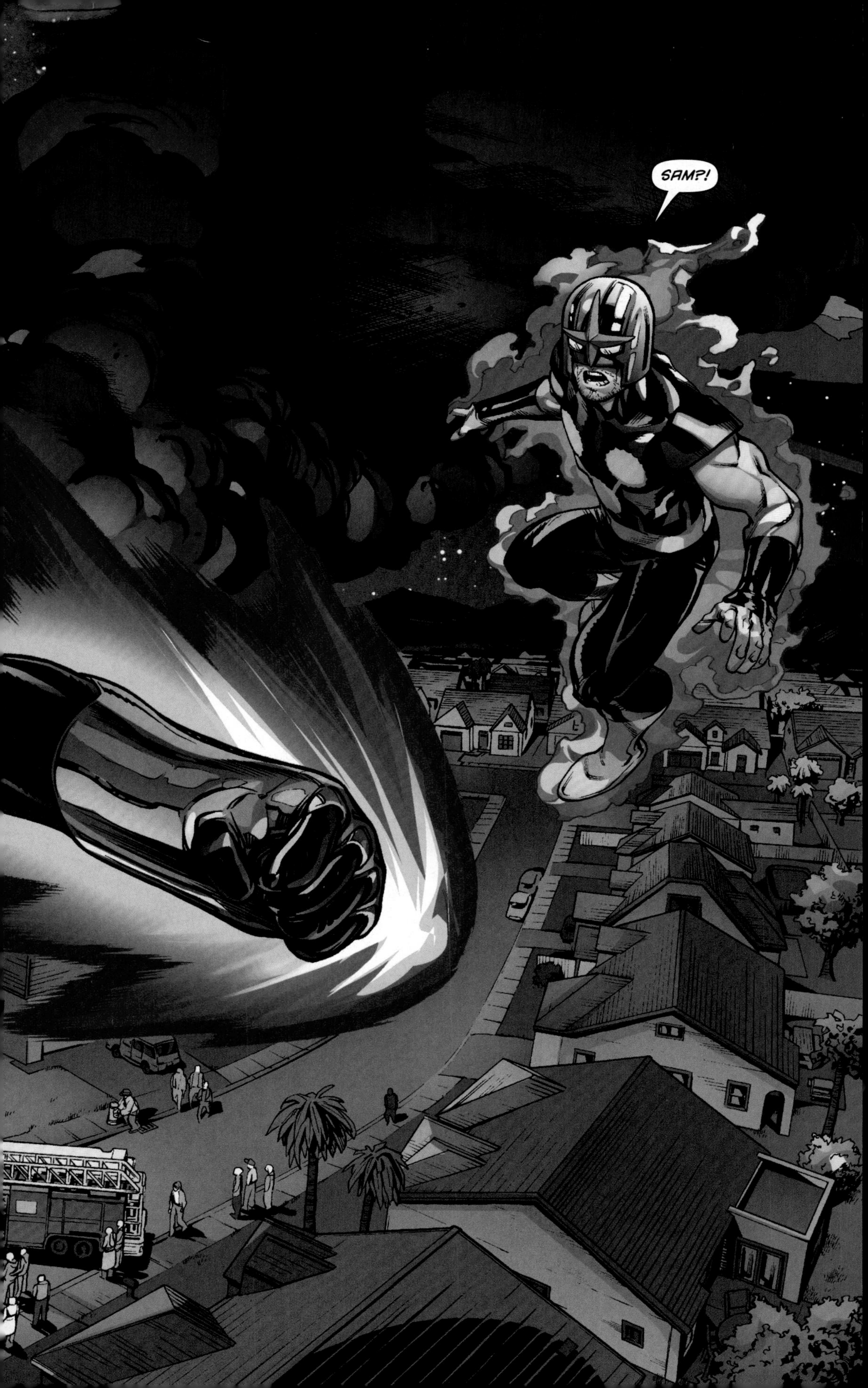
SAM?!

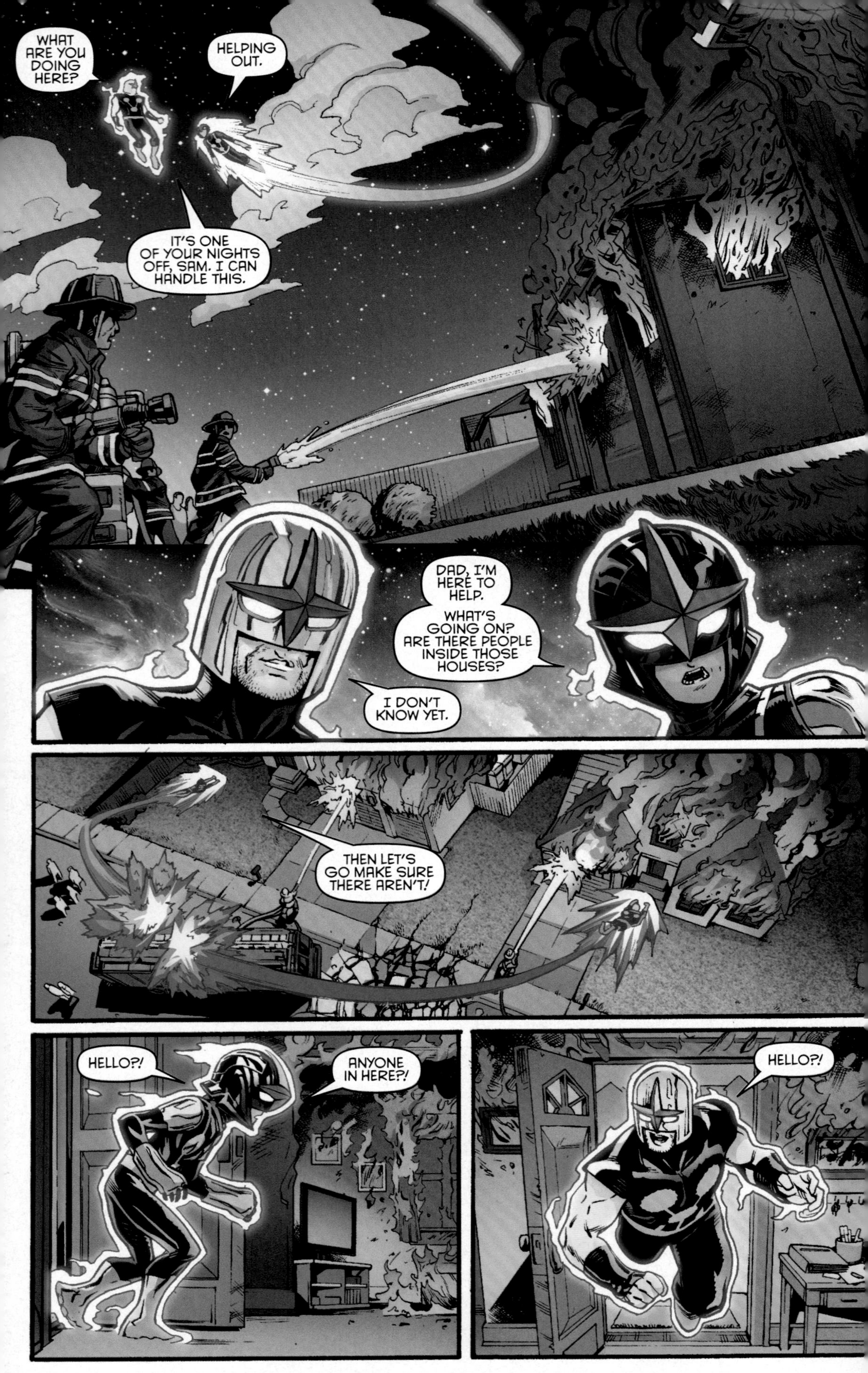
WHAT ARE YOU DOING HERE?
HELPING OUT.
IT'S ONE OF YOUR NIGHTS OFF, SAM. I CAN HANDLE THIS.
DAD, I'M HERE TO HELP.
WHAT'S GOING ON? ARE THERE PEOPLE INSIDE THOSE HOUSES?
I DON'T KNOW YET.
THEN LET'S GO MAKE SURE THERE AREN'T!
HELLO?!
ANYONE IN HERE?!
HELLO?!

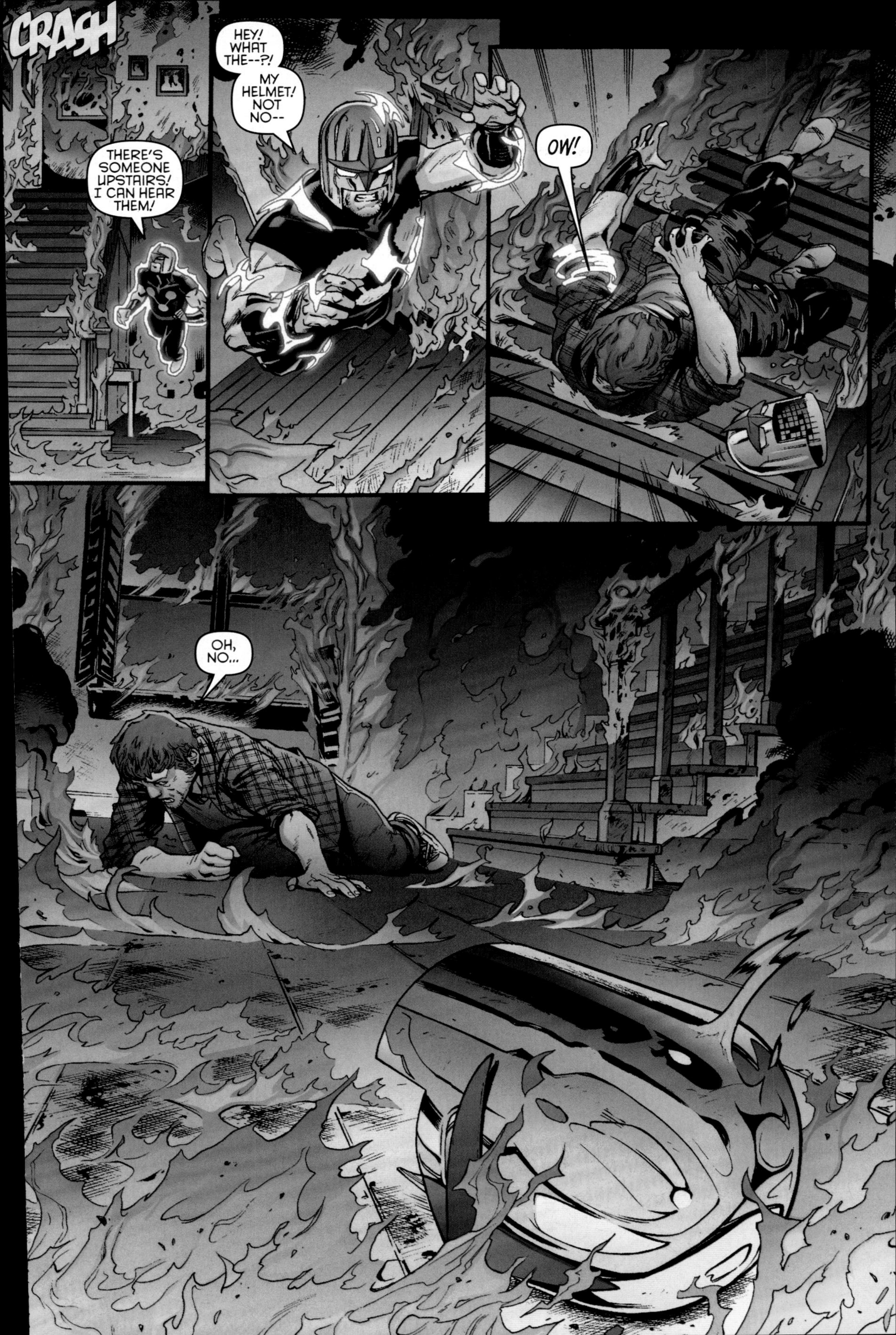
CRASH
THERE'S SOMEONE UPSTAIRS! I CAN HEAR THEM!
HEY! WHAT THE--?!
MY HELMET! NOT NO--
OW!
OH, NO...

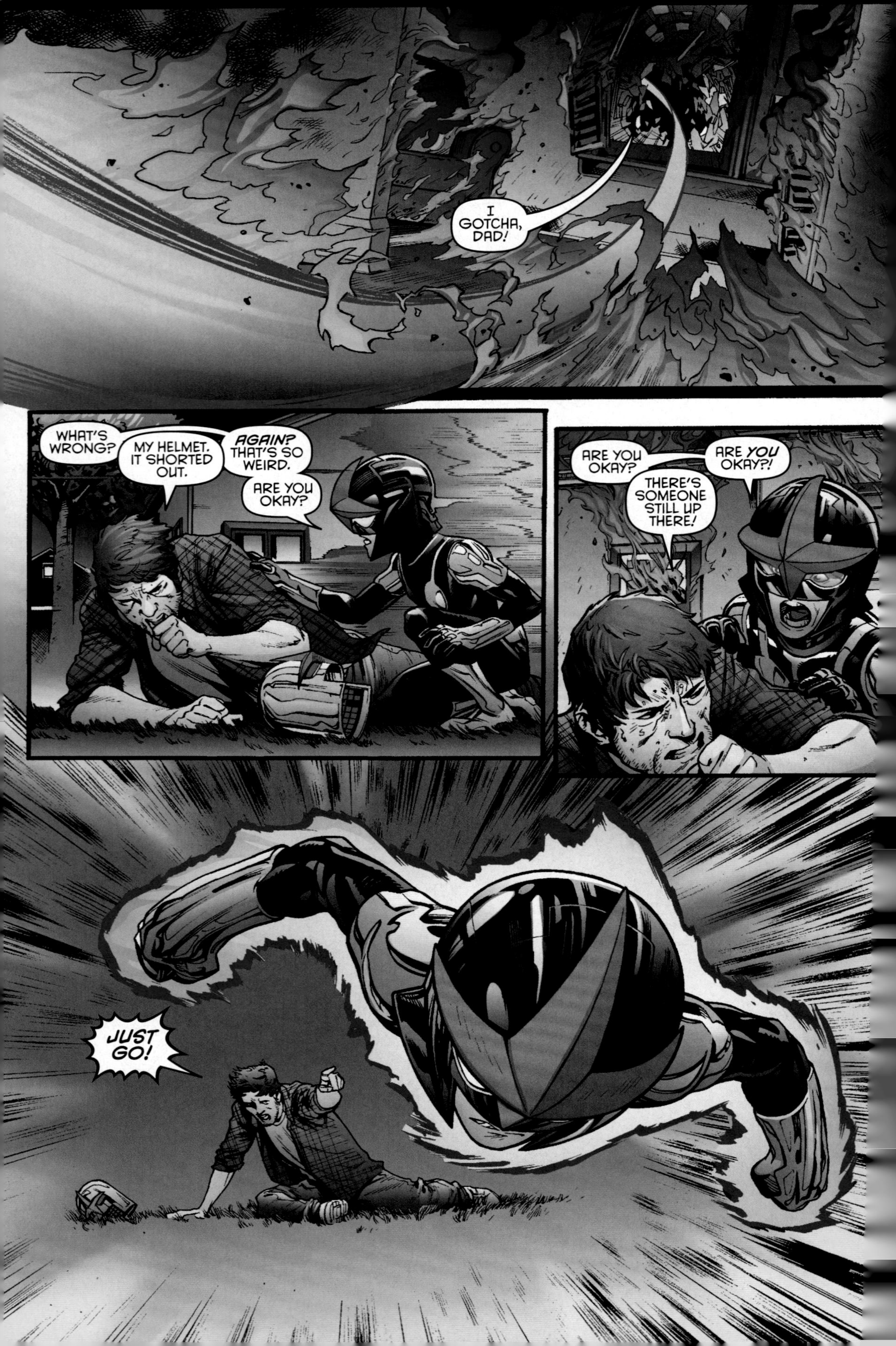
I GOTCHA, DAD!
WHAT'S WRONG?
MY HELMET. IT SHORTED OUT.
AGAIN? THAT'S SO WEIRD.
ARE YOU OKAY?
ARE YOU OKAY?
ARE YOU OKAY?!
THERE'S SOMEONE STILL UP THERE!
JUST GO!

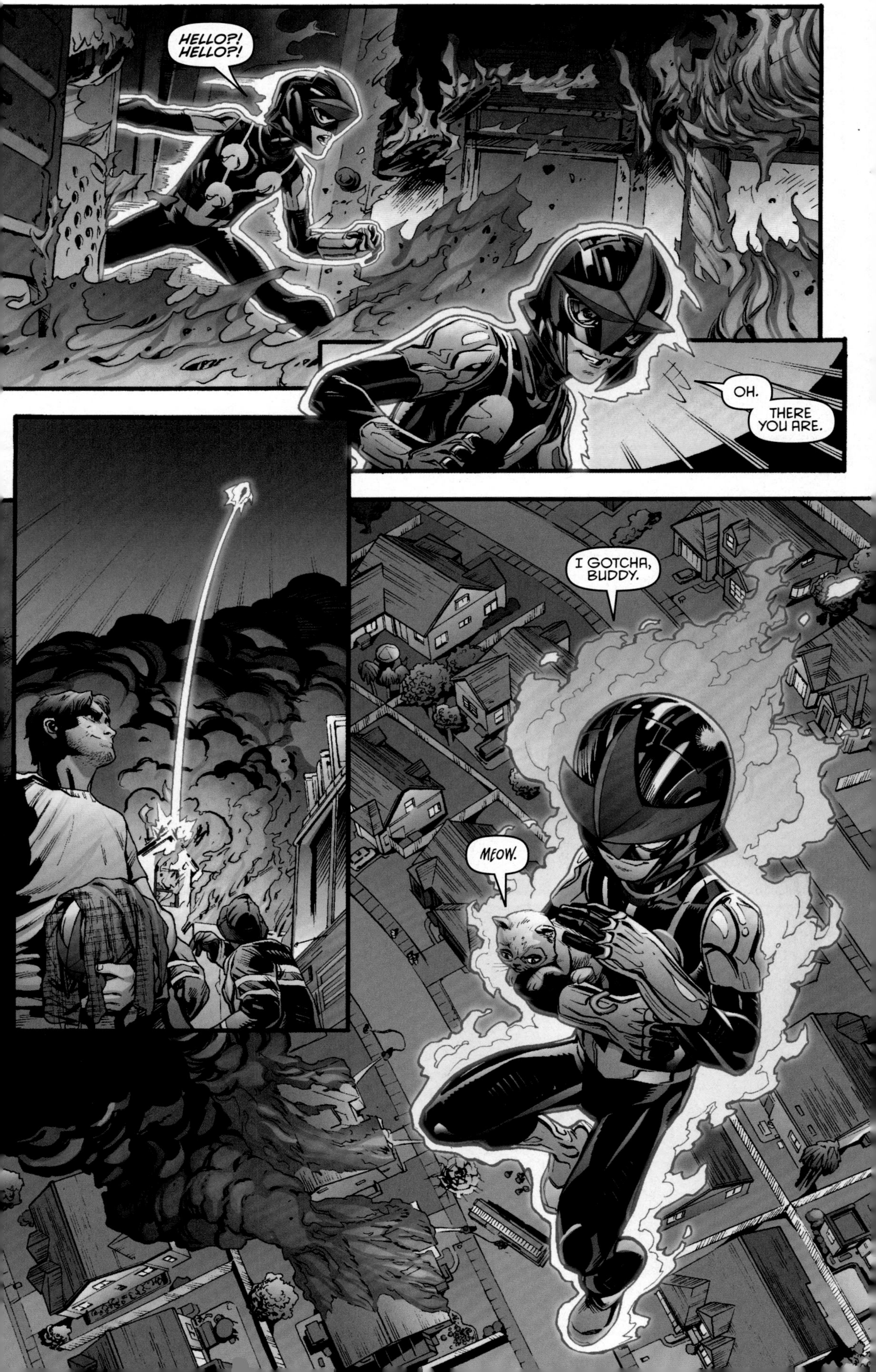
HELLO?! HELLO?!
OH.
THERE YOU ARE.
I GOTCHA, BUDDY.
MEOW.

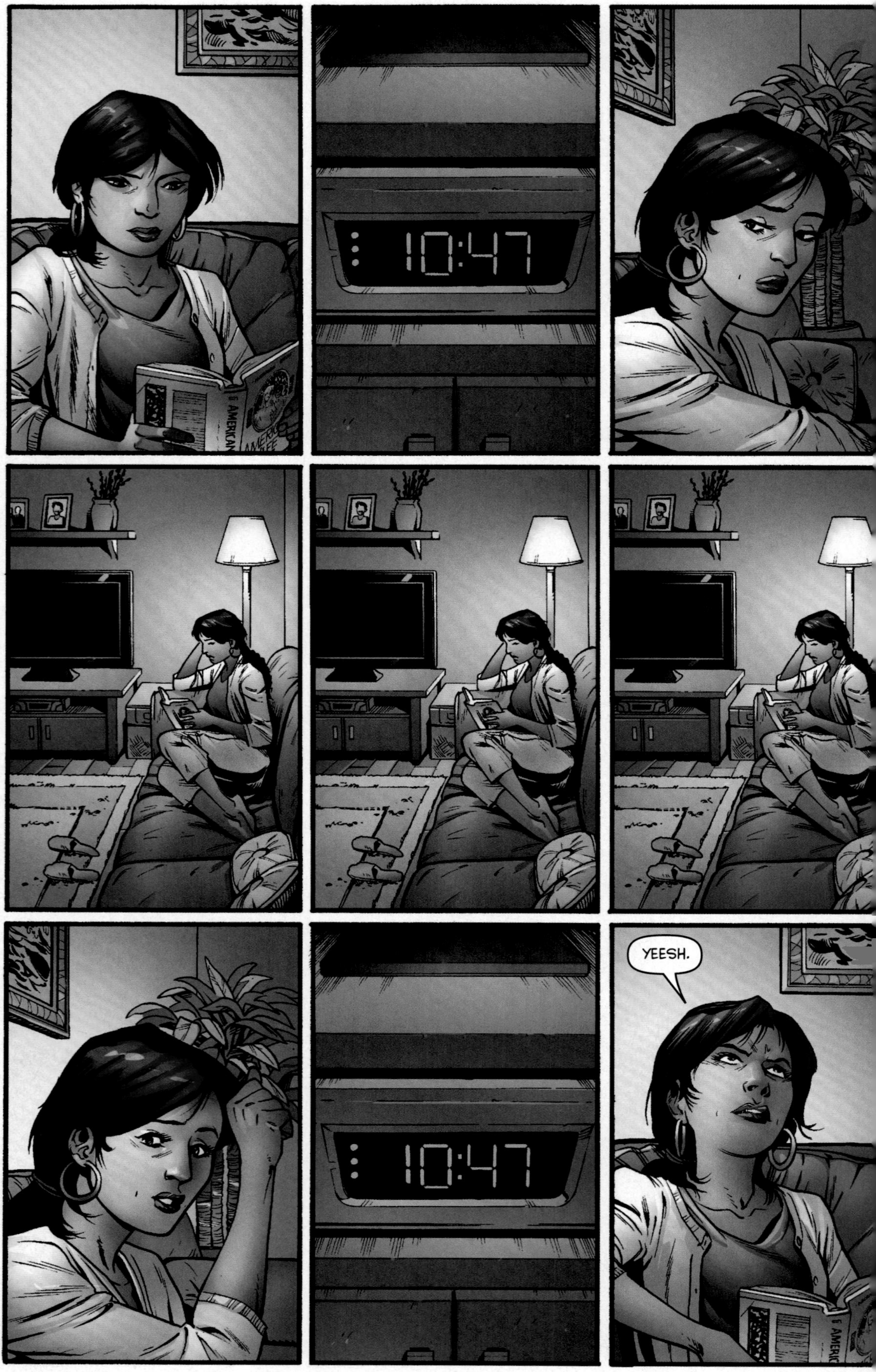
10:47
10:47
YEESH.

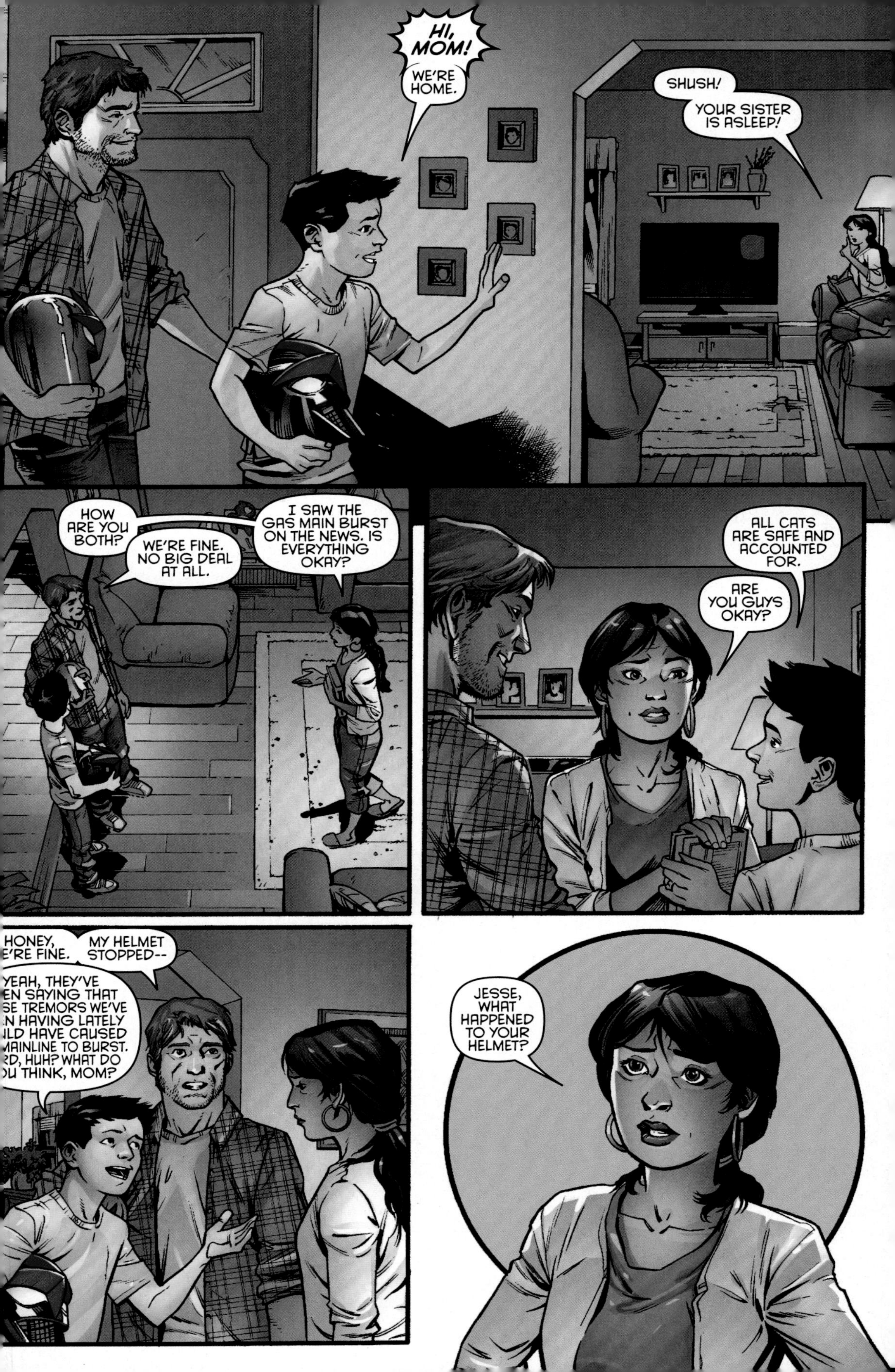
HI, MOM!
WE'RE HOME.
SHUSH!
YOUR SISTER IS ASLEEP!
HOW ARE YOU BOTH?
WE'RE FINE. NO BIG DEAL AT ALL.
I SAW THE GAS MAIN BURST ON THE NEWS. IS EVERYTHING OKAY?
ALL CATS ARE SAFE AND ACCOUNTED FOR.
ARE YOU GUYS OKAY?
HONEY, 'E'RE FINE.
MY HELMET STOPPED--
YEAH, THEY'VE EN SAYING THAT SE TREMORS WE'VE N HAVING LATELY ULD HAVE CAUSED MAINLINE TO BURST. RD, HUH? WHAT DO OU THINK, MOM?
JESSE, WHAT HAPPENED TO YOUR HELMET?

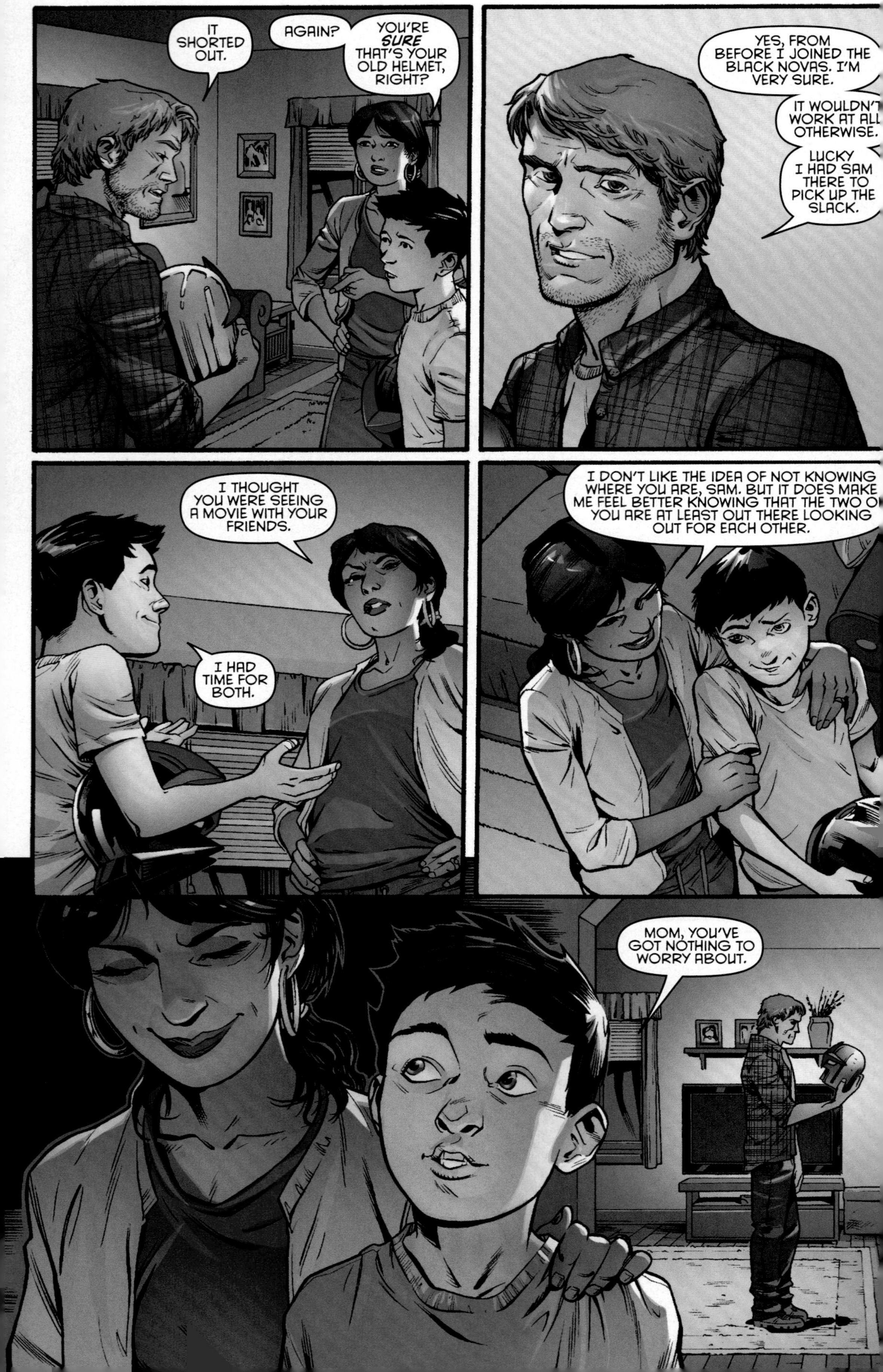
IT SHORTED OUT.
AGAIN?
YOU'RE SURE THAT'S YOUR OLD HELMET, RIGHT?
YES, FROM BEFORE I JOINED THE BLACK NOVAS. I'M VERY SURE.
IT WOULDN'T WORK AT ALL OTHERWISE.
LUCKY I HAD SAM THERE TO PICK UP THE SLACK.
I THOUGHT YOU WERE SEEING A MOVIE WITH YOUR FRIENDS.
I HAD TIME FOR BOTH.
I DON'T LIKE THE IDEA OF NOT KNOWING WHERE YOU ARE, SAM. BUT IT DOES MAKE ME FEEL BETTER KNOWING THAT THE TWO OF YOU ARE AT LEAST OUT THERE LOOKING OUT FOR EACH OTHER.
MOM, YOU'VE GOT NOTHING TO WORRY ABOUT.

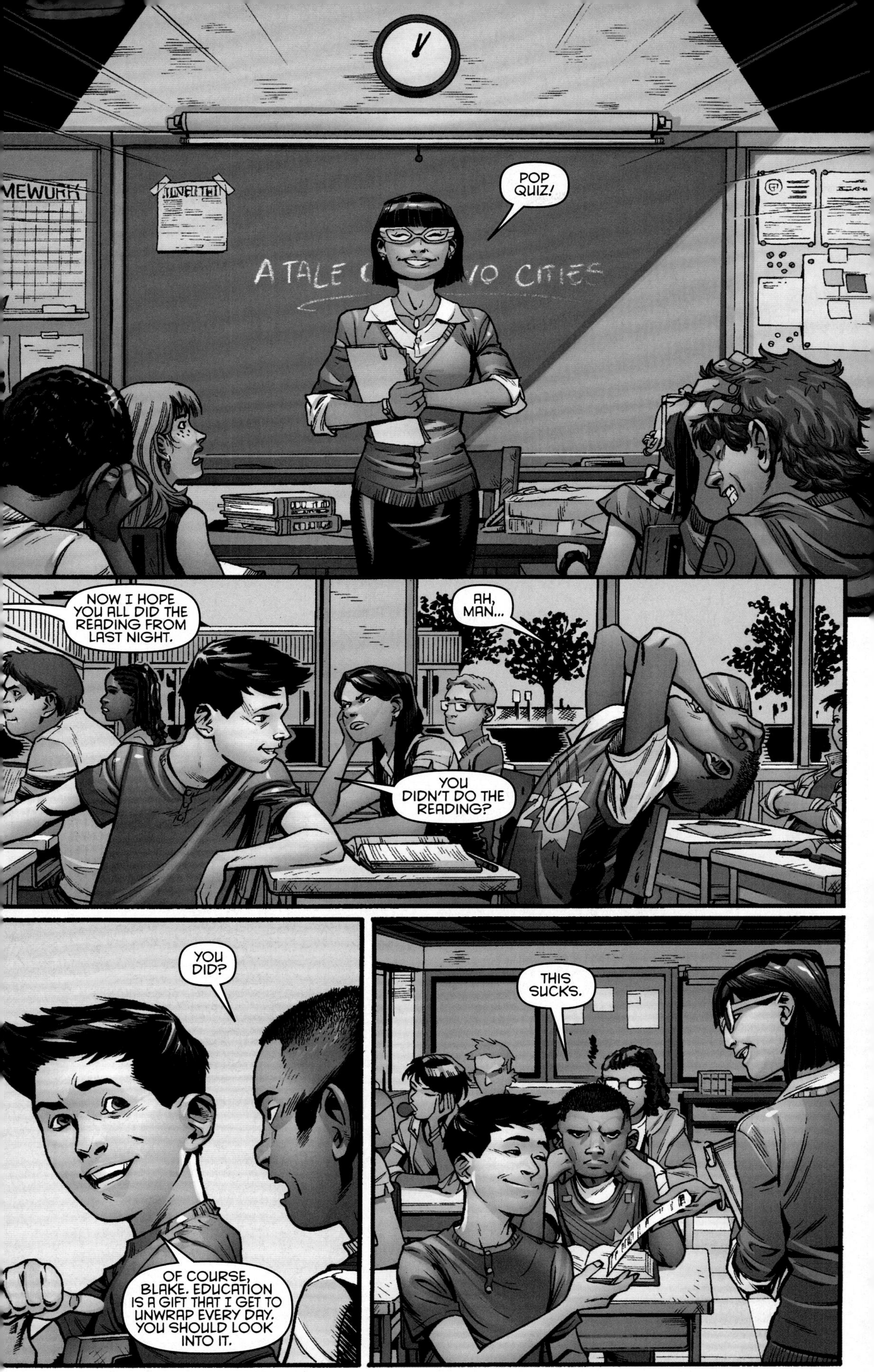
POP QUIZ!
NOW I HOPE YOU ALL DID THE READING FROM LAST NIGHT.
AH, MAN...
YOU DIDN'T DO THE READING?
YOU DID?
OF COURSE, BLAKE. EDUCATION IS A GIFT THAT I GET TO UNWRAP EVERY DAY. YOU SHOULD LOOK INTO IT.
THIS SUCKS.

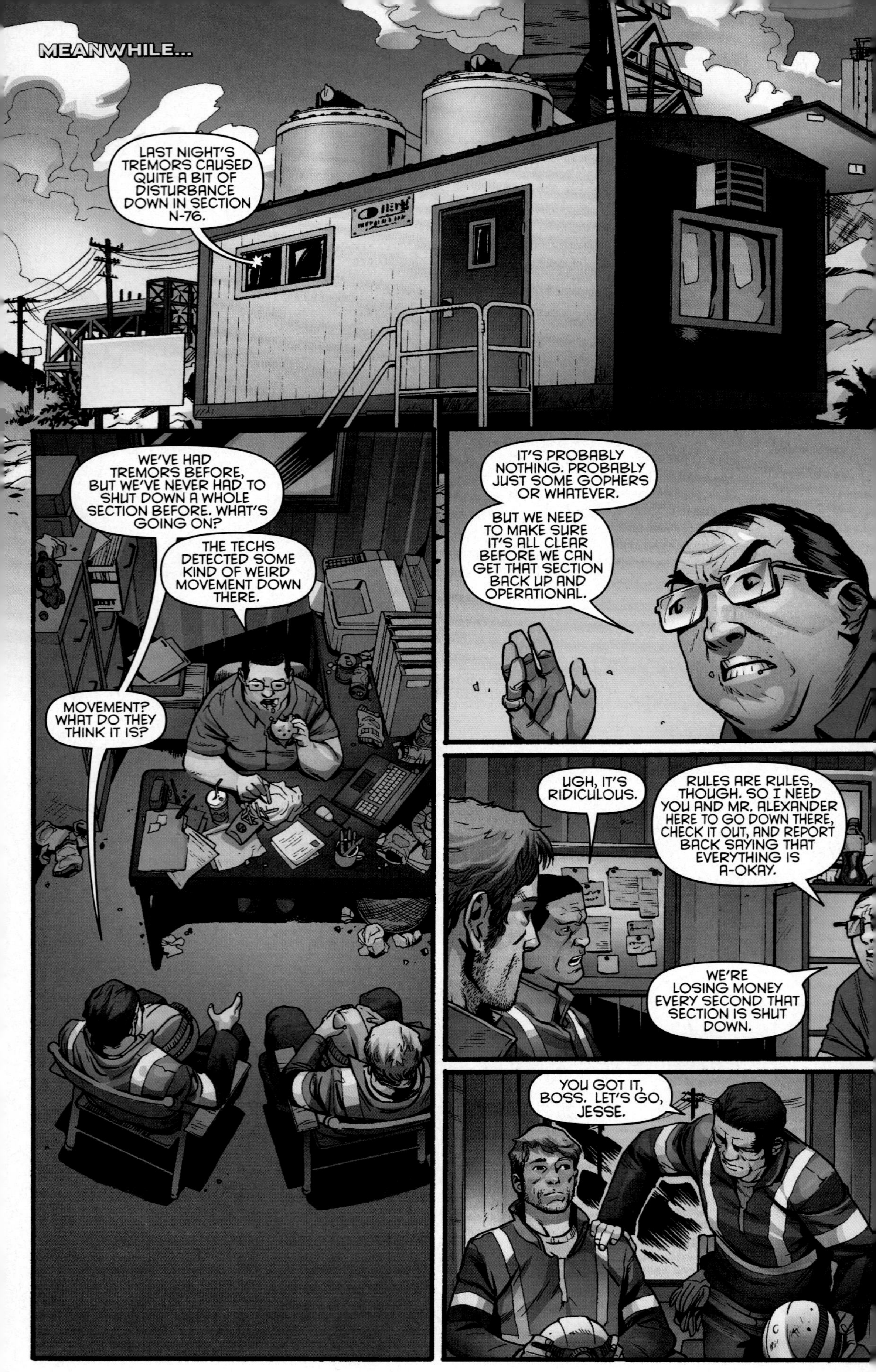
MEANWHILE...
LAST NIGHT'S TREMORS CAUSED QUITE A BIT OF DISTURBANCE DOWN IN SECTION N-76.
WE'VE HAD TREMORS BEFORE, BUT WE'VE NEVER HAD TO SHUT DOWN A WHOLE SECTION BEFORE. WHAT'S GOING ON?
THE TECHS DETECTED SOME KIND OF WEIRD MOVEMENT DOWN THERE.
MOVEMENT? WHAT DO THEY THINK IT IS?
IT'S PROBABLY NOTHING. PROBABLY JUST SOME GOPHERS OR WHATEVER.
BUT WE NEED TO MAKE SURE IT'S ALL CLEAR BEFORE WE CAN GET THAT SECTION BACK UP AND OPERATIONAL.
UGH, IT'S RIDICULOUS.
RULES ARE RULES, THOUGH. SO I NEED YOU AND MR. ALEXANDER HERE TO GO DOWN THERE, CHECK IT OUT, AND REPORT BACK SAYING THAT EVERYTHING IS A-OKAY.
WE'RE LOSING MONEY EVERY SECOND THAT SECTION IS SHUT DOWN.
YOU GOT IT, BOSS. LET'S GO, JESSE.

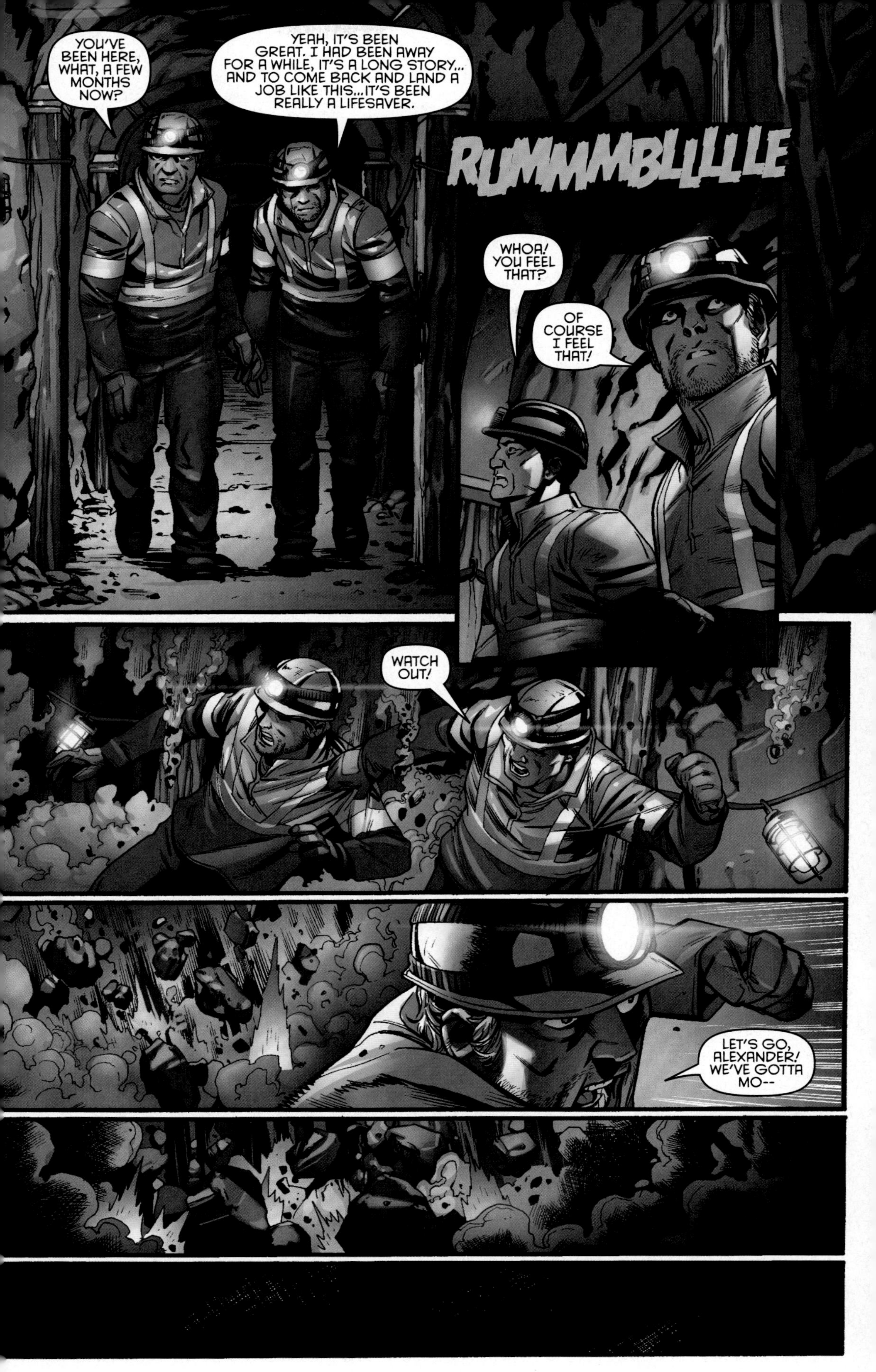

YOU'VE BEEN HERE, WHAT, A FEW MONTHS NOW?
YEAH, IT'S BEEN GREAT. I HAD BEEN AWAY FOR A WHILE, IT'S A LONG STORY... AND TO COME BACK AND LAND A JOB LIKE THIS...IT'S BEEN REALLY A LIFESAVER.
RUMMMBLLLLLE
WHOA! YOU FEEL THAT?
OF COURSE I FEEL THAT!
WATCH OUT!
LET'S GO, ALEXANDER! WE'VE GOTTA MO--

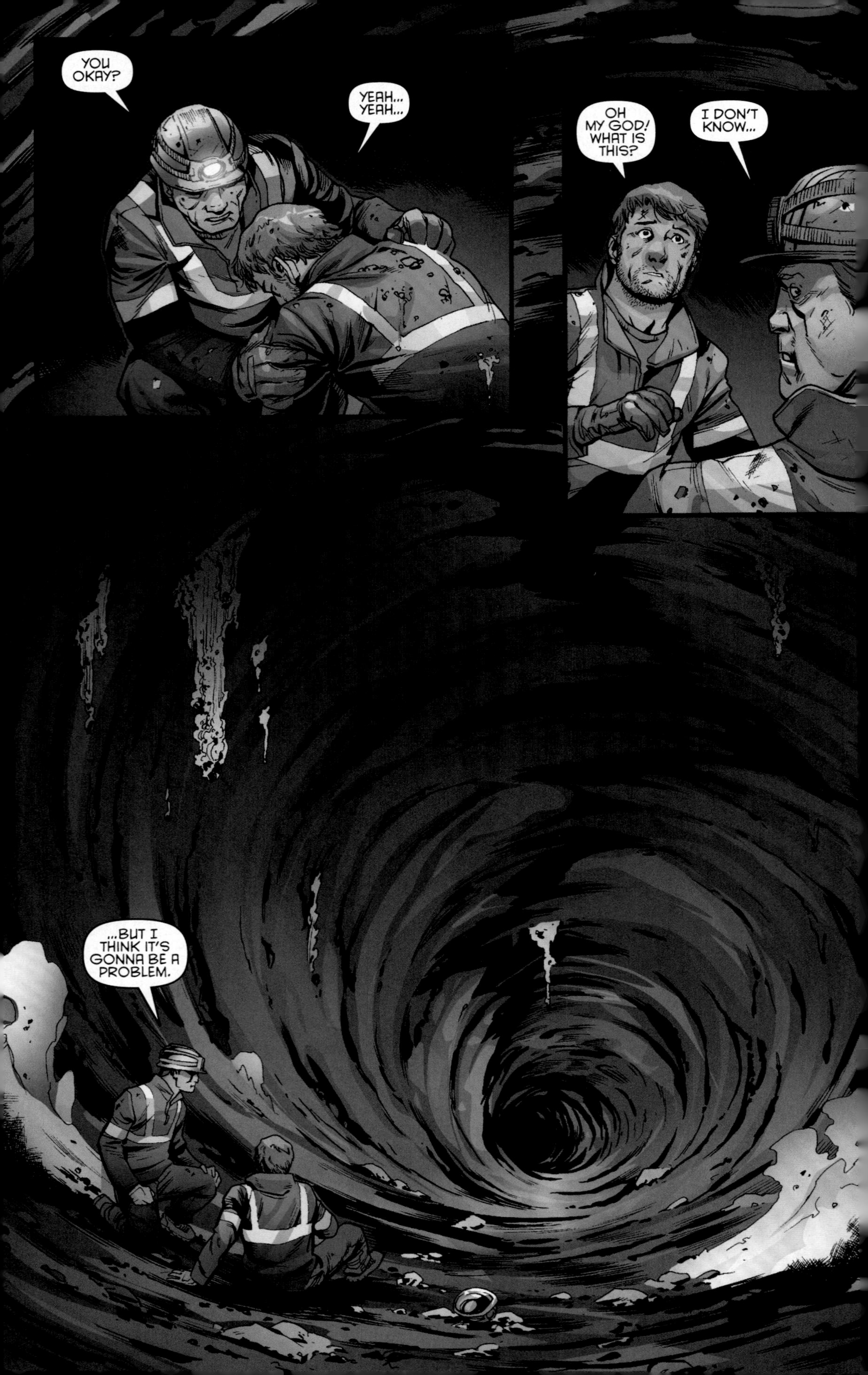
YOU OKAY?
YEAH... YEAH...
OH MY GOD! WHAT IS THIS?
I DON'T KNOW...
...BUT I THINK IT'S GONNA BE A PROBLEM.

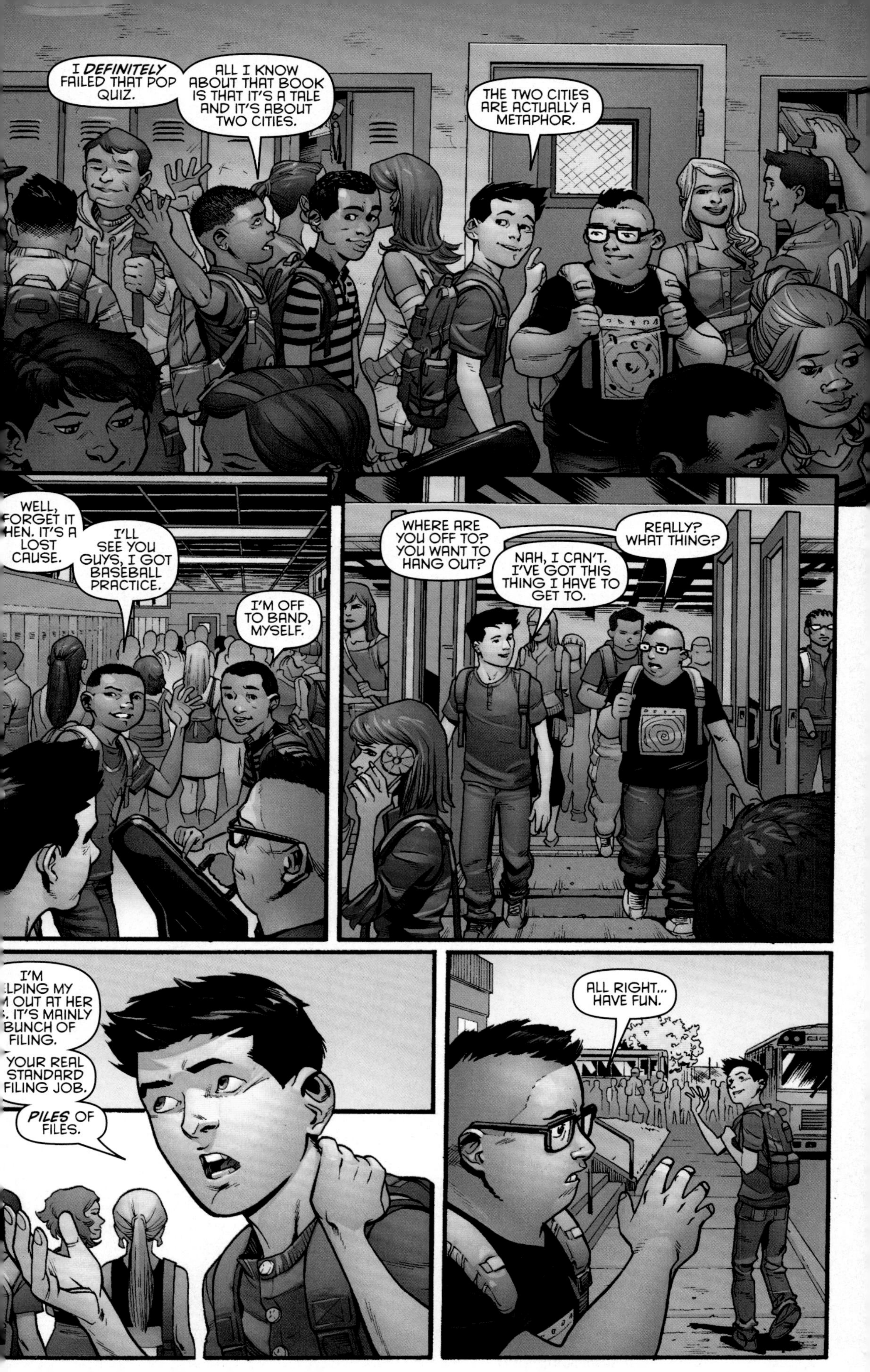

I DEFINITELY FAILED THAT POP QUIZ.
ALL I KNOW ABOUT THAT BOOK IS THAT IT'S A TALE AND IT'S ABOUT TWO CITIES.
THE TWO CITIES ARE ACTUALLY A METAPHOR.
WELL, FORGET IT HEN. IT'S A LOST CAUSE.
I'LL SEE YOU GUYS, I GOT BASEBALL PRACTICE.
I'M OFF TO BAND, MYSELF.
WHERE ARE YOU OFF TO? YOU WANT TO HANG OUT?
NAH, I CAN'T. I'VE GOT THIS THING I HAVE TO GET TO.
REALLY? WHAT THING?
I'M ELPING MY M OUT AT HER . IT'S MAINLY BUNCH OF FILING.
YOUR REAL STANDARD FILING JOB.
PILES OF FILES.
ALL RIGHT... HAVE FUN.

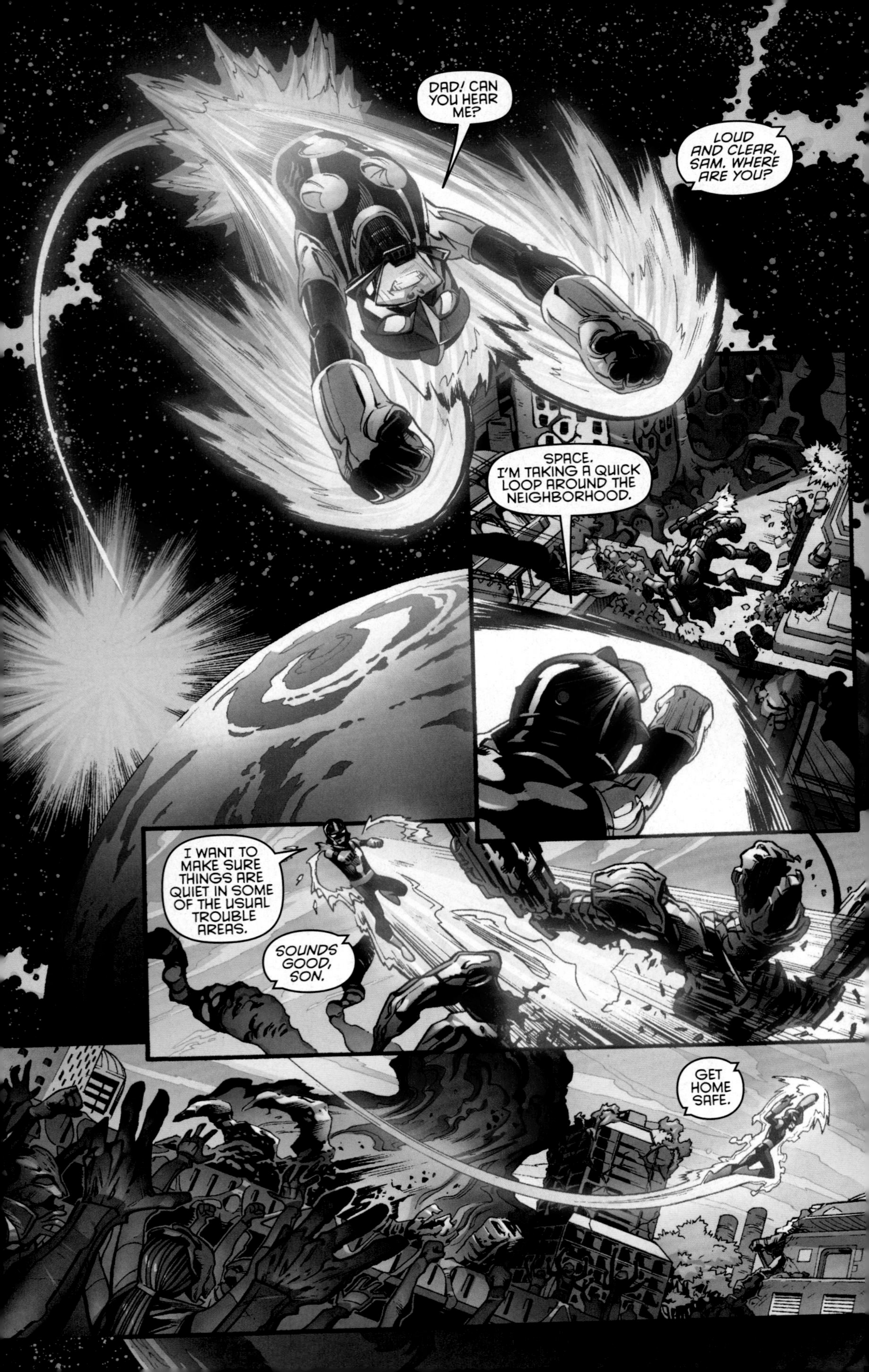
DAD! CAN YOU HEAR ME?
LOUD AND CLEAR, SAM. WHERE ARE YOU?
SPACE. I'M TAKING A QUICK LOOP AROUND THE NEIGHBORHOOD.
I WANT TO MAKE SURE THINGS ARE QUIET IN SOME OF THE USUAL TROUBLE AREAS.
SOUNDS GOOD, SON.
GET HOME SAFE.

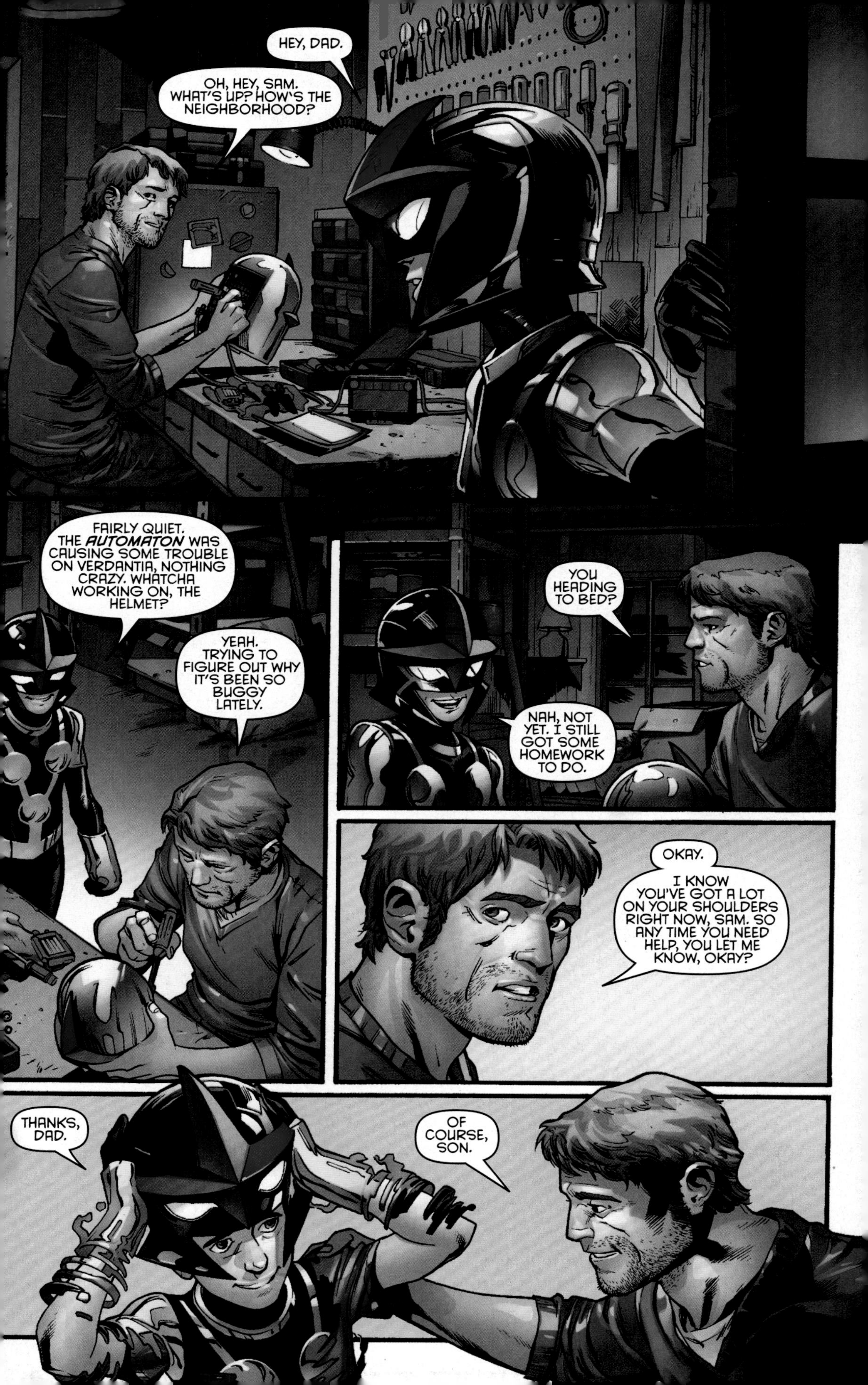
HEY, DAD.
OH, HEY, SAM. WHAT'S UP? HOW'S THE NEIGHBORHOOD?
FAIRLY QUIET. THE *AUTOMATON* WAS CAUSING SOME TROUBLE ON VERDANTIA, NOTHING CRAZY. WHATCHA WORKING ON, THE HELMET?
YEAH. TRYING TO FIGURE OUT WHY IT'S BEEN SO BUGGY LATELY.
YOU HEADING TO BED?
NAH, NOT YET. I STILL GOT SOME HOMEWORK TO DO.
OKAY.
I KNOW YOU'VE GOT A LOT ON YOUR SHOULDERS RIGHT NOW, SAM. SO ANY TIME YOU NEED HELP, YOU LET ME KNOW, OKAY?
THANKS, DAD.
OF COURSE, SON.

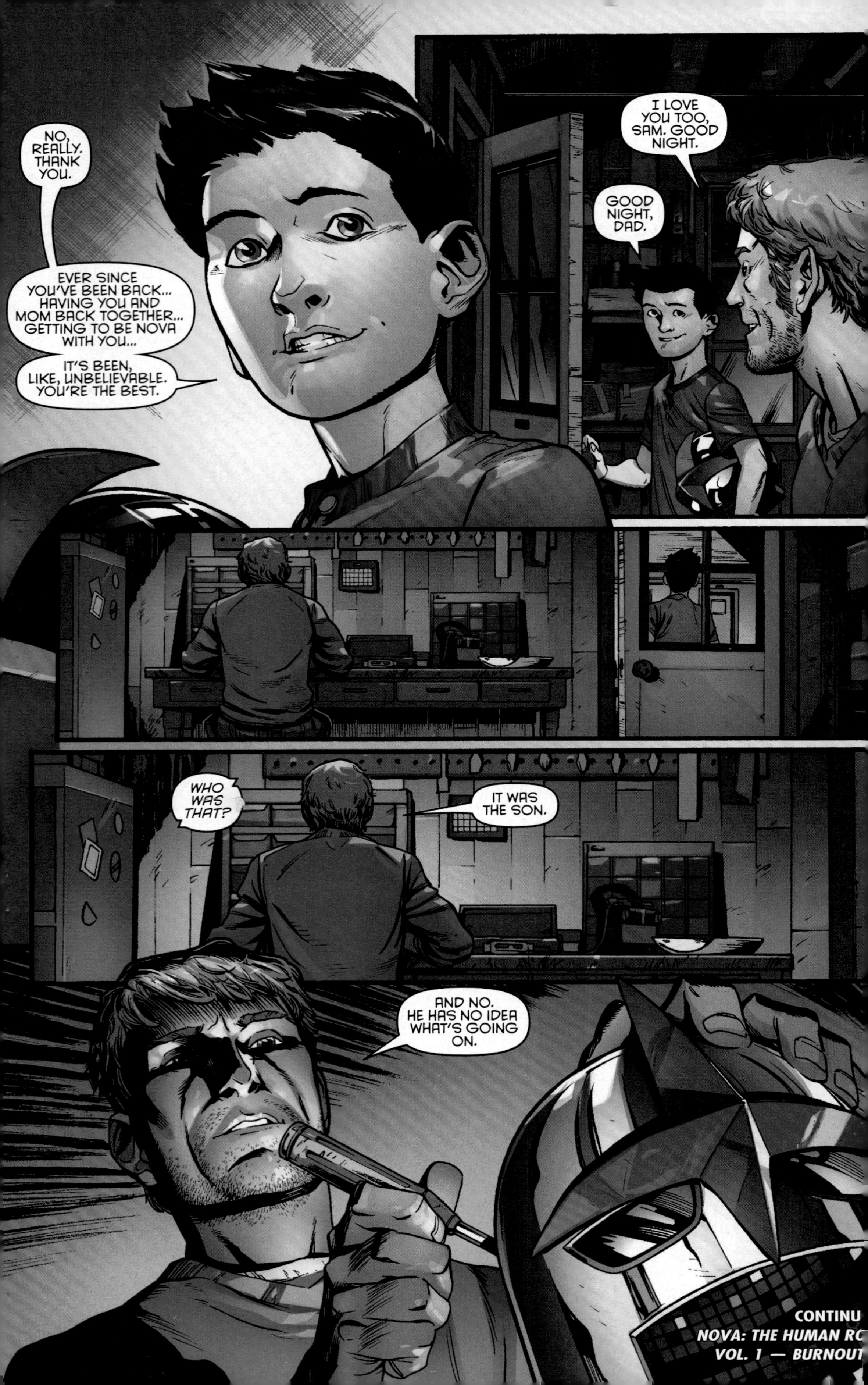
NO, REALLY. THANK YOU.
EVER SINCE YOU'VE BEEN BACK... HAVING YOU AND MOM BACK TOGETHER... GETTING TO BE NOVA WITH YOU...
IT'S BEEN, LIKE, UNBELIEVABLE. YOU'RE THE BEST.
I LOVE YOU TOO, SAM. GOOD NIGHT.
GOOD NIGHT, DAD.
WHO WAS THAT?
IT WAS THE SON.
AND NO. HE HAS NO IDEA WHAT'S GOING ON.
CONTINU
NOVA: THE HUMAN RO
VOL. 1 — BURNOUT